ORIGINS OF
THE SECOND WORLD WAR

MANCHESTER STUDIES IN MODERN HISTORY
General editor Jeremy Black

ALREADY PUBLISHED

British foreign policy 1919–39
Paul W. Doerr

Poverty and welfare in England 1700–1850
Steven King

Making sense of the Industrial Revolution
Steven King and Geoffrey Timmins

British fascism 1918–39
Thomas Linehan

ORIGINS OF THE
SECOND WORLD WAR

Victor Rothwell

MANCHESTER
UNIVERSITY PRESS
Manchester and New York
distributed exclusively in the USA by Palgrave

Published by Manchester University Press
Oxford Road, Manchester M13 9NR, UK
and Room 400, 175 Fifth Avenue, New York, NY 10010, USA
http://www.manchesteruniversitypress.co.uk

Distributed exclusively in the USA by
Palgrave, 175 Fifth Avenue, New York,
NY 10010, USA

Distributed exclusively in Canada by
UBC Press, University of British Columbia, 2029 West Mall,
Vancouver, BC, Canada V6T 1Z2

British Library Cataloguing-in-Publication Data
A catalogue record for this book is available from the British Library

Library of Congress Cataloging-in-Publication Data applied for

ISBN 0 7190 5957 7 *hardback*
ISBN 0 7190 5958 5 *paperback*

First published 2001

10 09 08 07 06 05 04 03 02 01   10 9 8 7 6 5 4 3 2 1

Typeset by Freelance Publishing Services, Brinscall, Lancs.
www.freelancepublishingservices.co.uk
Printed in Great Britain by
Bell and Bain Ltd, Glasgow

CONTENTS

Contents

INTRODUCTION

In 1955 a then prominent historian wrote that a case could be argued that too many historians were writing about the origins of the Second World War.[1] If this was advice to neglect the subject, it was, fortunately, not taken. Since the 1950s almost innumerable studies of almost every aspect of international relations between the two world wars have been published; the relevance of domestic politics and of economic developments to the origins of the Second World War has been much more fully considered than used to be the case; and the basic causes for both the European war of 1939 and the world war of 1941 have been much reassessed. Some historians, perhaps most notably Donald Cameron Watt and Richard Overy,[2] have discussed the general crisis in European society that constituted the background against which Europe descended into war. Watt showed how the shared values that had kept the continent largely at peace during the nineteenth century after Napoleon's defeat and which had become eroded by 1914, were not restored after 1918, or at least not in a form in which they could serve their old purpose. At the same time, new ideologies – fascism, Nazism and communism – that abhorred the status quo became important. Overy (and others) have stressed the failures and retreats between the wars of liberal democracy, the form of social organisation most conducive to the peaceful settlement of disputes. Many of the traditionally conservative social groups had no faith in it and, in its economic form, it came close to being fatally discredited by the world economic crisis of 1929–32 from which recovery was very slow.

Though it is essential to understand these considerations, they should not be allowed to distract attention from the fact that the actions of a narrow group of countries were of paramount importance

1

and it is to them that the major share of attention must be devoted. These countries were Germany and, to a much lesser extent, Italy and Japan on one side and Britain and, to a much lesser extent, France on the other. These states became locked in a contest for political supremacy in which economic considerations were, to an important extent, rationalisations.

The country that must be singled out for the most detailed consideration is Germany and interpretations of its development leading up to 1939 have been anything but consensual. At their most extreme, Germanophil explanations have depicted the German people as almost as much victims of Nazism as Dutch, Poles and Russians. Hitler, the argument runs, took control of their country under the most extraordinary circumstances and then used his power to pursue dreams of an empire founded on racism, mass murder and exploitation of non-Germans. Evidence to support this view is not hard to find. A few days before Hitler invaded Poland, the British ambassador in Berlin, Nevile Henderson, wrote to a friend in a third country: 'This is madness. The Germans do not want war.'[3] Two years earlier, the rightwing British politician, Lord Londonderry, had noted, after conferring with the gamekeepers on the estate of his host, Hermann Goering, that: 'They seemed to want to give up almost everything rather than pass through the tribulation of another war.'[4] Another interpretation, which can degenerate into Germanophobia, sees the Germans as a people seeking European, if not world, hegemony from some time after national unification in 1871, and recalls the annexationist war aims drawn up by the imperial German government in September 1914 and the fact that the leaders of the German left, the Social Democratic Party, were informed of these aims and supported them.[5] It is important to add that one theme – extermination – was absent from imperial German war aims. Two French scholars have produced a substantial collection of photographs of Jewish life in the first quarter of the twentieth century in the 'Pale of Settlement' in what are now western Ukraine and eastern Poland, many of them taken during the period of German wartime occupation.[6] The numerous photographs of Jewish people going about their normal business, manifestly untroubled by the presence of German soldiers on the streets of their towns and villages, must disprove any theory of complete continuity in German 'eastern' policy linking the two world wars. What can be asserted with least risk of contradiction is that the origins of the 1939 war make no sense without an understanding of the attitudes prevalent among the German people after the end of the First World War. They were unreconciled to defeat because the war had hardly impinged on to German soil, and the German army had not suffered obvious defeat. Many Germans sincerely believed that they had been fighting a war of self defence between 1914 and 1918, and that their losses in the treaty of Versailles embodied a vindictiveness that had to be reversed. And any chance that they might settle down to live in peace was lessened by an unworkably ultra-democratic constitution and by economic catastrophe in the form of the great inflation of 1923 that its victims blamed on the peace settlement.

The argument of chapter one of this book is that, despite the mood in Germany, undoubted flaws in the 1919 peace settlement and the fact that the ostensible main instrument for preserving peace, the League of Nations, was never taken seriously by the major powers as a means of regulating disputes among themselves as distinct from disputes involving small countries, leaders of the three major European powers, Britain, France and Germany, were actually on the road to rectifying the inadequacies in the peace settlement in the mid and late 1920s. If their work had continued, it would have led to some very large changes, including, for example, the almost certain emasculation of Poland and its reduction to, at best, an enfeebled rump state. But there would not have been another great war. The preconditions for the continuation of this 'peace process' were economic prosperity and a dynamic, outward looking American capitalism that sought a virtual economic special relationship with Germany. The Wall Street crash in October 1929 not only made the United States economically as well as politically and militarily isolationist, but also triggered a world economic depression without which Nazism could not possibly have gained power in Germany. The thesis that the entire period from 1914 to 1945 was a 'second Thirty Years War' cannot be sustained.

Nazism, and specifically the aims and beliefs of Adolf Hitler, which are discussed in chapter two of this book, go far towards explaining why a new war between Germany and at least some of the other major powers was as inevitable as anything in history can be. There was of course nothing inevitable about the precise form that that war would take, and Hitler only had limited control over many of the factors inside Germany – such as public opinion and the economic situation – of which he had to take account, let alone over international events. On the other hand, the very fact that Hitler was able to take power in Germany, no matter how unusual the circumstances, must say something very significant about that country. There was a tendency towards rightwing dictatorships or autocracies in inter-war Europe in response to economic problems, social tensions and unfulfilled nationalist ambitions, but it is a truism that someone with Hitler's wildly extravagant objectives and a relish for accomplishing them by the most brutal means, could only have come to power in Germany. To that extent, the widespread belief in allied countries during the Second World War that Germany was uniquely a troublemaker among the nations of the world still looks persuasive.

There has been a greater shift of interpretation in relation to Germany's enemies of 1939, Britain and France. After that date – during the war and afterwards – their policies were widely condemned in moralising terms; they were held to have failed until almost too late to oppose an obvious and immeasurably dangerous evil. Very little in early post-war historical study escaped the distortions that this produced. It was deplorable, as A. J. P. Taylor noted while he was gathering together his initial thoughts for his assault on accepted interpretations of Second World War origins, that this approach coloured the selection of inter-war British Foreign Office documents for publication with their 'unavowed slant that the Foreign Office was always right, appeasement always wrong'.[7] Few would now disagree that it was always preposterous to imagine that British, French or any other leaders might have considered the Nazi challenge in terms of morality and not power politics. It is less unrealistic to regret that for long these leaders, and especially the British, fashioned their response to Hitler's Germany as only one of a number of domestic and international problems, many of the latter outside Europe, that they had to consider. When they did respond to this challenge their answer was the policy of appeasement which is discussed in chapters four and five of this book.

To understand the reasons for the adoption of the appeasement policy, it is necessary to examine the history of international relations from the late nineteenth century. Britain and France both greatly expanded their colonial empires during this period, but there was an essential difference between them. There were relatively few threats to the French empire from outside Europe but France itself was vulnerable to German attack. If such an attack were to be successful, the French empire might then be largely lost to Germany, to nationalist elements in some places, and to powers outside Europe (including even the United States) that posed no threat while France remained an undefeated great power. Therefore France had an interest in continental European power politics that Britain, the stronger of the two great West European liberal democracies, did not feel to the same degree. The existence of threats to the pre-1914 British empire – from Russia and from internal revolts (especially in India if nationalists perceived British world power to have weakened) – led to a policy of appeasing those potential enemies and concentrating on imperial Germany as the one country that threatened both the European balance and British imperial and commercial worldwide interests.[8]

After the First World War and the signing of Versailles and the other peace treaties in 1919–20, the pre-war dichotomy between the two most important supporters of the new status quo, Britain and France, reasserted itself. France feared a German resurgence that might threaten its independence and yet, having recovered the provinces of Alsace and Lorraine that Germany had annexed in 1871, and having lost its great ally in the east, tsarist Russia, it was ready, in a faltering sort of way, to consider a process of accommodation in place of confrontation with Germany. It was in this environment that appeasement first became an important political word. A Franco-German dialogue, with some British input, was an outstanding feature of European international relations during the mid- to late-1920s. France's relatively robust performance during the world economic depression after 1929 gave a new lease to its international importance. It was, for instance, instrumental in 1931 in preventing Germany and Austria from forming a customs union that the French feared would be the precursor to a full *Anschluss* or union between the two German-speaking states. The watershed in French decline was Hitler's remilitarising of the Rhineland in 1936 which carried German military power to the border with France.

This diminution of French power propelled Britain to the fore and inter-war Britain needs always to be considered as an imperial state. Whether the inter-war British empire was a true superpower or a colossus with feet of clay,[9] Britain long gave priority to safeguarding it and other interests outside Europe. This was partly because most of the old dangers persisted and were joined by a new one from Japan, previously seen usually as a valuable ally, and partly because of disillusionment with the results of the earlier concentration on European problems. Dabbling with alliance politics had drawn Britain into what was increasingly looked upon as an unnecessary war in 1914. When the idea of alliance politics was reborn in the 1930s under the euphemism of collective security, its attractions were for a long time easily resistible. Early gestures of apparent interest in joining with other countries to prevent aggression, perhaps most notably the 'Stresa front' with France and Italy in 1935, were almost wholly insincere; while Britain and France vied with one another later in 1935 and in 1936 over their frustration at their obligations as members of the League of Nations that threatened at worst to involve them in what they regarded as a war over Ethiopia that would have been senseless or, at best, to alienate their partner, Italy, in that very Stresa alignment, however modest its substance had been.

The high casualties and other costs of the 'Great War' were another powerful argument for avoiding a new contest on the continent and against a policy of deterring potential aggressors because that could hardly be done without collective security. To the extent that there was deterrence there was a tendency to define it as self defence under which other countries would have to defend themselves. Only under the shock of the discovery that, in the words of Foreign Secretary Lord Halifax, Germany was less interested in 'racial efforts' than in 'a lust for conquest on a Napoleonic scale' from which Britain and its empire would not be exempt, did a reassessment of British policy take place.[10] This change, in which the key events were the failure of the Munich agreement of 1938 and the extinction of the independence of rump Czechoslovakia and the British guarantee of Poland in March 1939, set the stage for the European war that started in September 1939. A. J. P. Taylor once issued a wise warning against 'the perhaps misleading impression that international relations between the wars were an Anglo-German dialogue'.[11] Even so, the outbreak of war really was the result of the breakdown of that particular dialogue among all the others of the 1930s that contributed to the sum total of the international relations of that decade.

The overall international structure becomes more important, and Germany and Britain become less important, in explaining the transition from European to world war. A separate crisis from the one in Europe came about in the Far East from 1931 when self-styled 'double patriots' – all Japanese were supposed to be patriotic but the 'doubles' even more so – began to gain the upper hand in that oriental empire. This will be traced in detail later in this book. The European and Far Eastern crises did not seriously interconnect until after war had started in Europe in 1939 except in one important respect. The determination to defend its interests in east Asia and the Pacific dominions of Australia and New Zealand constituted for Britain a strong additional inducement to pursue the policy of the appeasement of Germany.

The essentially marginal roles of the Soviet Union and the United States in the events of the 1930s that took much of Europe into war will be discussed separately in chapters nine and eleven. The Soviet Union was excluded from great power dealings until the summer of 1939 when Germany and the Western powers made their bids for Stalin's favour and the German offer proved the more tempting. The United States, politically isolationist and economically depressed despite immense potential, excluded itself not only from exercising almost any influence in Europe but also from the war that Japan embarked upon against China in 1937. After 1939 the contrast between the positions of the Soviet Union and the United States continued. Just as the Soviet Union had for so long been denied the choice to participate seriously in international affairs, so in 1941 its entry into war was also involuntary; out of a mix of ideological and economic-strategic motives Hitler decided to invade Russia and nothing that Stalin did could make him change his mind. By comparison, the United States's road to war, beginning at Pearl Harbor, resulted partly from choices that the ruling administration made. The fact that the United States became a belligerent may have resulted from a Machiavellian strategy by Franklin D. Roosevelt to manipulate the country into war with Germany, or with both Germany and Japan. (One thing that is certain is that he regarded war with Japan alone as an undesirable proposition, though that might have happened if Hitler had tried to remain neutral after Pearl Harbor.) It is more likely that it occurred because the President miscalculated. Firstly, that he could force Japan to back down from expansion into south-east Asia and the Pacific and even into retreating from many of its conquests in China. Secondly, that he could embark on a limited and undeclared naval war with Germany to keep open the trans-Atlantic supply routes without which British resistance could not have continued. When Hitler promised in the late autumn of 1941 to make common cause with a Japan that had no intention of abandoning imperialism the Second World War lay only days in the future. The German declaration of war on the United States after the Japanese attack on Pearl Harbor was to be the final step in the bringing about of the Second World War.

Notes

1 See T. Desmond Williams (ed.), *Historical Studies: I: Papers Read to the Second Irish Conference of Historians* (London, Bowes and Bowes, 1958), p. 33.

2 Donald Cameron Watt, *Too Serious A Business: European Armed Forces and the Approach to the Second World War* (London, Temple Smith, 1975); R. J. Overy, *The Inter-War Crisis 1919–1939* (London, Longman, 1994).

3 Richard Bassett, *Balkan Hours: Travels in the Other Europe* (London, Murray, 1990), p. 8.

4 Marquess of Londonderry, *Ourselves and Germany* (London, Hale, 1938), p. 152.

5 Fritz Fischer, *Germany's Aims in the First World War* (London, Chatto & Windus, 1967) remains fundamental.

6 Gérard Silvain and Henri Minczyles, *Yiddishland* (Paris, Hazan, 1999).

7 *Manchester Guardian*, 27 May 1958.

8 Paul Kennedy, 'The tradition of appeasement in British foreign policy, 1865–1939' in his *Strategy and Diplomacy 1870–1945: Eight Studies* (London, Allen & Unwin, 1983), pp. 13–39.

9 Cf. Correlli Barnett, *The Collapse of British Power* (Gloucester, Sutton, 1984 edn.) and Anthony Clayton, *The British Empire as a Superpower 1919–39* (London, Macmillan, 1986).

10 Gaines Post, Jr., *Dilemmas of Appeasement: British Deterrence and Defense, 1934–1937* (Ithaca, NY, Cornell University Press, 1993), pp. 19, 169, 173, 248, 340.

11 A. J. P. Taylor, *The Origins of the Second World War* (Harmondsworth, Penguin, 1964 edn.), p. 38.

CHAPTER ONE

THE PEACE SETTLEMENT AND THE 1920S

The fundamental importance of the facts that most of the German people were not reconciled to defeat after 1918 and that even fewer of them were willing to accept that there could be any justification for imposing harsh peace terms on them has already been noted.[1] Before examining the 'continuity' debate in German history, the resented peace settlement of 1919 therefore needs to be analysed. During the First World War the allied powers were guided by the conviction that imperial Germany was an aggressor nation, wholly responsible for starting the war and intent on world domination, and also by the desire to turn it into a peaceful nation concerned with economic well-being and not aggressive power politics.[2] This implied that there should be a conciliatory peace settlement of a kind that was not actually achieved. In explaining this failure the notion of a sharp contrast between France – determined to impose a harsh peace and then to maintain it by indefinite repression of Germany – and Britain and the United States – dedicated to a peace sufficiently mild to win grudging German acquiescence – is no longer taken seriously by historians. France did not wholly ignore German sensitivities. Even if only on the basis of wishful thinking, the French leader, Georges Clemenceau, thought that the boldest French demand, for the Rhineland to be detached and made a buffer state under French protection, could be made to work by fostering a mass-based Rhenish separatist movement that would resist the restoration of German sovereignty in the area.[3] In any case, the ambition was temporarily abandoned as work on the peace treaty proceeded. On reparations, France was willing to accept less than Britain, and, unlike either Britain or the United States, was willing to discuss with the Germans what they could pay.[4] If the final reparations package,

9

agreed by the allies in 1921, was not 'mad' in a purely economic sense, that owed most to France.[5]

The peace treaty imposed on Germany a swathe of economic penalties that were bound to provoke continuing resentment, ranging from large, even if technically feasible, reparations to the confiscation of German private, as well as public, property in allied and neutral countries that even the staunchest defender of the economic side of the treaty of Versailles admitted could not be justified.[6] Germany lost all but a minuscule fragment of its navy, which was inevitable after the Anglo-German naval tensions prior to 1914, but also was restricted to a small army as the result of pressures from, again, Britain which wished to complement its own voluntary dissolution of its huge wartime army with an enforced German equivalent.[7]

On territory, the peacemakers made a more serious effort at justice. Germany lost 15 per cent of its 1914 territory and a somewhat smaller percentage of population: 6.5 million people of whom only 1.9 million were ethnic Germans according to pre-war German census figures, and these included the 315,000 Germans of Danzig and its district who were constituted a self-governing free city as a compromise between leaving them in Germany and ceding the area to Poland. In the case of the especially sensitive German–Polish border the working principle was that Poland should not receive an area without a plebiscite unless German census returns showed a non-German majority.[8] Only in the south did the victorious allies deny all equity by rejecting the recommendation of their own experts that some almost exclusively ethnic German border areas of the new Czechoslovakia should be ceded to Germany, while at the same time they detached from Germany a small piece of land whose population was mostly Czech and gave it to the new state.[9] In addition, the rump German-speaking Austrian republic left over from the dissolution of the Austro-Hungarian Dual Monarchy was denied the right to choose union with Germany.

In this way the decisions of the conference in Paris laid the ground for the three situations that Hitler was to manipulate in 1938 and 1939, leading up to the outbreak of war. A country, Austria, was subjected to an enforced independence. Czechoslovakia was left with a larger population of Germans than of Slovaks who gave the state the second half of its name. None of this could be justified in terms of the democratic principles that the peacemakers claimed to uphold, and yet the crises in 1938 over Austria and Czechoslovakia were to pass without involving Europe in war. It was the principled settlement imposed on Germany and Poland that was to prove the occasion for war in 1939. A British leader had warned of the risks. In the summer of 1918 Arthur Balfour, the Foreign Secretary, had recommended against ceding German territory to Poland as politically unwise, even if morally sound.[10] The loss of West Prussia, Posen and part of Upper Silesia to Poland and the detachment of Danzig did more than any other foreign policy issues to excite a durable bitterness in Germany that Hitler was to exploit.

At the time in 1919 Germany singled out the peace treaty provisions for the trial of its wartime leaders and the so-called 'war guilt' clause in the treaty as being particularly objectionable. The former faded away with no trials of political or military leaders being held.[11] The latter rankled for years, despite the fact that the relevant clause did not mention the words 'war guilt', and despite the fact that the German government, which denounced the clause in 1919 as 'a lie', had received expert advice that a preliminary study of official documents indicated that they would provide evidence to support the allied charge.[12]

As the United States retreated into isolation, the leaders of the other two countries that had largely drawn up the settlement, Britain and France, had an uneasy premonition of the sorts of judgement on their work that would eventually be made, for instance that 'the one major peace dictated solely by the great democracies was also the most unstable peace in European history.'[13] Any hopes of preventing the settlement from unravelling in ways that might lead to renewed war rested on an organisation, the League of Nations, and on two powers, Britain and France. The League was conceived as a substitute for the pre–1914 system, novel in its day, of long-term peacetime alliances as a means of ensuring security. The mostly British and American authors of the League's constitution or 'Covenant' defined its purposes in terms of mediation, not coercion. From Paris, President Woodrow Wilson wrote excitedly to his wife after discussions on the Covenant had concluded: 'This is our first real step forward, for I now realise, more than ever before, that once established, the League can arbitrate and correct mistakes which are inevitable in the treaty ... the League will act as a permanent clearing house where every nation can come, the small as well as the great.'[14] Every nation, that is, except for the United States which withdrew from the League project.

Partly because of the United States's withdrawal there was a steady retreat from this grand vision. It proved impossible to attract a major international political figure to head the League machinery and the designation for the post was downgraded from chancellor to secretary-general.[15] The idea of any real equality between large and small League members proved unfounded. The Spanish League official, Salvador de Madariaga, even went so far as to declare, 'When Great Britain stops, the League stops; when Great Britain goes forward, the League goes forward too.' Austen Chamberlain, British Foreign Secretary from 1924 to 1929, was indeed blunt in telling the League representatives of small countries about their unimportance.[16] The League was able to enforce settlements in several disputes involving only small countries. The first time a large country was a party to a dispute, when Italy seized the Greek island of Corfu in 1923, the League virtually handed over the ultimately successful quest for a formula to cause Italy to withdraw, to another body, the Conference of Ambassadors, which the allied powers had set up in 1921 following the formal coming into force of the treaty of Versailles to oversee the practical implementations of its territorial provisions. This was despite the fact that Corfu had not figured in the peace settlement. For sixty years the island had been universally recognised as part of Greece.[17] An important part of the responsibility for deflecting the League from Corfu rested with France, which did not wish to set a precedent for League interference in French policy in Germany. Primary credit for causing Mussolini to abandon his aggression belonged to Britain which threatened naval action unless he evacuated the island.[18]

International crises like Corfu took place in a Europe in which there were many deep-rooted causes of instability, including the fact that many Europeans were open to persuasion from extremist doctrines; the existence of 12,500 extra miles of borders; the disruption of many natural economic arrangements; and the absence of means to give any security arrangements an economic bedrock. For example, Britain and France had no use for food imports from Eastern Europe, Britain because it imported food from the empire and France because it produced its own food.[19] Despite this, the majority of historians no longer regard the 1920s as the age of 'the illusion of peace'[20] in which there was the sharpest contrast between the appearance of durable peace and the reality of a Europe and in particular a Germany whose grievances and ambitions would inevitably lead to a new war. The decade after the treaty of Versailles can more accurately be divided into a first half, in which there was an all too apparent as well as real survival of earlier hatreds and tensions, and a second half in which there was both apparent and real progress towards achieving durable peace.

The inadequacies of the League of Nations had, as indicated, been demonstrated by 1923 in its dealings with Italy, a country that, at most, was on the fringe of being a great power. Among the three great status quo powers, the United States had retreated into political and military, though not economic, isolation. Even so, the combination of Britain and France, plus minor allies, was in a position to preserve the peace by coercion or an admixture of coercion and conciliation. The observation by Orme Sargent of the Foreign Office in 1937 that, 'We are the power which occasions Germany the most uneasiness'[21] had some force throughout the inter-war period. But an effective British role in European international relations was impeded by a number of factors. These included defects in the machinery for deciding foreign and security policy that were evident during Lloyd George's premiership after the war and which were not to be resolved under his successors.[22] They also included a refusal to spend heavily on defence. British military expenditure was reduced from £604 million in 1919 to £111 million in 1922,[23] and hovered around that figure for the next ten years during which there was an actual Ten Year Rule under whose terms the services were instructed to rule out British participation in a major war for at least that length of time. As a result the Chiefs of Staff of the three forces warned in 1930 and again in 1931 that Britain's actual military capacity to intervene in a war on the continent was nil.[24]

British relations with France were embittered by unsuccessful negotiations in 1921–22 for a security pact that few in Britain wanted and which collapsed in recriminations about whether Britain should take on obligations of some kind to French allies in eastern Europe, Britain being only willing to offer help in the event of a 'direct attack on the soil of France'. The two countries could also not agree about the duration of a pact, with France demanding thirty years and Britain offering only ten. With conscious or unconscious humour, the British timescale coincided exactly with the period of time in which a major war was ruled out in their strategic discussions.[25] This niggardliness towards France contrasts with Britain's generous post-war relationship with the effectively independent dominions of Canada,

Australia, South Africa and New Zealand under which Britain was pledged to come to their aid under all circumstances, while they were under no such obligation to Britain. Except for Australia, their defence budgets per head of population made British defence expenditure look astronomical.[26] Both politically and in terms of the allocation of Britain's limited armed forces, the Dominions and the colonial empire were a massive impediment to a serious British role in collective security in Europe.

Underlying all this was a national mood of unwillingness to assume obligations as a result of which the horrors of the First World War might be repeated or even magnified. To give an illustration from an utterly non-pacifist source, in 1922 the professor of military history at, and Conservative member of Parliament for, the University of Oxford, Sir Charles Oman, wrote: 'For my own part, I believe that as the world realises more and more what the horrors of the next war would be, everyone save a Bolshevik, must see that such a war ought never to be allowed to come about.'[27] Though one must always be cautious about such generalisations, it has been argued with some plausibility that Britain's mature liberal society of the 1920s and 1930s made the country unfitted to cope with the problems of an increasingly illiberal world and that Stanley Baldwin, the most durably successful politician of the inter-war period, was the personification of this national characteristic.[28] Symptomatic of the British mood was a vast outpouring between 1929 and 1933 of 'trench literature', published reminiscences of fighting in the recent war, almost always with an anti-war theme. By contrast, in Germany during the same period there was an equally vast output of Great War memoirs, but with the difference that 90 per cent of it took a positive view of the war experience. (The towering exception was the novel *All Quiet on the Western Front*, but it was an exception and the film version was banned by the Weimar German government as being likely to bring Germany into international disrepute.[29]) On a more concrete level, complacency about Germany was inevitably fostered by the disappearance of the naval and colonial issues that, in addition to imperial Germany's threat to the balance of power, had poisoned Anglo-German relations before 1914. Germany had lost its large navy and colonies as a result of the war. Germany in the 1920s appeared relatively reconciled to these losses, though there was a slight shudder in Britain when the former enemy embarked on building technically legal 'pocket battleships' in 1928.[30]

The greater share of responsibility for preventing a new war lay therefore in the 1920s with France. After the peace conference France developed both military and political-economic strategies for that purpose. Contemplating what they regarded as the continuing German threat to their security, the French, as a contemporary observer expressed it, were a nation that 'was rather in the situation of a boxer who has laid out the former champion by a well-planted blow, but is still too dazed to be certain whether his opponent has been or will be "counted out".'[31]

Spurned and even betrayed, as it thought, by Britain and the United States and with its old ally, Russia, now presenting an additional set of dangers, France sought new allies in the revived state of Poland and the new state of Czechoslovakia, Germany's eastern neighbours. But the treaties concluded with them scarcely amounted to a genuine alliance. The treaty with Poland in 1921 promised French technical assistance but not troops if Poland was attacked. The treaty with Czechoslovakia in 1924 was even weaker, guaranteeing only staff contacts if there was war. France was conscious of the weaknesses of these two countries, and was understandably dismayed by their mutual hostility, centring on a territorial dispute over ownership of the Teschen area of Czechoslovakia – a 'racial jungle'[32] whose fauna was partly Polish.

It is now known that most French policymakers in the 1920s thought that Poland's position, if not Czechoslovakia's, was untenable in the long term, and that it would have to return to the Reich the 'corridor' that gave it a short coastline on the Baltic while also consenting to the return of the Free City of Danzig to Germany. They hoped that this could take the form of *révision à froid*, that is not at the point of a gun, and with Germany offering a quid pro quo that would benefit France more than its eastern allies in the form of arms limitations.[33] It would be easy to sneer at the element of dishonesty in French policy towards eastern Europe. The British were commendably lacking in hypocrisy in making clear their rejection of any thesis that they had vital security interests in east or central Europe.[34] However, awareness of the weakness of the new, small states in that area and of the many hatreds between and within them produced all too comprehensible cynicism in the French. In the early 1920s a British diplomat reported the none-too-bright former Habsburg emperor, Karl, as declaring that the fragments into which his realm had divided were 'calculated to give the greatest satisfaction to Germany and her future aspirations to control the whole of Central Europe.'[35] What was morally deplorable in French policy was their intention that any new war including France and Germany should be fought in central Europe, using central Europeans as cannon-fodder, while the territory of France remained unscathed. The French sometimes hinted at all this to the Germans, as in 1925 when Aristide Briand said to Gustav Stresemann that if France and Germany could settle their differences 'the Poles would become very uninteresting' to France.[36]

France's initial political-economic strategy was directed towards western Germany and sought the reverse of what it expected in the east: whereas Germany's eastern borders might well expand, its western should, in a sense, contract. After Germany's reparations burden was formally fixed in 1921, France looked for defaults in its implementation and used even minor ones to extend its power into western Germany by setting up economic and other controls whose ostensible purpose was reparations collection, but which were really intended to give France a permanent share in sovereignty over the Rhineland, the Ruhr and the Saar, turning them effectively into a Franco-German condominium, rather than integral parts of Germany. In that way the disparity in economic and other matters between France and Germany would diminish and the economies of the two countries would become so interlocked that a future war would become technically impossible.[37] This over-ambitious aim caused France to over-reach itself grotesquely with its disastrous occupation of the Ruhr in 1923. The French vision should not, however, be dismissed as pure fantasy. In the early 1920s there were discussions between French and German industrialists on closer links between their enterprises, though they did not proceed far owing to French stress on reparations and German on cartels.[38] Realistically, though, France's only hope would have been a socialist takeover and consolidation of power in Berlin, in which case some west German rightwingers had contingency plans to proclaim a Catholic Republic of the Rhineland which would have had to look to France for support.[39] By 1923 the chances of such a development appeared gone. The idea of winning popular support in western Germany for French schemes was finally revealed as a delusion by the bitterness of German passive resistance to the Ruhr occupation. The French would have benefited from listening to the British politician Bonar Law's response to a remark by Marshal Foch in 1919 that France would win over the Rhinelanders by conciliating them: 'We ourselves had tried for years to conciliate the Irish.'[40] The failure of the Ruhr occupation gave the initiative in French policy to politicians like Aristide Briand, former Prime Minister and Foreign Minister from 1925 to his death in 1932, and officials like Philippe Berthelot who wished to set aside notions that there were serious centrifugal forces in Germany, and to concentrate on creating what he described to Briand in 1923 as a German republic hostile to war without which 'we are doomed.'[41]

Under these circumstances French security policy shifted radically in 1924 and 1925. They accepted the Dawes plan for somewhat reduced reparations and, at a conference in London in 1924, agreed to end the occupation of the Ruhr and not to carry out any more territorial incursions into Germany without the consent, obviously unlikely to be forthcoming, of the League. The treaty of Versailles effectively ended in 1924 in the sense that there was no longer the will to use force to deal with anything but outright German aggression. A British and also American and indeed German concept of conciliation and peaceful change replaced the earlier concept of 'fulfilment'.[42] This found its greatest expression in the Locarno treaties of October 1925, stemming from a German initiative that had found favour first with Britain and then France. These countries, and Belgium, Italy, Poland and Czechoslovakia, signed various pacts which guaranteed Germany's borders in the west but in the east only laid down arbitration procedures; Germany refused to accept as sacrosanct its borders with Poland or even Czechoslovakia.[43]

A year later Germany joined the League of Nations with the prestige feature of a permanent seat on its governing Council. If the treaty of Versailles had been no more than 'a prolonged and sometimes even a precarious armistice' as a British Foreign Office memorandum characterised it in 1926,[44] then these developments were hopeful: Germany was gaining a profitable and honourable stake in a peaceful world order. The way was open to the negotiated restoration of many, even most, of its losses under the peace settlement. Germany became the recipient of huge American investment funds, and there was the glittering prospect of becoming a global partner of the dynamic, expansionist United States of the later 1920s – but only if Germany pursued a strictly peaceful foreign policy.[45] Besides these incentives, Weimar German leaders were also aware that if they did threaten to resort to force there was a bedrock of Anglo-French solidarity that would probably cause the two countries to make common cause with one another again. Foreign Secretary Austen Chamberlain, admittedly a Francophile, told his officials in 1925 that Britain would have to enter any war between France and Germany, regardless of who had caused it, 'for we cannot afford to see France crushed, to have Germany or an eventual Russo-German combination supreme on the Continent'.[46]

Britain certainly wanted a strong and economically prosperous Germany.[47] Then the two countries could go their own separate ways in matters other than trade. It must have been delightful to Baldwin and his colleagues that between December 1926 and September 1928 Anglo-German relations needed to be included on the Cabinet's agenda only once.[48] But all was contingent on reasonable German political behaviour such as was fostered by Gustav Stresemann, the outstanding figure in Weimar foreign policy until his death in 1929. He thought that the recovery of Germany's main loss in the west, of Alsace-Lorraine to France, and the pan-German nationalist dream of annexing Austria to the Reich, were unattainable and probably undesirable.[49]

If relations between Germany and its western neighbours in the late 1920s lacked excitement, that was precisely because they were not the stuff of which future wars were made. Germany's main immediate aim was to secure the withdrawal of foreign occupation troops from the Rhineland well ahead of the scheduled date in 1935. With some help from a Britain that was increasingly anxious to end its role in the area,[50] this was agreed to in 1929 and evacuation was completed the following year. On reparations, French policy changed from seeking increased payments in return for political concessions to Germany at the expense of third parties in the abortive Thoiry proposals of 1926, to accepting their further scaling-down in the Young Plan in 1930 under which 75 per cent of all reparations payments were to finance the repayment of west European debts to the United States.[51]

Between 1919 and 1925 a new war involving the major European powers appeared probable in the long term on an objective analysis. Between 1925 and 1929 it increasingly appeared more and more probable that peace could be made permanent. This impression is not lessened by consideration of the position of the successor to another traditional European great power, the Soviet Union that had replaced the Russian Empire. The Bolsheviks, who seized power in Petrograd in 1917, expected their revolution to be repeated throughout Europe and perhaps also in parts of Asia, at first within two or three years and then within a longer and unpredictable timespan. They quickly acquired a readiness to use the Red Army to help spread communism outside their borders. Even in the 1930s Stalin, by then Soviet dictator, was to proclaim the legitimacy of using the Red Army to add more republics to the Soviet Union, along any lines of least resistance that might present themselves.[52] This went hand in hand with a renascent Russian nationalism that, fatefully, gave the Bolshevik rulers a bond with Weimar Germany in 'their common hatred of Poland'[53] which they would cheerfully have partitioned between themselves and Germany in the 1920s if they had had the chance. If that had happened and if Germany and Russia had again become contiguous, or had only been separated by a weak, rump Polish buffer state, some sort of Russo-German clash would have been likely. More moderate opinion in the Weimar political establishment would have been content with a privileged economic position in Russia. Others, including the military strongman, General von Seekt, envisaged the crushing of Poland as only the preliminary to a contest with Russia in which the gains made in the treaty of Brest-Litovsk in March 1918 would be restored.[54] That would inevitably have provoked Russian resistance. In the world as it was in the 1920s, Poland could survive and the Western powers merely worried, without considering practical action, about the possibility of Germany and Russia combining, albeit from obviously differing motives, to upset the entire peace settlement by force. Hence the exaggerated Western reaction when the two countries signed a very limited agreement at the Italian resort of Rapallo in 1922. This was not an alliance, nor even a promise to observe neutrality if the other country was attacked, though that latter provision did figure in the treaty of Berlin four years later. In the words of Walter Laqueur: 'It was simply a political manifestation of the need for self-assertion on the part of two European powers which had been ostracised by the rest.'[55]

The Soviets adorned their relationship with Germany with such curiosities as giving explicit endorsement to the German complaint in 1923, the year after Rapallo, that the French occupation of the Ruhr was bad enough in itself but that their use of non-white colonial troops added unpardonable insult.[56] This solicitude cut little ice with the German ambassador in Moscow who hoped that Rapallo would be shortlived because the Soviet rulers were 'a gang of criminals'.[57] The reality of extremely limited German–Soviet common ground was not always clear to Western statesmen like Austen Chamberlain, who told his cabinet colleagues that the beauty of a pact such as he was hoping would be signed at Locarno was that it would deter Germany from 'throwing herself into the arms of Russia, so that together they made an anti-Western block'.[58] Chamberlain responded with alarm and indignation to the supplementary Soviet–German treaty of 1926, which the Germans agreed to mainly as a lever to prise concessions from the West.[59] 'I had looked forward to steady progress in the path of concession and conciliation', he wrote. Soon, however, he concluded that the treaty was not a serious threat to international security after all.[60] Chamberlain's second thoughts were sound. Soviet Russia had the will but lacked the means to threaten peace without running suicidal risks. In any case, by the late 1920s the limited Soviet–German relationship was in decay,[61] and at the beginning of the next decade the Soviet rulers became deeply worried about the security of their eastern territories from Japanese aggression, giving them a stake in peace in Europe.[62]

And yet there was a very big difference between perceiving the Soviet Union as virtually a neutral force for preventing war and valuing it as a positive factor. The difficulties lay with the western democracies as well as with the Soviets. In the former, repugnance against any political cooperation with 'Bolshevik' Russia was by no means confined to the backwards-looking right. In an age that was not used to state-sponsored sadism and lawlessness, the often bestial cruelty of the Bolsheviks received a justifiably bad press.[63] In 1935 one of the ablest of all Western journalists ever to report from Moscow summed up their rule as 'a tragedy of cruelty'.[64] In 1927 the British Trades Union Congress passed a resolution expressing 'the fervent hope that the practice of executing persons for political offences, with or without trial, will cease'.[65] In the 1920s in Britain leftwing dissent from official foreign policy was heavily pro-German, not pro-Soviet.[66] In the case of the Soviets, the late 1920s witnessed a shift in headship of their foreign ministry from the doctrinaire Anglophobe, Georgii Chicherin, to the more well disposed Maxim Litvinov.[67] And yet in a speech at Geneva in 1931 to the League that Russia did not yet deign to join, Litvinov, intent both on ingratiating himself with his 'bourgeois' audience and preserving ideological honesty, could not bring himself to say more than that peaceful coexistence between his 'proletarian' state and those that were 'capitalist' was only something that applied at a 'given historical stage'.[68] He thus informed his listeners that they were ultimately doomed, a point that the British diplomat, Robert Vansittart, shrewdly noted.[69]

Notes

1 These points are discussed by both of the following: Keith Eubank, *The Origins of World War II* (Arlington Heights, IL, Harlan Davidson, 1990), pp. 2–9; and Gordon Martel (ed.), *The Origins of the Second World War Reconsidered: The A. J. P. Taylor Debate After Twenty-five Years* (London, Allen & Unwin, 1986), pp. 23–5.

2 For the British perspective, see V. H. Rothwell, *British War Aims and Peace Diplomacy 1914–1918* (Oxford, Clarendon, 1971).

3 Alan Sharp, *The Versailles Settlement: Peacemaking in Paris, 1919* (London, Macmillan, 1991), pp. 105–13.

4 Marc Trachtenberg, 'Versailles after sixty years', *Journal of Contemporary History*, 17: 3 (1982), 487–506.

5 Sharp, *Versailles*, pp. 97–9; Bruce Kent, *The Spoils of War: The Politics, Economics, and Diplomacy of Reparations 1918–1932* (Oxford, Clarendon, 1989), Part one and pp. 374–5; Sally Marks '1918 and After: the Postwar Era' and Stephen A. Shuker 'The End of Versailles' in Martel (ed.), *Origins of the Second World War Reconsidered*, pp. 37 and 55–6.

6 Etienne Mantoux, *The Carthaginian Peace – Or the Economic Consequences of Mr. Keynes* (London, Oxford University Press, 1946), pp. 88–9.

7 Lorna S. Jaffe, *The Decision to Disarm Germany: British Policy towards Postwar German Disarmament, 1914–1919* (London, Allen & Unwin, 1985).

8 Mantoux, *Carthaginian*, p. 70; and Harold I. Nelson, *Land and Power: British and Allied Policy on Germany's Frontier 1916–19* (London, Routledge & Kegan Paul, 1963), p. 118.

9 Nelson, *Land and Power*, pp. 293–304.

10 *Ibid.*, pp. 43–5.

11 James F. Willis, *Prologue to Nuremberg: The Politics and Diplomacy of Punishing War Criminals of the First World War* (Westport, CT, Greenwood Press, 1982).

12 Gerhard Schulz, *Revolutions and Peace Treaties, 1917–1920* (London, Methuen, 1972), pp. 184–5.

13 Trachtenberg, 'Versailles', p. 503.

14 Seth P. Tillman, *Anglo-American Relations at the Paris Peace Conference of 1919* (Princeton, NJ, Princeton University Press, 1961), p. 133.

15 Sharp, *Versailles*, pp. 58–9.

16   George Scott, *The Rise and Fall of the League of Nations* (London, Hutchinson, 1973), pp. 165–6, 179.

17   J. Barros, *The Corfu Incident of 1923* (Princeton, NJ, Princeton University Press, 1965); Byron Dexter, *The Years of Opportunity: The League of Nations, 1920–1926* (New York, The Viking Press, 1967), pp. 121–5; and F. P. Walters, *A History of the League of Nations* (London, Oxford University Press, 1952), pp. 244–55.

18   Alan Cassels 'The Corfu Crisis' in Philip V. Cannistraro (ed.), *Historical Dictionary of Fascist Italy* (Westport, CT, Greenwood Press, 1982), p. 137.

19   Paul Kennedy, *The Rise and Fall of the Great Powers: Economic Change and Military Conflict from 1500 to 2000* (London, Unwin Hyman, 1988), pp. 284–6, 289.

20   *The Illusion of Peace* is the title of a book by Sally Marks (London, Macmillan, 1976).

21   Anthony Adamthwaite, 'War origins again', *Journal of Modern History*, 56 (1984), 100–15.

22   Alan J. Sharp, 'The Foreign Office in eclipse, 1919–22', *History*, 61:202 (1976), 198–218.

23   Kenneth O. Morgan, *Consensus and Disunity: The Lloyd George Coalition Government 1918–1922* (Oxford, Clarendon Press, 1979), p. 146.

24   Correlli Barnett, *The Collapse of British Power* (Gloucester, Sutton, 1984 edn.), pp. 337–43.

25   Anne Orde, *Great Britain and International Security 1920–26* (London, Royal Historical Society, 1978), pp. 18, 28; and Arnold Wolfers, *Britain and France between Two Wars: Conflicting Strategies of Peace since Versailles.* (Hamden, CT, Archon Books, 1963 reprint), p. 204.

26   Barnett, *Collapse*, pp. 186–96, 201–5, 211, 232–3; and Orde, *Great Britain*, p. 164.

27   Charles Oman, *The Unfortunate Colonel Despard and Other Studies* (London, Arnold, 1922), p. 178.

28   Barnett, *Collapse*, pp. 159–68, 186.

29   W. Deist, M. Messerschmidt, H-E. Volkmann and W. Wette, *Germany and the Second World War: Vol. I, The Build-up of German Aggression* (Oxford, Clarendon Press, 1990), pp. 33, 77–9.

30   F. L. Carsten, *Britain and the Weimar Republic* (London, Batsford, 1984), pp. 236–7.

31   G. M. Gathorne-Hardy, *A Short History of International Affairs 1920 to 1934* (London, Oxford University Press, 1934), p. 21.

32   Elizabeth Wiskemann, *Prologue to War* (London, Constable, 1939), pp. 180–1.

33   Nicole Jordan, *The Popular Front and Central Europe: The Dilemmas*

of French Impotence, 1918–1940 (Cambridge, Cambridge University Press, 1992), pp. 7–8, 13, 17.

34 See Douglas Johnson 'The Locarno Treaties' in Neville Waites (ed.), *Troubled Neighbours: Franco-British Relations in the Twentieth Century* (London, Weidenfeld & Nicolson, 1971), pp. 111–12, for a typical expression.

35 A. Lentin, 'Decline and fall of the Versailles settlement', *Diplomacy and Statecraft*, 4:2 (1993), 359–75.

36 Harvey Leonard Dyck, *Weimar Germany and Soviet Russia 1926–1933* (London, Chatto & Windus, 1966), p. 29.

37 Jon Jacobson, 'Is there a new international history of the 1920s?', *American Historical Review*, 88:3 (1983), pp. 627–9.

38 Marshall M. Lee and Wolfgang Michalka, *German Foreign Policy 1917–1933: Continuity or Break?* (Leamington Spa, Berg, 1987), pp. 36–40.

39 Kees van der Pijl, *The Making of an Atlantic Ruling Class* (London, Verso, 1984), p. 71.

40 David G. Williamson, *The British in Germany 1918–1930* (Oxford, Berg, 1991), p. 25.

41 Jordan, *Popular Front*, p. 10.

42 Jacobson, 'Is there?', pp. 639–40.

43 Jon Jacobson, *Locarno Diplomacy: Germany and the West 1925–1929* (Princeton, NJ, Princeton University Press, 1972), Part one.

44 Barnett, *Collapse,* p. 332.

45 Jacobson, 'Is there?', pp. 634–5; van des Pijl, *The Making,* pp. 62–3; and Lee and Michalka, *German Foreign Policy,* pp. 68–71.

46 Johnson in Waites (ed.), *Troubled,* p. 109.

47 Williamson, *British in Germany,* pp. 193–8, 247.

48 Jacobson, *Locarno Diplomacy,* p. 127.

49 Michael Laffan (ed.), *The Burden of German History 1919–45* (London, Methuen, 1989), p. 85; Lee and Michalka, *German Foreign Policy,* pp. 74–80, 126; but see also Deist et al: *Germany and the Second World War,* pp. 54–7 and 557, for the view that Stresemann retained immense annexationist aims.

50 Williamson, *British in Germany,* pp. 287, 300–1, 347–8.

51 Jacobson, *Locarno Diplomacy*; and Jon Jacobson and J. T. Walker, 'The impulse for a Franco-German entente: the origins of the Thoiry conference, 1926', *Journal of Contemporary History*, 10:1 (1975), 157–81.

52 Elliot R. Goodman, *The Soviet Design for a World State* (New York, Columbia University Press, 1960), pp. 25–33, 130–3, 293–9, 303–8.

53 Josef Korbel, *Poland between East and West: Soviet and German Diplomacy toward Poland, 1919–1933* (Princeton, NJ, Princeton University Press, 1963), p. 114.

54 Lee and Michalka, *German Foreign Policy*, pp. 52–4, 58–9.
55 Walter Laqueur, *Russia and Germany: A Century of Conflict* (London, Weidenfeld & Nicolson, 1965), p. 129.
56 Louis Fischer, *The Soviets in World Affairs, 1917–1929* (New York, Vintage Books, 1960), p. 323.
57 Pierre Renouvin, *Histoire des Relations Internationales: VII; Les Crises du XXe Siècle. I, de 1914 à 1929* (Paris, Hachette, 1957), p. 270.
58 Lionel Kochan, *The Struggle for Germany 1914–1945* (Edinburgh, Edinburgh University Press, 1963), p. 42; see also Orde, *Great Britain*, pp. 124–30.
59 Dyck, *Weimar Germany*, pp. 13–19.
60 Jacobson, *Locarno Diplomacy*, p. 80; Gabriel Gorodetsky, *The Precarious Truce: Anglo-Soviet Relations 1924–27* (Cambridge, Cambridge University Press, 1977), pp. 134–5.
61 See for example, Dyck, *Weimar Germany*, p. 118.
62 William Henry Chamberlin, *Russia's Iron Age* (London, Duckworth, 1935), pp. 205–6, 209–10, 221.
63 Raymond J. Sontag, *A Broken World 1919–1939* (New York, Harper, 1971), p. 36.
64 Chamberlin, *Iron Age,* p. 374.
65 Gorodetsky, *Precarious Truce*, p. 249.
66 A. J. P. Taylor, *The Troublemakers: Dissent over Foreign Policy 1792–1939* (London, Hamish Hamilton, 1957), pp. 161–4, 174–7.
67 Teddy J. Uldricks, *Diplomacy and Ideology: The Origins of Soviet Foreign Relations, 1917–1930* (London, Sage, 1979), pp. 87–90.
68 Goodman, *Soviet Design*, p. 174.
69 Lord Vansittart, *The Mist Procession* (London, Hutchinson, 1958), pp. 455–6.

CHAPTER TWO

HITLERISM AND THE
DEPRESSION YEARS

In 1925 the State Secretary at the German foreign ministry, Carl von Schubert, a man gifted with a 'shrewd understanding of the subtleties of Germany's postwar situation',[1] dismissed Hitler to a British colleague with the comment 'what an idiot'.[2] About the same time the British ambassador in Berlin noted with satisfaction that Hitler was 'fading into oblivion'.[3] Hitler was in fact the last and most disastrous in a line of exponents of 'irrational revolutionary reaction' in German history.[4] It is necessary to examine his ideology and the process by which the impersonal circumstances of Germany in the early 1930s and the all too personal mistakes of politicians such as Heinrich Bruning, Chancellor from 1930 to 1932 who thought that he could use Hitler for his cherished aim of restoring the monarchy,[5] combined to bring this man to the headship of the German government in January 1933. His rise to be absolute, unquestioned autocrat in the Nazi Party had been slow. Many Nazis in the 1920s had been reluctant to call him 'Fuhrer' and had preferred 'Heil Deutschland' to 'Heil Hitler'.[6] Hitler himself initially saw his role with relative modesty as a kind of revolutionary ayatollah, or 'drummer' to use his own word, who would provide ideological guidance while the 'Republic of Versailles' as he called Weimar was overthrown and in the purified Germany that would follow, while leaving the detailed work of government to others. This reflected both a certain early modesty and his understanding of politics as, primarily, a matter of propaganda.[7] It took his successful performance in the 1930 Reichstag election campaign to convince him that he could and should be the all-powerful leader in policy as well as ideology. Most party members acquiesced if only because they realised that they would fall into hopeless squabbling among themselves if they did not recognise an omnipotent leader who could only be Hitler.[8]

Ideology was of supreme and transcendent importance in Nazism. It was a 'composite ideology'[9] in which previously separate and exclusive varieties of German imperialist ambition and thought, including *Lebensraum* territorial expansion to the east and *Weltpolitik* or a position of power for Germany in almost every part of the world, were combined, to be achieved in stages.[10] The stage in the middle – between power in Germany and central Europe and *Weltpolitik* – that of *Lebensraum*, to be achieved mainly at the expense of the Soviet Union, was the most cherished one to Hitler. His pre-1914 political inspiration owed much to observation of ethnic conflict between Austrian-Germans and Czech Slavs in the Habsburg Monarchy in which the former were obsessed with race and living space as they competed with the latter to be the largest ethnic group in various areas. 'Hitler raised the politics of the industrial slums of northern Bohemia to a European level.'[11] *Lebensraum* also seemed to Hitler to be likely to be easily accomplished if only Russia could be isolated, because he thought that Russia was a country in decay under its racially and ideologically inferior 'Jewish-Bolshevik' rulers. He also believed *Lebensraum* to be necessary because only by colonisation and expansion could the Germans retain their racial superiority and only in that way could Germany's problem of having too little living space for its population be solved.[12] This was despite the birth rate in Germany having fallen by one third between 1923 and 1933, but that was of no more interest to Hitler than the fact that many of the lands that he sought to acquire for Germany were suffering from rural overpopulation.

The Nazi *Weltpolitik* programme was more ambitious than anything contemplated by any sane person in Wilhelmine Germany before it collapsed in 1918 because it would be nothing less than some form of German world domination. Hitler seems to have been uncertain about its precise nature: somewhere between British world power at its nineteenth century peak and the absolute power of a new Roman empire.[13] By 1938–39 he was undoubtedly leaning towards the latter, if only to provide security for a Europe in which only Germany would be fully independent, though some other countries would be allowed degrees of freedom dictated by Nazi calculation of their racial value.[14] In any case, to speak of finite Nazi aims is somewhat misleading. Nazism believed in struggle as an end in itself.

Hitler had much in common with those German intellectual nihilists in the Weimar Republic who advocated war as an end in itself.[15] At the height of their victories in the early part of the Second World War, when there was least need for concealment, the indoctrination programme for the Hitler Youth included no concrete list of 'war aims' but stressed instead the inevitability of 'eternal struggle'.[16] In the words of the late Timothy Mason: 'To put it another way, a Third Reich "at peace" is an unimaginable contradiction in terms.'[17]

Hitler's attitudes to the other European great powers can be summarised briefly. Italy was racially suspect and the absence of anti-Semitism from the policies of the fascist regime strengthened that suspicion. Even so, Italy was worth having as an ally, and to the extent of not demanding the return of the South Tyrol with its ethnic German population that had been detached from Austria in 1919, though in that Hitler merely continued a Weimar policy of sacrificing the South Tyrolese.[18] France was most probably a foe which would have to be crushed before Germany turned eastwards, because it had shown itself to be an inveterate enemy of Germany, intent on annexing the Rhineland and retaining it 'by keeping Germany broken up and in ruins' as Hitler put it in *Mein Kampf*; because, in Nazi mythology, its revolution of 1789 had initiated a Jewish bid for world domination that was still going on; and because it had allowed black people to gain a foothold in Europe.[19] Britain was a desirable ally in the short and medium term, during which there appeared to be no irreconcilable differences. Hitler interpreted the relatively pro-German strain in British foreign policy from the time of the French occupation of the Ruhr to traditional Anglo-French rivalry and, with a characteristic lapse into the irrational, to a waning of Jewish influences in Britain. The belief that those influences were becoming ever stronger in the United States and were increasingly manipulating American policy turned Hitler's attitude to that country into one bordering on total contempt.[20] A book published in Leipzig in 1935 was to set the tone for Nazi descriptions of the United States by referring to it as 'the most primitive and shallow of European civilisations'.[21] Hitler had to abandon some ideas in the light of their sheer unreality: most notably in this context, his acceptance by 1937 that Britain would not become his ally, which he could only attribute to 'hate'.[22] Hitler was somewhat unusual on the German radical right in not being an Anglophobe almost by nature,[23] but the British were, even if they had acted only from the most selfish motives, right to reject his overtures. In the ultimate *Weltpolitik* stage of the Hitlerian programme conflict would have been inevitable with Britain, the United States and even Japan, not because of any ill-feeling towards them, or at least not towards Britain, but simply because such conflict was in the nature of things in the Nazi view of the world.

Hitler had no 'blueprint' for implementing his ideas, but was to justify von Schubert's description of him as an idiot (*Naar*) in the sense that he 'ignored sober calculations of national interest in order to put his manic ideas into practice',[24] to say nothing of the sheer bestiality of his mindset and aims. In this context, it is important that those historians who have tried to argue that Nazi foreign policy was a product of the way in which the Nazi regime functioned and not a result of Hitler consciously seeking to realise his intentions have not persuaded many of their colleagues of their thesis.[25] What they have usefully done is to divert some attention from Hitler to German society in relation to foreign policy during the Third Reich. Between 1933 and 1939 most Germans gave broad approval to the unfolding of Hitler's foreign policy aims as they (very imperfectly) understood them,[26] that is in terms of the bloodless achievement of limited objectives. What is more difficult to comprehend is that this approval was also given by some Germans who were both well educated and decent. Historians may still share the distress and bewilderment of those British intellectuals in the 1930s whose German friends found much to admire in Hitler's domestic and foreign policies.[27]

German and international history between 1929 and 1933 contained a number of features relevant to this study of war origins. One was the rise of an ultra nationalist party, the Nazis, that tried studiously to avoid saying a word in public about war. Another was a democratic German republic whose foreign policy became so truculent that the surviving democracies could regard the ultimate Nazi advent to power as potentially a blessed relief. The year 1930 was a breakthrough year for the Nazi Party. Its share of the vote in Reichstag elections was 6.4 million compared with only 800,000 in the previous elections in 1928. However, the essential feature of a breakthrough is that it can only be achieved by a movement that has already built up much force, and, in explaining that, the importance of the previous war cannot be stressed too much. The bitterness of German defeat in November 1918 combined with sweet memories of the euphoria that accompanied the outbreak of war in August 1914 to give birth to a rightwing populist nationalism not deferential to traditional authority. (This helps to account for the ease with which monarchy was abolished in Germany: the left had always been republican; the new right regarded monarchy as an anachronism.) Hitler rode on this wave. His public meetings after he was released from prison in 1925 were consistently packed to capacity. Many who would not yet vote for him were already prepared to listen to a politician who 'gave sharp political definition to imprecisely held affinities and frustrated expectations'.[28] The Nazis made big electoral strides between their dismal Reichstag performance in 1928 and even the start of economic problems in local elections. This was achieved by stressing domestic and mostly non-racist themes. War and *Lebensraum* expansion were not mentioned in public at all. The emphasis was on saving Germany itself from communism and socialism. The Nazis relied heavily on 'negative campaigning' in which their opponents were vilified and yet, between 1928 and 1932, only 5 per cent of Nazi electoral posters attacked Jews and none advocated war.[29] This compared favourably with the German communists' unrestrained advocacy of revolutionary violence with its unconcealed aim of unleashing a red terror.[30] The result was that the Nazis' opponents issued very few warnings to German voters that voting for Hitler meant voting for war. There were one or two exceptions, most notably the future West German president, Theodor Heuss, but most democratic German politicians simply did not know how seriously to treat the war and *Lebensraum* ideas expounded in *Mein Kampf* and preferred to concentrate on the more immediate issue of the threat that Nazism posed to German democracy.[31] The electorate in late Weimar Germany was denied the opportunity to vote, in any meaningful sense, on whether it wanted war and *Lebensraum* expansion.

The Nazi concentration on domestic politics owed something to the fact that, from a nationalist standpoint, it would not have been easy to criticise late Weimar foreign policy. If the second half of the 1920s was a time when there was a tendency 'to regard goodwill as an adequate substitute for specific commitments',[32] then at least there was some goodwill present. This changed with the spread to Europe of the economic collapse that began in New York in October 1929. Faced with a slump in the economy for which they had no quick or painless remedies, successive German governments turned to foreign policy for victories. Personalities were important. Bruning, Chancellor from 1930 to 1932, was impatient for big foreign policy gains (and also pursued deflationary policies that worsened unemployment and, consequently, increased support for the anti-democratic parties). Another key change in personnel was the replacement as State Secretary at the foreign ministry of von Schubert by the crudely nationalistic Bernhard Wilhelm von Bulow who was to retain the job under the Nazis until his death in 1936. Germany at the start of the 1930s exhibited the paradox that the treaty of Versailles was no longer such an aching wound but also that there was less revulsion than ever about resorting to threatened or actual force to undo it if circumstances were favourable.[33]

Under Bruning, besides demands for treaty revision, the army budget was fully protected, and there was expansion of the navy with a programme of building 'pocket battleships' that kept within the letter, though hardly the spirit, of the peace treaty. Some Western attention may have been deflected from this by the fact that Britain and France were deadlocked in an argument over the size of their navies.[34] Even so, there was some alarm. In 1931 the British Prime Minister, Ramsay MacDonald (who in 1928, when Leader of the Opposition, had been the first foreign statesman to address the Reichstag) initiated all-party discussions that agreed that there should be no further cuts in British defence spending except as part of international agreements.[35] Actual increases in the almost minute level of defence spending were a different matter. In 1932 the three most powerful officials serving the government, Warren Fisher (Treasury), Maurice Hankey (Cabinet Secretariat) and Robert Vansittart (Foreign Office), urged the Royal Air Force chiefs to apply for an additional twenty-five squadrons, but they only dared to request five, though they did join with the other service chiefs to warn of Britain's complete military impotence to intervene on the continent of Europe.[36] British politicians were actually fixated on air power and were beginning to have a vision of the Royal Air Force as the strongest in the world.[37] This might provide a shield behind which problems in which Britain was not directly involved could be ignored. One prerequisite would be the ending of the ten year rule on defence spending. This was done in 1932 but in circumstances that illustrated that it might be difficult for Britain stay clear of conflicts in distant places – a Japanese threat to the International Settlement at Shanghai.

In 1932 an international conference on disarmament met at Geneva under the chairmanship of a former British Foreign Secretary, Arthur

Henderson. It had a doomed air from the start. It was unable even to agree on statistics for existing numbers of military personnel and armaments. This produced a Gallic witticism from French Prime Minister Edouard Herriot that the verb 'to disarm' was the most irregular of all because it was conjugated only in the future tense and used only in the second person.[38] Elsewhere, there seemed to be more progress on the economic front. War debt and reparation payments were suspended by the wartime allies, by the United States in the Hoover moratorium and by Germany in the spring of 1931, and in December the British cabinet resolved that there should be a British initiative for a permanent 'all-round settlement in reparations and disarmament'. France was not particularly responsive and early in the new year moved troops to its border with Germany after the Germans had clumsily 'leaked' information to Britain that it would never resume reparations payments. This unfortunately coincided with a resolution by the United States Congress that the Hoover moratorium was to be precisely that: strictly temporary.[39]

For Britain this initiative, including a readiness to make concessions to Germany on the agreed levels to which its military and naval establishments might rise,[40] involved an act of faith because by that time suspicions of Weimar intentions ran deep.[41] They were justified. Under Bruning and his successors, the last two Weimar Chancellors, German foreign policy alternated between visions of a pact with the Soviet Union under which Poland would be erased from the map, and an economic link-up with France in which Germany would be dominant. A goal of economic domination in East Central Europe remained constant. In this way the Weimar Republic between 1930 and 1933 provided Hitler with a perfect springboard not for his ultimate aims, a *Lebensraum* empire in Russia and then some form of German world domination, but for the more limited aims that he was to pursue before the outbreak of war.[42] In June 1932 Britain and, with ill-grace, France,[43] agreed to the effective abandonment of reparations, and also resolved that they would simply not resume debt payments to the United States since agreement with the United States was manifestly impossible. After gaining what amounted to the end of its reparations obligations at a conference at Lausanne, at the end of the summer, Germany temporarily withdrew from the disarmament conference when it reconvened, causing the British ambassador in Berlin to speculate on what the Germans thought that they could achieve by such a display of boorish nastiness.[44] Germany did actually obtain from the Western powers an arms offer of 'equality of rights in a system which would provide security for all nations'.[45] This was the sort of verbiage under which they could make sweeping claims, as Ramsay MacDonald realised while hoping that major concessions would bring Germany back to the path of 'trust and cooperation'.[46] The British and French awareness of how far the Weimar Republic had strayed from that path in its last years can hardly be exaggerated as a factor in explaining the element of complacency in their initial responses to the Nazi regime. It would have had to behave very badly to outdo Weimar.

If Hitler was even more ungracious to the last Weimar rulers than they had been to the western powers, even to the point of murdering some of them in the Long Knives massacre in 1934, he could plead that the basis for Nazi aims that they had bequeathed to him was, even if reasonable in the purely foreign policy field, flawed in the matter of armaments. On taking office he ordered military spending to rise to 1900 million marks from 800 million in 1932, but the former figure was still only 3 per cent of national income.[47] In 1931 the German army command had advised the government that, in the event of war with Poland, the most that it would be able to do offensively would be to occupy the narrow coastal plain of the 'Polish Corridor' that separated East Prussia from the rest of the Reich.[48] The army's first rearmament plan in December 1933 envisaged an army of 300,000 men, a reasonable defensive force for a country the size of Germany.[49] In rearmament the new Nazi Germany had a very long way indeed to travel. To begin with, it had to contrive to present arms inequality as the Reich's main grievance, while fending off any proposals to give it equality with the other great powers and no more. Hitler realised the need for patience and cunning in dealing with the outside world, but reaffirmed to military chiefs at a meeting on 3 February 1933 that he would not rest until he had achieved 'the conquest and ruthless Germanisation of new living space in the east'.[50] In this game of disguising intentions, it was not difficult for Hitler to improve on his immediate predecessors. Since the departure of Stresemann and von Schubert German diplomacy had shown all the finesse of a herd of trampling elephants. An example of how Hitler could be a Bismarck in comparison with them is provided by German–Soviet relations. The Fuhrer's policy towards Russia was to be unambiguously cold for several years, to be followed by an equally unambiguous overture when he felt that this was required in

1939. By contrast, late Weimar could only fumble. When Foreign Minister Litvinov visited Berlin a few weeks before the fall of the republic, the German government assured him of their goodwill, which was genuine in the case of the Chancellor, Kurt von Schleicher,[51] but kept him from seeing anyone else who mattered by taking him from one Berlin cinema to another.[52] What Litvinov can have made of that is not recorded.

Notes

1 Marshall M. Lee and Wolfgang Michalka, *German Foreign Policy 1919–1933: Continuity or Break?* (Leamington Spa, Berg, 1987), p. 110.

2 Patrick Howarth, *Intelligence Chief Extraordinary: The Life of the Ninth Duke of Portland* (London, The Bodley Head, 1986), p. 67.

3 Lord D'Abernon, *An Ambassador of Peace* (London, Hodder & Stoughton, 1929), vol. I, p. 52.

4 Rohan D'O. Butler, *The Roots of National Socialism 1783–1933* (London, Faber, 1941), p. 244.

5 Robert G. L. Waite, *The Psychopathic God: Adolf Hitler* (London, Basis Books, 1977), pp. 345–6.

6 Otto Strasser, *Hitler et moi* (Paris, Grasset, 1940), pp. 115, 140.

7 D. Aigner 'Hitler's ultimate aims – a programme of world domination?' in H. W. Koch (ed.), *Aspects of the Third Reich* (London, Macmillan, 1985), p. 260; and Ian Kershaw, *Hitler 1889–1936: Hubris* (London, Penguin Press, 1998), pp. 169–70.

8 William Carr, *Hitler: A Study in Personality and Politics* (London, Arnold, 1978), pp. 19–22, 28; Kershaw, *Hitler*, pp. 260–1; see also Strasser, *Hitler et moi*, pp. 15, 35.

9 Woodruff D. Smith, *The Ideological Origins of Nazi Imperialism* (New York, Oxford University Press, 1986), p. 253.

10 *Ibid.*, especially chapter 10.

11 Z. A. B. Zeman, *Pursued by a Bear: The Making of Eastern Europe* (London, Chatto & Windus, 1989), p. 107.

12 William Carr, *Arms, Autarky and Aggression: A Study in German Foreign Policy: 1933–1939* (London, Arnold, 1972), pp. 11–15; Gerhard L. Weinberg, *The Foreign Policy of Hitler's Germany: Diplomatic Revolution in Europe, 1933–36* (Chicago, IL, University of Chicago Press, 1970), pp. 6–7, 12–13, 310; Geoffrey Stoakes 'The evolution of Hitler's ideas on foreign policy, 1919–1925' in Peter Stachura (ed.), *The Shaping of the Nazi State* (London, Croom Helm, 1978), pp. 23–5, 38–41; Geoffrey Stoakes, *Hitler and the Quest for World Dominion* (Leamington Spa, Berg, 1986), pp. 110–39.

13 Stoakes, *Hitler*, pp. 165–70; Ian Kershaw, *The Nazi Dictatorship* (London, Arnold, 1985), pp. 126–8.

14 E. M. Robertson 'Hitler's planning for war and the response of the great powers' in Koch (ed.), *Aspects*, pp. 198–200; Robert Edwin Herzstein, *When Nazi Dreams Come True* (London, Abacus, 1982), pp. 21–3.

15 W. Deist, M. Messerschmidt, H-E. Volkmann and W. Wette; *Germany and the Second World War: Vol. I, The Build-up of German Aggression*, (Oxford, Clarendon Press, 1990), pp. 35–7.

16 Aigner in Koch (ed.), *Aspects*, pp. 264–5.

17 Thomas Childers and Jane Caplan (eds), *Reevaluating the Third Reich* (New York, Holmes & Meier, 1993), p. 180.

18 Stoakes, *Hitler*, pp. 103–10; Weinberg, *Foreign Policy* pp. 17–18; G. M. Gathorne Hardy, *A Short History of International Affairs 1920 to 1934* (London, Oxford University Press, 1934), pp. 161–2.

19 Weinberg, *Foreign Policy*, pp. 4–5, 14–17; Stoakes, *Hitler* p. 97.

20 Stoakes in Stachura (ed.), *Shaping*, pp. 23–35; Stoakes, *Hitler*, pp. 90–103; Weinberg, *Foreign Policy*, pp. 21–2; Strasser, *Hitler et moi*, pp. 125, 225–6; Andreas Hillgruber, 'England's place in Hitler's plans for world dominion', *Journal of Contemporary History*, 9:1 (1974), 5–22.

21 Max Weinreich, *Hitler's Professors* (New Haven, CT, Yale University Press, 1999 edn.), p. 101.

22 John Hiden and John Farquharson, *Explaining Hitler's Germany: Historians and the Third Reich* (London, Batsford, 1989), pp. 118–21.

23 Smith, *Ideological Origins*, pp. 245–7.

24 Norman Rich 'Hitler's foreign policy' in Gordon Martel (ed.), *The Origins of the Second World War Reconsidered: The A. J. P. Taylor Debate After Twenty-five Years* (London, Allen & Unwin, 1986), p. 124.

25 Hiden and Farquharson (eds.), *Explaining*, chapter 5.

26 Ian Kershaw, *The 'Hitler Myth': Image and Reality in the Third Reich* (Oxford, Oxford University Press, 1987).

27 Shiela Grant Duff, *The Parting of the Ways: A Personal Account of the Thirties* (London, Peter Owen, 1982) is a particularly evocative Anglo-German memoir.

28 Peter Fritzche, *Germans into Nazis* (Cambridge, MA, Harvard University Press, 1998), p. 190.

29 Donny Gluckstein, *The Nazis, Capitalism and the Working Class* (London, Bookmarks, 1999), p. 76.

30 Deist et al., *Germany and the Second World War*, pp. 76n, 83–7.

31 *Ibid.*, pp. 22, 67–9, 81–2.

32 W. Norton Medlicott, *British Foreign Policy since Versailles 1919–*

63 (London, Methuen, 1968), p. 74.

33 Eberhard Kolb, *The Weimar Republic* (London, Unwin Hyman, 1988), p. 170; Pierre Renouvin, *Histoire des Relations Internationales: VII, Les Crises du XXe Siècle. I, de 1914 à 1929* (Paris, Hachette, 1957), pp. 226–9, 340, 350–1; Deist et al., *Germany and the Second World War*, p. 579.

34 David Carlton, *MacDonald versus Henderson: The Foreign Policy of the Second Labour Government* (London, Macmillan, 1970), pp. 133–43.

35 Viscount Templewood, *Nine Troubled Years* (London, Collins, 1954), pp. 117–19.

36 Lord Vansittart, *The Mist Procession* (London, Hutchinson, 1958), p. 443; and Correlli Barnett, *The Collapse of British Power* (Gloucester, Sutton, 1984), pp. 337, 342–3.

37 Dick Richardson 'The Geneva disarmament conference, 1932–34' in Dick Richardson and Glyn Stone (eds.), *Decisions and Diplomacy: Essays in Twentieth Century International History* (London, Routledge, 1994), chapter 3.

38 Renouvin, *Crises*, p. 346; John F. Naylor, *Labour's International Policy* (London, Weidenfeld & Nicolson, 1969), p. 36.

39 Neville Waites 'The Depression years' in Neville Waites (ed.), *Troubled Neighbours: Franco-British Relations in the Twentieth Century* (London, Weidenfeld & Nicolson, 1971), pp. 135–6.

40 Martin Gilbert, *The Roots of Appeasement* (London, Weidenfeld & Nicolson, 1966), pp. 132–3.

41 John Jacobson, *Locarno Diplomacy: Germany and the West, 1925–1929* (Princeton, NJ, Princeton University Press, 1972), pp. 212–14, 245–6, 293.

42 Lee and Michalka, *German Foreign Policy*, pp. 130–48, 156.

43 John Wheeler-Bennett, *Knaves, Fools and Heroes* (London, Macmillan, 1974), p. 47.

44 Martin Gilbert, *Sir Horace Humbold* (London, Heinemann, 1973), pp. 331–2.

45 Lee and Michalka, *German Foreign Policy*, p. 132.

46 Waites, *Troubled,* p. 142.

47 Carr, *Arms*, p. 27.

48 Donald Cameron Watt, *Too Serious A Business: European Armed Forces and the Approach to the Second World War* (London, Temple Smith, 1975), pp. 103–4.

49 Wilhelm Deist, *The Wehrmacht and German Rearmament* (London, Macmillan, 1981), p. viii.

50 *Ibid.,* p. 105.

51 Harvey Leondard Dyck, *Weimar Germany and Soviet Russia, 1926–*

1933 (London, Chatto & Windus, 1966), pp. 254–5.

52   Armand Bérard, *Au Temps du Danger Allemand: un Ambassadeur se Souvient* (Paris, Plon, 1976), p. 215.

CHAPTER THREE

GERMAN WAR PREPARATIONS: AN OVERVIEW

From the moment he came to power Hitler's overriding aim was to prepare Germany for war, no matter how uncertain he was about the exact form war would take. The preparations were psychological (to inculcate the German people with a warrior spirit), economic and military, of which the last was the most important. Coercion and the use of terror against opponents were, after the brutalities of the initial 'seizure of power' period, regarded as almost a last resort, partly because of the difficulty of concealing them from the outside world. Thus the number of inmates in the concentration camps fell to only 10,000 in the winter of 1936–37 and some of those were petty criminal or workshy types.[1] The Nazi propaganda machine under Goebbels had to tread warily because of the necessity that propaganda addressed to the domestic audience was not openly contradictory to propaganda addressed to the outside world, which constantly trumpeted Germany's peaceful intentions, though also, from 1936, with an undertone that Germany was not to be trifled with now that it had again become strong. Propaganda for the domestic audience combined protestations of peaceful intentions with an admixture of militarism by 'preaching old-fashioned heroic and authoritarian ideals in somewhat general, emotional terms, avoiding the mention of specific targets of aggression'.[2]

Even more important was the instilling of the 'national community' concept which stressed national solidarity, the transcendent importance of the simple fact of being German and the infallibility of the Fuhrer's decisions, including, by implication, ones for war. How successful this was can never be fully known. All that can be said with confidence is that it was not a complete failure and that it was particularly successful with youth. German boys and young men, compulsorily in the Hitler Youth from the ages of fourteen to eighteen, were given a carefully measured amount of political and racist-militarist indoctrination in a general setting of apolitical 'campfire romanticism'.[3] There were, of course, elements in German youth who required restraint rather than persuasion. These included the organisations of Nazi university students who, on a night in May 1933, publicly burnt books, some of them by their own recently dismissed Jewish professors, at university towns across Germany, to the mild embarrassment of Goebbels.[4] Hitler's difficulties with public opinion will be discussed further in later chapters.

Nazi economic policy had two main aims: the first was to make Germany as self-sufficient as possible – the concept of autarky; while the second was to maximise the share of the national wealth that could be devoted to rearmament without unduly depressing the German standard of living. Before attaining power, Hitler ruled out in advance any policy of squeezing living standards that he feared might lead to 'attempts at subversion'.[5] It proved possible to make great progress with both these objectives. After what had happened on Wall Street in October 1929 there was a general yearning in Germany in the early 1930s to make the country independent of the vagaries of the New York Stock Exchange. There was widespread support for the idea of Germany acquiring a semi-exclusive economic sphere in which the food and raw material exports of the 'lesser' members would be exchanged for German manufactured goods. Such links were cultivated with considerable success by Germany after 1933 in its trade relations with many Central and East European countries and could be presented as being no more questionable than the British empire economic bloc, that of the United States in the Western Hemisphere and the apparently emerging Japanese economic sphere in China. That was sufficient during most of the 1930s and was a useful waystation to the later goal of *Lebensraum*, about which hints were dropped for internal consumption as the Third Reich grew stronger. In 1939 one Nazi theoretician wrote: 'The nation's manifestation of life emerges most conspicuously from the flexibility of the living space boundary which ... by its nature is a genuine boundary of movement.'[6] By then there were many in Germany who understood what this apparent semi-gibberish meant, while few in the outside world, including the Soviet leadership in Moscow, were likely to comprehend. Domestically, a relatively painless shift in resources from consumption to investment in rearmament was achieved by a variety of policies, including prices for basic foods that were often lower than in the 1920s. This inevitably meant real depression of farm incomes. Before 1933 many rural areas had voted massively for the Nazis; after 1933 they were rewarded with cuts in income. The Nazis calculated that rural discontent could be dealt with more easily than urban unrest.

Nearly 90 per cent of investment into the German economy even in the early Nazi years from 1933 to 1936 went into rearmament. Most of it was absorbed directly into armaments production; the rest went into road building and other civil engineering projects with direct military significance.[7] Such concentration could only be achieved by some enfeeblement of the civilian and export producing economy, in particular by starving it of imports so that foreign exchange could be spent on purchasing raw materials for rearmament. For instance, the average annual importation of foodstuffs for farm animals had been 734,000 tonnes in 1931–33, in 1934 this fell abruptly to 144,000 tonnes.[8] It was the realisation that such distortions were resulting in unsustainable burdens on the economy that caused Hitler in the late summer of 1936 to decide on a four year plan of which more will be related later. Here it is enough to state that it practically obliged Germany to resort to war within that four year period to acquire foreign territory to exploit with few of the restraints that the Nazis observed in the treatment of their own *Volk*. The hope was that these early wars would be against weak opponents who could easily be crushed.

It soon became clear that the rearmament effort could not be sustained for a period of time anything like as long as four years. Within a year, by the summer of 1937, Germany had few foreign currency reserves left to pay for imports that could not be obtained by barter. Yet it was decided to continue spending until there was nothing left. That stage had very nearly been reached by early 1938 so that the acquisition of foreign territory in Austria and Czechoslovakia became an imperative necessity, simply to provide resources with which the four year plan could be continued for a little longer. The takeover of those countries still left Germany living economically from hand to mouth. In September 1939 its gold and foreign currency reserves were RM 500 million which was barely one seventieth the combined reserves of the British Commonwealth and France.[9]

Under the four year plan the purpose of rearmament expenditure was to create, from an army of only 100,000 men in 1933, one of 3.6

million men by October 1940, though with probably no more than one third the desirable number of officers. This might be compared with the German army of 1914 of 2.15 million men which had been built up during four decades of uninterrupted development.[10] Besides the army, there were, of course, also the navy and the air force. No machinery was set up for coordination between this inflated army and those other two services which were also being massively expanded other than Hitler himself in his capacity, from February 1938, as supreme commander of the armed forces. Not willing to trust the leadership of the armed forces until some distant day when senior officers would have been trained in the Hitler Youth, he encouraged the normal tendency of the three services to squabble with one another and discouraged independent thought, except of a technical sort within an officer's designated area of competence. Long before 1939 the senior commanders accepted this limitation and, in the case of the army, the setting up of a separate SS army.[11] The result of all this was that in September 1939 Germany had armed forces that were vast and formidable but which also had serious flaws.

Turning to foreign policy, for five years Hitler used the traditional machinery of German foreign policy to pursue what was initially a more moderate version of the foreign policy of the Weimar Republic during its later years. The services of the last Weimar Foreign Minister, Constantin von Neurath, were retained in that role until as late as 1938, though at first with the supreme irony that Hitler had considerable difficulty in impressing on von Neurath that he was being too flattering in thinking that the mere fact that Hitler had become Chancellor meant that the time was ripe for showdowns with France and Poland. These were traditional enemies and it suited Hitler's purposes admirably that Germany should continue for a few years to be represented by professional diplomats who had no real understanding of the fact that German foreign policy was now fundamentally determined by racial ideology. The nazification of the Foreign Ministry only really began after Hitler appointed a disciple, Joachim von Ribbentrop, to replace von Neurath in 1938, four years after Ribbentrop's earlier appointment as 'Disarmament Commissioner'.[12] Even after Ribbentrop became Foreign Minister, his top official, the State Secretary, was Ernst von Weizsacker, a cautious conservative who was to record the day on which the Munich agreement was signed as the happiest of his life because it appeared to have saved Germany from a war that he was convinced it could not win.[13]

Hitler was alarmed by the chorus of foreign disapproval that greeted his advent to power. One of the strongest denunciations was made in the British parliament in April 1933 by Austen Chamberlain, a former Foreign Secretary and half brother of the future Prime Minister Neville Chamberlain. He argued against concessions to a Germany in which, 'It is a crime to be in favour of peace and a crime to be a Jew ... That is not a Germany to which Europe can afford to give equality.'[14] This was a reference to equality in armaments, and Hitler responded to the chorus by embarking on a campaign, which was to be as sustained as it was mendacious, to present himself as a man of peace. He cancelled his initial decision to leave the disarmament conference in Geneva. Then British Prime Minister Ramsay MacDonald proposed a plan under which Germany would have been allowed limited rearmament: a doubling of its army to 200,000 men and a small air force.[15] Hitler's response was two-fold with the aim of buying time while Germany rearmed to the maximum extent of its physical capacity. It consisted of peaceful protestations and spurious offers, and hindsight must not be allowed to obscure the fact that there were many in the democracies who were ready to give genuine credence to both. In a speech in May 1933 he denounced war as utterly evil and declared that he would 'never attempt to conquer foreigners who hate us by a process which requires that we sacrifice millions who are dear to us and whom we love, on the field of battle'.[16] The offer on this occasion was a plan under which decisions on arms equality for Germany would be postponed for five years, coupled with an immediate renunciation of the use of offensive weapons under any circumstances.[17]

When Hitler did take Germany out of the conference and also out of the League of Nations, in October 1933, his government mounted an elaborate propaganda offensive in which it claimed that the step was being taken more in sorrow than in anger and that Germany would return when France in particular was willing to treat it as an equal.[18] This was given some similitude of justification by the fact that other countries continued to show disdain for the new German regime. Foreign visitors of high rank could not be attracted – the first was the Foreign Minister of Hungary in June 1933, though only unofficially. In Italy Mussolini's initially unfavourable reaction to the new rightwing dictatorship north of the Alps was expressed in his offer of temporary refuge to fleeing German Jews. The Nazi media, especially in Bavaria, responded and made matters worse by drawing explicit attention to the racial inferiority of Italians in National Socialist ideology.[19] There was no real change on the Duce's part in 1934 when he invited Hitler to visit Italy – the accommodation with which he was provided would hardly have been adequate for an ordinary tourist. Hitler suppressed any sense of humiliation that he might have felt and began a patient and ultimately successful cultivation of Mussolini.[20] This display of moderation showed signs of producing even more rapid dividends in the other country that Hitler had identified as a desirable ally – Britain. In February 1934 the Foreign Secretary, Sir John Simon, pronounced in Parliament that the German claim to equality in armaments neither could nor should be resisted.[21]

Hitler's fears were actually exaggerated. The country that he feared most in his first years in power was France, without which there could have been no preemptive military action against the Nazi regime. To deny the French any pretext for intervening while Germany remained weak, Hitler reassured them on the most sensitive issue, that of the provinces of Alsace and Lorraine that they had recovered at Versailles. He accepted their return to France as final and ordered the Nazi Party not to set up branches in them. Until the spring of 1934 he also kept up desultory arms negotiations with France, and, even after those lapsed, he laid down that the air force programme should take the form of a small 'risk Luftwaffe', big enough to give a potential enemy pause for thought but not so big that France could claim justification for attacking to nip its development in the bud. Gradually, however, he sensed that France was not likely to attack the new Reich under any circumstances.[22] From this starting point, Hitler began to entertain a great hope. This was that both France and Britain could be won over to neutrality when he eventually attacked the Soviet Union. The German dictator found it irritating to contemplate having to fight them first, given that he regarded them as infinitely more formidable military opponents than the Soviet Red Army. Invading Russia without first having to defeat France and Britain was Hitler's fondest hope during the peacetime Third Reich.[23] To understand why it was not to be realised we must turn to the policies of the Western powers and especially to the policy of appeasement.

Notes

1 W. Deist, M. Messerschmidt, H-E. Volkman and W. Witte, *Germany and the Second World War: Vol. I, The Build-up of German Aggression* (Oxford, Clarendon Press, 1990), pp. 137–8, 146–8.
2 *Ibid.*, p. 109.
3 *Ibid.*, p. 153.
4 David Irving, *Goebbels: Mastermind of the Third Reich* (London, Focal Point Publications, 1996), pp. 166–7; on the popularity of Nazism among university students see Deist et al., *Germany and the Second World War*, pp. 37–40.
5 Deist et al., *Germany and the Second World War*, p. 131.
6 *Ibid.*, p. 182.
7 Avraham Barkai, *Nazi Economics: Ideology, Theory and Policy* (Oxford, Berg, 1990), p. 217.
8 Deist et al., *Germany and the Second World War*, p. 259.
9 *Ibid.*, p. 365.
10 *Ibid.*, pp. 438–9.
11 *Ibid.*, pp. 443–4, 520–6, 538–40.
12 Martin Broszat, *The Hitler State* (London, Longman, 1981), pp. 296–9, 352; Gerhard L. Weinberg, *The Foreign Policy of Hitler's Germany: Diplomatic Revolution in Europe, 1933–36* (Chicago, IL, University of Chicago Press, 1970), p. 175.
13 Leonidas Hill, 'Three crises, 1938–39', *Journal of Contemporary History*, 3: 1 (1968), 113–44.
14 Charles Petrie, *Life and Letters of the Rt. Hon. Sir Austen Chamberlain* (London, Cassell, 1940), Vol. II, pp. 391–2; see also Austen Chamberlain, *Down the Years* (London, Cassell, 1935), pp. 228–9.
15 Deist et al., *Germany and the Second World War*, pp. 584–6.
16 Gerhard L. Weinberg, *Germany, Hitler, and World War II* (Cambridge, Cambridge University Press, 1995), p. 72.
17 Raymond J. Sontag, *A Broken World 1919–1939* (New York, Harper, 1971), pp. 248–9; Gordon A. Craig, *Germany 1866–1945* (Oxford, Clarendon Press, 1978), p. 677.
18 Armand Bérard, *Au Temps du Danger Allemand: un Ambassadeur se Souvient* (Paris, Plon, 1976), p. 207; Weinberg, *Diplomatic Revolution*, pp. 159–67.
19 Esmonde M. Robertson, *Mussolini as Empire-Builder: Europe and Africa 1932–36* (London, Macmillan, 1977), pp. 35–43, 133.
20 Weinberg, *Diplomatic Revolution*, pp. 112–14; David Irving, *The War Path: Hitler's Germany 1933–9* (London, Joseph, 1978), p. 94; Anthony T. Komjathy, *The Crises of France's East Central European Diplomacy 1933–1938* (New York, Columbia University Press, 1976), pp. 61–4.
21 John F. Kennedy, *Why England Slept* (London, May Fair Books, 1962

edn.), p. 62.

22 Pierre Renouvin, *Histoire des Relations Internationales: VIII, Les Crises du XXe Siècle. II, de 1929 à 1945* (Paris, Hachette, 1958), pp. 72–5; Weinberg, *Diplomatic Revolution*, pp. 170–4; Irving, *War Path*, p. 30.

23 Deist et al., *Germany and the Second World War*, pp. 595–6.

CHAPTER FOUR

THE WESTERN POWERS
AND APPEASEMENT

It is now known that Poland did twice suggest to France a preventive war to crush the infant Third Reich, the first time after Hitler took office and the second after he took Germany out of the League of Nations. The recriminations surrounding France's refusals reduced the Franco-Polish semi-alliance to little more than a piece of paper, though France did not write off Czechoslovakia in the same way that it now did Poland. The latter, for its part, turned to reaching an accommodation of its own with Germany, leading to the two countries' non-aggression declaration of January 1934 and to Poland informing Germany that it would have no objection to the remilitarisation of the Rhineland.[1] At the root of France's caution lay, possibly, moral decay which one British observer detected setting in rapidly after the Stavisky scandal early in 1934,[2] and, much more definitely, economic weakness which afflicted France badly in the mid 1930s until an improvement in the economic situation in 1938–39 at least coincided with a resurgence in the will to resist aggression, though that had other stimulants as well, as will be discussed later.[3]

Militarily, the French army in the 1930s was not under real political or any other control. Chaos prevailed in many spheres, including military technology in which there were seventeen different engines to power the main battle tank.[4] Those who presided over this shambles had a healthy reluctance to take risks. Even so, France did have a strategy for fighting a war. It was based on the premise that it would be rash to expect anything more than benevolent neutrality from Britain which had advised France in September 1933 that if Germany made agreements and then broke them London could only guarantee to join in 'the moral condemnation of the world'. Britain also rejected French proposals for the two countries and Belgium to conduct military staff talks.[5] British readiness to participate in French security proposals for Eastern Europe was contingent, with embarrassing transparency, on their being without means of enforcement.[6] Under these circumstances, France sought to form a geographically linked alliance with Italy and the anti-revisionist, Danubian 'Little Entente' countries of Czechoslovakia, Romania and Yugoslavia, with a neutral Britain on its western flank being complemented by a likewise benevolently neutral Soviet Union to the east.

Under Pierre Laval, who succeeded the assassinated Louis Barthou as Foreign Minister in October 1934, the quest to win over Italy became an obsession, while a theatrical and almost insignificant security pact was concluded with Russia in 1935.[7] How little the pact meant to France was shown by its private disapproval of the pact that Czechoslovakia signed with Russia the same year and by its rebuffing of Soviet overtures for staff talks and for the sale of military equipment, except for some obsolete stock which France did sell.[8] Poland and the two Little Entente members not directly threatened by Germany, Romania and Yugoslavia, regarded Paris's wooing of Moscow as evidence of desperate French weakness, and it stimulated in them more thoughts of deals with Hitler whose anti-communism seemed uncompromising and who, in a notable public gesture in 1934, sacked his ambassador to Russia, Rudolf Nadolny, who was a well known advocate of German–Soviet collaboration.[9] In yet another false move at this time, France bought oil from the Middle East simply because it was cheaper than Romanian.[10] Hitler cannot, therefore, have felt much apprehension about possible adverse consequences when, in September 1934, he rejected French proposals for an 'Eastern Locarno' pact in which the European great powers and the East European states would have united to guarantee the status quo in the east on the lines of the 1925 Locarno agreements for Western Europe which Hitler professed to be intent on honouring.[11]

More signs of confidence were Hitler's announcements in quick succession in March 1935 of the existence of the German air force and then that conscription was to be reintroduced. With less fanfare, a plenipotentiary for war economy was appointed and the entire country was divided into defence areas with a group of officials in each to ensure that their area made its proper contribution to the rearmament effort. In 1936–37 there was a flowering of unconcealed economic preparations for war. Several institutions researching problems of total war were founded. 'Annual Reports on War Economy' were published from 1936. In August 1937 a law was issued for the compulsory registration of all persons knowing foreign languages (and not only those who taught them) and all such persons were served notice that the state might call upon their services.[12]

One of the features of the international scene least satisfactory to Hitler even as he carried out these measures was the failure of Britain to show any interest in becoming his ally. Britain's international importance, already huge, was to grow during the 1930s and especially after Germany remilitarised the Rhineland in 1936. Even before that French diplomats in Berlin had the impression that the Nazis were more concerned with British than with French reactions to their moves. Thus Germany surely announced the reintroduction of conscription on a Saturday, the French thought, because everything in Britain, notoriously in continental eyes, ground to a complete halt over the weekend. After Rhineland remilitarisation the Germans seemed exclusively interested in Britain.[13] Even if this was much exaggerated, as it was, the issue of European war or peace was eventually to centre round Anglo-German relations. The motives behind, and the development of, British policy towards Nazi Germany therefore merit detailed treatment.

In 1932–33 the British mood was introspective and anti-French, though also anti-Weimar German, as we have seen. The world depression was at its deepest in Britain in 1932. It appeared self evident to the most important department of state, the Treasury, that 'today financial and economic risks are by far the most serious that the country has to face',[14] and not ones relating to national security. The Nazi advent to power produced no immediate widespread change in perceptions. Most early British criticisms of the Nazi regime concentrated on its domestic excesses, as the young John F. Kennedy was to note shrewdly,[15] and a country's domestic policy could not be a reason for a liberal democracy to go to war with it. Reports from the departing British ambassador in Berlin, Horace Rumbold, were at first soothing, even to the extent of finding Hitler on first personal acquaintance not unpleasant, though Rumbold's final note was one of alarm.[16] The reports of his successor, Eric Phipps, were at first adverse to the regime but had little impact, though Baldwin did resist pressure for Phipps to be recalled on the grounds that his hostile tone made him unsuitable for the job.[17] Before long, Phipps mellowed and could even write days after Germany left the disarmament conference and the League in October 1933 that 'a sound disarmament convention with present day Germany is, perhaps, not an entirely Utopian idea'.[18] Even if these ambassadorial reports had been published in the press, which was, of course, unthinkable, it is not certain how much attention they would have attracted. The spell cast by domestic concerns over most people, including opinion-formers, showed signs of being unbreakable. When a group of the country's brightest public figures, drawn from across the political spectrum, founded a Next Five Years group in 1935 they were concerned with how the economy could be improved over that time and in particular how unemployment could be reduced, not with focusing on threats to peace between 1935 and 1940.[19]

It is not, then, surprising that, as the British economy began to recover in 1933, the most pressing item on the Anglo-German agenda was seen to be the stabilisation of trade and financial links between the two countries so that, at the minimum, they did not fall below the depressed level of 1931–32 under a new regime in Germany that could be expected to find attractions in economic isolationism. In 1934 Britain and Germany signed a trade and payments agreement whose terms were favourable to the former and which was to be renewed annually until 1939.[20] This achievement contrasted not only with the nervous nastiness of late Weimar, but also with the poor state of British relations with France. Those two countries quarrelled bitterly in the early 1930s over limits on the size of navies in a dispute in which Germany was not involved.[21] There were even more bitter and protracted Anglo-French altercations over economics and finance that did not start to diminish in bitterness until 1934.[22] Despite doubts about ultimate German ambitions, British leaders in the mid 1930s found French attempts to retain some of the inequalities imposed on Germany at Versailles unrealistic. This applied particularly to armaments, despite a revulsion against weaponry, whoever owned it. Britain in the early 1930s was ruled by politicians who were a generation older than the Nazi elite and to whom the 'Great War' had been a shattering experience after they had reached maturity in the peaceful conditions of the late nineteenth century.[23]

Besides this generational factor, Hitler's advent to power coincided with a climax of semi-pacifist emotion affecting all age groups of the British population as horror about the sacrifices in the 1914–18 war was aroused by a flood tide of anti-war 'trench' reminiscences that began in 1927 and only started to slow down in 1931.[24] There was a widespread belief that any new war would bring with it a new catastrophe in the form of mass bombing of cities and civilians, and in late 1932 Stanley Baldwin, the joint leader of the 'National Government', appeared to endorse this with his remark that the bomber would always get through. Fear about bombing was strong in the Foreign Office,[25] and a study of the British periodical press in the 1930s has identified a fear of aerial attack so intense as to lead to the conclusion that 'belief in the Luftwaffe's potency ... was probably the single most important determinant of appeasement in the thirties'.[26]

On the right there was a widespread belief that democracy could only work for a few nations and that Germany was not one of them and might fare as well under Hitler as Italy was supposedly doing under Mussolini. Apart from the joy of actual anti-Semites, there was much readiness among British rightwingers from the Prince of Wales downwards to find excuses for the Nazis' much publicised anti-Semitism, though usually on the assumption that anti-Jewish excesses would gradually reduce and not, as they did, escalate to diabolical levels.[27] In 1936 Lord Londonderry, the most rightwing politician to achieve ministerial rank in Britain in the 1930s, advised Ribbentrop that the Nazi movement should abandon anti-Semitism altogether and concentrate on 'your most proper and legitimate aspirations'.[28]

On the left, pure pacifism in some quarters and widespread suspicion that the government were only rearming because they had a secret agenda to use the arms against the working class,[29] reinforced the entrenched Francophobia of even the moderate left to cause a refusal to detect dangers in Nazi foreign policy aims as distinct from their reviled domestic policies. In March 1935 the official Labour Party newspaper, the *Daily Herald,* editorialised that, as a result of the reintroduction of conscription in Germany, 'Europe is bright with hope'. As late as 1938 there were those on the left who could not easily sympathise with Czechoslovakia because it was 'a vassal of French imperialism'.[30] Attitudes in the Labour Party only even began to change in late 1935,[31] and it required the Spanish Civil War, in which leftwingers were fighting for their lives against a rightwing insurgency, to produce a real, though still incomplete, shift.[32] The craving for disarmament remained never far below the surface of Labour politics,[33] and it also did not encourage the government to be bold against Germany having an opposition which sometimes saw more merit in the actions of the Soviet government than in those of the British, a tendency in Labour that peaked in 1938–39 between Munich and the Nazi–Soviet pact.[34]

The attitude of political opponents, since the government polled only 15 per cent more votes than they did in the general election of November 1935, was one aspect of the domestic scene that the British government had to consider. More generally, until 1938 their 'aim was to prevent British politics from becoming completely swept up in the dynamic of foreign affairs'.[35] This was partly because a stable society was regarded as a foreign policy asset in itself, but chiefly it reflected a determination by almost all politicians in inter-war Britain to give precedence to domestic economic and social issues over foreign problems about which Prime Minister Stanley Baldwin was explicit in a speech in 1936. The convulsions in France after the election of the Popular Front government in that year were regarded as an object lesson in what to avoid.[36]

The formulation of a British policy to meet the responsibilities that were being thrust upon the country was additionally impeded by the manifold inadequacies of the British system of government by committees;[37] by the notorious amateurishness of British politicians, including cabinet ministers who often preferred to rely on their 'intuitions' and the 'fresh' impressions of acquaintances who had recently visited Germany or Italy;[38] and by divided counsels and waning prestige in the department for foreign policy, the Foreign Office. In the testimony of one witness, then a junior official, the Foreign Office in the 1930s did not have a 'conscious policy-forming machine'. Policy was expected to emerge from 'reams of minutes' that the department's senior men were expected to 'umpire correctly'.[39] This was not likely to be effective when, for instance, quite senior officials were hopelessly divided among themselves about whether Germany would be easier to deal with politically if it was economically favoured and made 'fat', or opposed and made 'lean', with some others admitting that they simply did not know.[40] From early 1936 the authority of the Foreign Office was to wane rapidly and an impatient Treasury was to gain preeminence in policymaking.[41] A department that appeared to its own future head in late 1936 as a 'mess of destroyed causes and smug, complacent incompetence'[42] was not well placed to influence events. This was unfortunate because it was the one branch of the British government in the 1930s in which there was high level support for 'collective security' – a term that came into wide public use in the mid 1930s.[43] Its official head until 1938, Robert Vansittart, warned as early as 1934 of a 'landslide' of European countries into the German camp if Britain did not give a lead in organising them to resist aggression.[44] This contrasted markedly with the tendency of the British military chiefs to oppose seeking allies.[45]

In summary, collective security was unattractive to ruling politicians. Under another name, that of alliance and entente politics, it had failed to prevent the catastrophe of the outbreak of war in 1914. Then there had at least been two roughly evenly matched camps. Now there was not even that, with the United States in isolation, Russia ideologically suspect and of doubtful value as an ally, and France problematical. Under all these circumstances, Britain, increasingly the one country that could effectively oppose Germany, turned to appeasement which was a total strategy for national survival rather than a foreign policy in any conventional sense. It involved a 'juggling act at the diplomatic level', coupled with ones 'at the domestic-political level (winning elections, preserving backbench support), and at the fiscal level (keeping a balance between rearmament and economic stability), and at the strategic level (adjusting resources among the services to the most threatened areas)'.[46]

Rearmament was the key to making the strategy work. At least as it developed in its early stages, it was intended to make Britain self-reliant for defence and so able, if desired or if it appeared necessary, to dispense with allies, and to make the country so strong as to be irresistible when it offered its services as a mediator, proposing for Germany mostly economic benefits in return for refraining from aggression and appealing to what Neville Chamberlain called the 'will to peace' of the 'common people' of Germany, plus moderate Nazis and even the Nazi leadership as a whole who would surely mellow with the passage of time and after generous but justifiable concessions from their former enemies.[47] All of this went hand in hand with a conviction that almost everything in the 1919 peace settlement that Germany objected to had become 'untenable and indefensible'; the disarmament clauses were even 'a putrefying corpse'.[48] This involved moving away from the earlier concept of the very official who made these remarks, Orme Sargent of the Foreign Office, that the need not to alienate France meant that there could only be 'a more or less platonic advocacy of Treaty revision'.[49] In November 1934 Foreign

Secretary Sir John Simon had argued that territorial changes in Germany's favour were as inevitable as ones relating to armaments. Britain could only influence their 'manner and form' by trying to keep them peaceful and reasonable, though earlier that year he had advocated the necessity to 'keep out of troubles in Central Europe at all costs. July twenty years ago stands out as an awful warning'.[50]

Notes

1 Anthony T. Komjathy, *The Crises of France's East Central European Diplomacy 1933–1938* (New York, Columbia University Press, 1976), pp. 19–20, 30–1, 42–3, 49–51, 50–1; Gerhard L. Weinberg, *The Foreign Policy of Hitler's Germany: Diplomatic Revolution in Europe, 1933–36* (Chicago, University of Chicago Press, 1970), pp. 185–92; and W. Deist, M. Messerschmidt, H-E. Volkmann and W. Wette, *Germany and the Second World War: Vol. I, The Build-up of German Aggression* (Oxford, Clarendon Press, 1990), pp. 616–17.

2 John Wheeler-Bennett, *Knaves, Fools and Heroes* (London, Macmillan, 1974), pp. 169–70.

3 Maurice Larkin, *Gathering Pace: Continental Europe 1870–1945* (London, Macmillan, 1969), pp. 340–2, for a summary of 1930s French economic history; René Girault 'The impact of the economic situation on the foreign policy of France, 1936–9' in Wolfgang J. Mommsen and Lothar Kettenacker (eds), *The Fascist Challenge and the Policy of Appeasement* (London, Allen & Unwin, 1983), pp. 209–26.

4 Donald Cameron Watt, *Too Serious A Business* (London, Temple Smith, 1975), pp. 53–4, 92; and Paul Kennedy, *The Rise and Fall of the Great Powers* (London, Unwin Hyman, 1988), pp. 310–14.

5 Paul Kennedy, *The Realities behind Diplomacy: Background Influences on British External Policy, 1865–1980* (Glasgow, Fontana, 1981), p. 271; Deist et al., *Germany and the Second World War*, p. 611.

6 Arnold Wolfers, *Britain and France between Two Wars* (Hamden, CT, Archon Books, 1963), pp. 274–9.

7 Pierre Renouvin, *Histoire des Relations Internationales: VIII, les Crises du XXe Siècle. II, de 1929 à 1945* (Paris, Hachette, 1958), pp. 82–4; Komjathy, *Crises*, pp. 80–2, 98–9; Nicole Jordan, *The Popular Front and Central Europe: The Dilemmas of French Impotence, 1918–1940* (Cambridge, Cambridge University Press, 1992), pp. 29–31, 37–9.

8 Jordan, *Dilemmas*, pp. 41–2; Michael Jabara Carley, *1939: The Alliance That Never Was and the Coming of World War II* (Chicago, IL, Dee, 1999), p. 24.

9 William Carr, *Arms, Autarky and Aggression* (London, Arnold, 1972),

pp. 117–19; John Hiden, *Germany and Europe 1919–1939* (London, Longman, 1977), p. 97; Johnnie von Herwarth, *Against Two Evils* (London, Collins, 1981), pp. 88–9, 112–15; Weinberg, *Diplomatic Revolution*, pp. 180–3.

10 Komjathy, *Crises*, pp. 25–6, 61–4.

11 Weinberg, *Diplomatic Revolution*, pp. 184–5.

12 Max Weinreich, *Hitler's Professors* (New Haven, CT, Yale University Press, 1999 edn.), p. 71.

13 Armand Bérard, *Au Temps du Danger Allemand: un Ambassadeur se Souvient* (Paris, Plon, 1976), pp. 263, 287–8, 307.

14 Robert P. Shay, Jr., *British Rearmament in the Thirties: Politics and Profits* (Princeton, NJ, Princeton University Press, 1977), p. 24.

15 John F. Kennedy, *Why England Slept* (London, May Fair Books, 1962 edn.), p. 92.

16 Martin Gilbert, *Sir Horace Rumbold* (London, Heinemann, 1973), pp. 331–2, 352, 367–8, 378–82, 393–6.

17 Martin Gilbert and Richard Gott, *The Appeasers* (London, Weidenfeld & Nicolson, 1967), p. 45.

18 Norton Medlicott, 'Britain and Germany: the search for agreement, 1930–37' in David Dilks (ed.), *Retreat from Power: Studies in Britain's Foreign Policy of the Twentieth Century, Vol. One 1906–1939* (London, Macmillan, 1981), p. 82.

19 Ben Pimlott, *Labour and the Left in the 1930s* (London, Allen & Unwin, 1986 edn.), p. 145.

20 Frederick Leith-Ross, *Money Talks: The Autobiography of Sir Frederick Leith-Ross* (London, Hutchinson, 1968), pp. 182–8; Berndt-Jurgen Wendt, '"Economic appeasement" – a crisis strategy' in Mommsen and Kettenacker (eds), *The Fascist Challenge*, pp. 157–62; Gustav Schmidt, *The Politics and Economics of Appeasement: British Foreign Policy in the 1930s* (Leamington Spa, Berg, 1986), p. 44.

21 David Carlton, *MacDonald Versus Henderson* (London, Macmillan, 1970), pp. 133–43.

22 Robert Boyce, 'World war, world depression: some economic origins of the Second World War' in Robert Boyce and Esmonde M. Robertson (eds), *Paths to War* (London, Macmillan, 1989), chapter 2.

23 John Mander, *Our German Cousins: Anglo-German Relations in the 19th and 20th Centuries* (London, Murray, 1974), pp. 247–50.

24 Correlli Barnett, *The Collapse of British Power* (Gloucester, Sutton, 1984), pp. 419, 426–35.

25 Martin Thomas, *Britain, France and Appeasement* (Oxford, Berg, 1996), p. 38.

26 Quoted in Alexander J. Groth, *Democracies against Hitler: Myth, Reality and Prologue* (Aldershot, Ashgate, 1999), p. 67.

27 Richard Griffiths, *Fellow Travellers of the Right: British Enthusiasts for Nazi Germany 1933–39* (London, Constable, 1980), chapters 1–3.

28 Marquess of Londonderry, *Ourselves and Germany* (London, Hale, 1938), p. 111.

29 John F. Naylor, *Labour's International Policy* (London, Weidenfeld & Nicolson, 1969), p. 70; Pimlott, *Labour and the Left*, pp. 150–1.

30 A. J. P. Taylor, *The Troublemakers* (London, Hamish Hamilton, 1957), pp. 187, 196–7; see also Michael R. Gordon, *Conflict and Consensus in Labour's Foreign Policy, 1914–1965* (Stanford, CA, Stanford University Press, 1969), pp. 23–4, 40–3, 66–72, 76–7, 81–2.

31 Naylor, *Labour's International Policy*, pp. 104–11.

32 *Ibid.*, pp. 181–96; Maurice Cowling, *The Impact of Hitler: British Politics and British Policy 1933–1940* (Chicago, IL, University of Chicago Press, 1977 edn.), pp. 115–17.

33 James Jupp, *The Radical Left in Britain 1931–1941* (London, Cass, 1982), pp. 164–6.

34 Bill Jones, *The Russia Complex: The British Labour Party and the Soviet Union* (Manchester, Manchester University Press, 1977), pp. 28–9.

35 Schmidt, *Politics of Appeasement*, pp. 5, 390.

36 *Ibid.*, pp. 228, 252–3, 388–9; see also Wolfers, *Britain and France*, p. 209.

37 A major theme of Gaines Post, Jr., *Dilemmas of Appeasement* (Ithaca, NY, Cornell University Press, 1993).

38 Schmidt, *Politics of Appeasement*, pp. 315–18.

39 Paul Gore-Booth, *With Great Truth and Respect* (London, Constable, 1974), pp. 61–2.

40 *The Memoirs of Lord Gladwyn* (London, Weidenfeld & Nicolson, 1972), pp. 63–5; and John Harvey (ed.), *The Diplomatic Diaries of Oliver Harvey 1937–40* (London, Collins, 1970), p. 403.

41 Post, *Dilemmas*, pp. 62, 316–17.

42 *Ibid.*, p. 306.

43 Taylor, *Troublemakers*, p. 180.

44 Michael L. Roi, *Alternative to Appeasement: Sir Robert Vansittart and Alliance Diplomacy, 1934–1937* (Westport, CT, Praeger, 1997), p. 45.

45 N. H. Gibbs, *Grand Strategy: Vol. I, Rearmament Policy* (London, HMSO, 1976), pp. 610–12, 627.

46 Paul Kennedy, 'The logic of appeasement', *TLS*, 28 May 1982, 585–6.

47 Schmidt, *Politics of Appeasement*; A. R. Peters, *Anthony Eden at the Foreign Office 1931–1938* (Aldershot, Gower, 1986), p. 44.

48 Medlicott in Dilks (ed.), *Retreat*, pp. 80 and 84.
49 Andrew J. Crozier, *Appeasement and Germany's Last Bid for Colonies* (London, Macmillan, 1988), p. 32.
50 Schmidt, *Politics of Appeasement*, pp. 300, 309.

CHAPTER FIVE

APPEASEMENT AND AGGRESSION, 1935–36

By 1936 Britain had worked out a definite policy of seeking to persuade Germany to agree to limits on its rearmament and to guarantee the political status quo in East and Central Europe which would thus be rendered safe without Britain having to accept commitments there. This partly embodied the views of Simon, who had left the Foreign Office in June 1935, but not yet his readiness for territorial changes. In return for accepting the British programme, Germany could claim its reward in economic concessions and, probably, the return of some of the colonies that it had lost in 1919, together with guaranteed supplies of raw materials from most of tropical Africa.[1] British hopes about what could be achieved from colonial appeasement were a particularly graphic illustration of the frequently deluded premises on which appeasement was based. Although in 1936 the Nazi regime did mount a propaganda campaign for colonial restitution and Hitler did suddenly stress its importance, for reasons that remain conjectural, after earlier playing it down to British visitors,[2] this was a smokescreen for the reality of Hitler's aggressive intentions in Europe. Public and much official opinion in Britain was, in any case, never really converted to colonial appeasement, and when Britain finally made an offer to Germany the bubble burst with Hitler's curt rejection of it in early 1938. He had no intention of being deflected from his European ambitions with the offer of a small colonial empire. In his 'secret book' in 1928 he had stated that he wanted *Lebensraum* in Russia, not 'in the Cameroons for instance', referring to a former German colony in west Africa.[3] This was not a case of Hitler being idiosyncratic. German official records of the time appear to contain no indication in favour of a colonial deal as opposed to unconditional return of all former colonies except those held by Japan.[4]

British economic appeasement was a more rational offshoot of the general policy than was colonial appeasement because it was intended to buy time for rearmament if it could not make a contribution to bringing about permanent peace.[5] It appealed powerfully to Chamberlain and to certain individuals in a Foreign Office generally lacking in economic expertise. (In the early 1930s its economic section comprised precisely two members of staff.[6]) The chief British economic negotiator with Germany, Frederick Leith-Ross of the Treasury, was an agnostic in this matter. By 1936–37 he regretted having to negotiate with the Germans unless they 'purged themselves of their present diseased mentality', while lamenting any tendency to pursue an 'unremitting vendetta against Germany'.[7] The Anglo-German negotiations about trade and finance during Chamberlain's premiership were regarded with some scepticism by most of his colleagues who may even have listened to the warnings of the commercial section in the British embassy in Berlin that the Nazis had no interest in trade liberalisation and simply wanted to acquire more foreign exchange from Britain to buy materials for rearmament.[8]

Turning from the 'carrot' policy of appeasement to the 'stick' fellow policy of rearmament, its role in the origins of the war is twofold. On the one hand, it was to prove insufficient to deter Hitler from aggression. On the other, rearmament (French and other countries' as well as British) was to make it possible for Nazi actions to be resisted with force with some chance of ultimate success. British rearmament began modestly in 1934 when it was proposed to spend an extra £82 million on defence over the following eight or nine years. That was little enough, especially considering the remarkably accurate prediction that, if there was to be war, it would be most likely to start in 1939. However, the government feared that more spending on rearmament simply would not be acceptable to the 'morally disarmed' British public.[9] At the same time, Germany was designated as Britain's 'ultimate enemy', though there were those, especially in the Royal Navy, who would have preferred Japan to receive that accolade and, to the Conservative leader, Stanley Baldwin, both were 'mad dogs'.[10] The Japanese threat was to parts of the empire and not to Britain itself. This highlights the fact that the value of rearmament as a means of limiting concessions to be made to Germany was lessened by the growing needs of imperial defence. The imperial factor was made even more important because of the doubts within the political elite about whether the empire could survive a war politically even if it was victorious militarily. Nobody felt these doubts more acutely than Neville Chamberlain who was to become Prime Minister. If there was a major politician who was oblivious to them it was Winston Churchill, but by 1933 he stood little chance of ever again becoming a cabinet minister unless a war started.[11]

As British rearmament actually took shape, it was heavily weighted in favour of expanding the air force. This was partly because air power offered the prospect of an effective deterrent to an aggressor that could be built up fairly rapidly. In 1936 Chamberlain almost waxed lyrical about converting the Royal Air Force 'from a defensive organ into a weapon of aggression with unprecedented powers of destruction.'[12] The army received little additional funding because the government did not envisage the use of British troops in large scale warfare. In 1936–37 the cabinet rejected chiefs of staff proposals for a 'continental field force' if Britain went to war. Instead much of the army was to remain in India and the colonies and the Territorial Army was to maintain internal order if air raids threatened to produce civil disorder.[13]

As for Britain's traditional instrument of power, the Navy, official Britain put its faith in an agreement with Germany, signed in June 1935, by which German naval expansion was not to exceed in size 35 per cent of the combined naval forces of the British Empire, though the inclusion of dominion naval forces meant little because they were small. This agreement was pressed for by two men: one of them was Hitler who hoped that it would be followed by a British disclaimer of any interest in East or Central Europe; the other was the First Sea Lord, Admiral Sir Ernle Chatfield, who had a 'bold and legitimate' plan of 'utter audacity' for restoring Britain's position as the world's premier naval power.[14] To a politician as inclined to conciliation as Simon, 35 per cent seemed an excessive figure.[15] To Chatfield it was irrelevant. The Admiralty did not think that Germany would have the capacity to build up to that size before 1942 or 1943. The British negotiated the agreement to include details that would prevent qualitative German naval expansion in areas such as commerce raiding in which the German navy would otherwise have been able to mount a formidable challenge to Britain long before the time, if it ever came, when the two navies reached quantitative equality.[16] Finally, the Admiralty hoped (in vain) that the naval agreement with Germany would convince Japan of the futility of refusing to conclude a new agreement on naval armaments limitations with Britain and the United States.[17]

For a few years the agreement worked fairly well in locking Germany into a symmetrical programme of naval building and preventing Germany from building more ships of the feared 'pocket battleship' type that Britain was not itself building. Politically, it had a disillusioning effect on both countries and made them readier to contemplate war with one another. Hitler became genuinely angry when he realised that the agreement was not going to be the precursor to Britain giving him a free hand in Central Europe. Politicians and diplomats on the British side also felt alienated when it became clear that the agreement would not be followed by others in which Germany would accept limits on its military and political ambitions. Remarkably, the one person without illusions about Hitler's motives in ordering his reluctant naval chiefs to accept the agreement was Chatfield.[18] The agreement thus gave both British and Germans the first indication that they might be on a collision course.

In 1935 there was an increase in British defence spending but the sums involved were still modest.[19] The next year the cabinet agreed that in public ministers should be evasive about rearmament costs, fearing a public and, in particular, a working class outcry in case the full costs became known.[20] The working classes made up around 70 per cent of the electorate in a Britain in which universal male suffrage was as new as votes for women, and the ruling politicians of the 1930s had only limited faith in their patriotism or capacity to reason, though a major effort was made to prepare them psychologically for the possibility of war through manipulation of cinema newsreels to give a more alarmist view of the international situation than the one in which the government actually believed.[21] Another decision of this time was that there should be no cuts in social welfare spending to help finance rearmament, and in 1936 it remained the case that spending on the National Debt exceeded defence spending. Most of that debt had been accumulated to pay for the First World War. Britain was therefore still spending more on the costs of a previous war than on preparations for a possible new one.[22]

Perhaps the most important element in British defence preparations concerned the timetable for possible war. From 1934 the service chiefs argued energetically for war to be ruled out until 1942, whatever political sacrifices that might entail.[23] By then Britain's defences were expected to be so formidable that Germany would not dare to make further demands that might in any way adversely affect British interests, though if it did Britain would be ready to resist. The two major international crises of the mid–1930s were to provide considerable support for this argument by threatening to involve Britain in war over issues seen as irrelevant to its security at a time when its defence preparations were not well advanced.

To British policymakers the international crisis caused by Mussolini's invasion and conquest in 1935–36 of the East African state of Ethiopia, then usually called Abyssinia, was the 'Mediterranean crisis'; to the French it was the 'Anglo-Italian crisis'.[24] It came as a particularly shattering blow to France because it began just after the French thought that they had concluded in principle a military alliance with Italy,[25] under which the two countries would fight together if Germany committed aggression. Italy would send troops into Austria and would allow passage through its own territory to two French divisions that would then proceed to Czechoslovakia, France's main ally in Central Europe. Much larger French forces would march unopposed into a Rhineland that Hitler was expected to leave conveniently demilitarised. That was a fantastic assumption on which to base a whole strategy, though perhaps no more than the belief that Mussolini could be trusted. But nothing could stop the French from ascribing the breakdown of this supposed agreement entirely to Anglo-Italian squabbles in East Africa. The British in reality had scarcely more time for Ethiopia than had the French, despite the existence of large British colonies and a small French colony on its borders. One of their prime reflections was bewilderment at the strategic madness of the Italian invasion that began in October 1935. For once Chamberlain's liberal rationalism did not play him false when he wrote in late 1935 that, by sending much of the Italian army to the Horn of Africa, Mussolini would be 'tying a noose round his own neck' for Britain, the country that controlled the Suez Canal, to pull,[26] as was to be demonstrated by the successful British campaign in 'Italian East Africa' in 1941. And yet, in the circumstances of 1935, that would have been small consolation to Britain and France for having to contemplate warfare in the Mediterranean, something that the British up to 1935 had considered to be utterly unlikely except for possible Japanese sabotage of the Suez Canal.[27] Disdain for Ethiopia in Britain and France in official circles was traditional and profound.[28] There were few British or French policymakers who could contemplate without horror a war for such a country to be fought primarily in an area of great strategic importance like the Mediterranean that had previously been thought safe.

Such contemplation was slow to occur. Britain in early 1935 was so much preoccupied with European and Far Eastern problems that for long the rumblings of trouble between Italy and Ethiopia were left to an overworked Foreign Office that itself regarded the matter as one to be virtually ignored.[29] The subject reached Cabinet level only in May 1935 and was particularly unwelcome in the wake of the conference at Stresa the previous month in which the heads of government of Britain, France and Italy had, after a leisurely six days together, proclaimed their intention to use 'all practical means' to oppose anything 'which may endanger the peace of Europe'. This was fine sounding, but, for the British at least, nothing of a practical nature was envisaged, while the reference to Europe appeared to rule Africa out of any consideration. A journalist who asked the Prime Minister, Ramsay MacDonald, whether Ethiopia had been mentioned at Stresa received the answer that his question was 'irrelevant'.[30] Even in the European context the Cabinet had resolved that there could be no question of an anti-German entente with France and Italy, and that the purpose of any three-power arrangement 'would be largely for the purpose of collating information'.[31]

Lukewarm in this way about obligations in Europe, it was unbearable for Britain (and still more so for France) to have to contemplate strong action over a problem in Africa. Visiting Mussolini in June, Anthony Eden, newly appointed Minister for League of Nations Affairs, pleaded in vain with him that Ethiopia was 'not worth' a quarrel between Britain and Italy. In Paris on the way home he told French ministers that the reasons why Britain could not simply ignore Ethiopia were 'chiefly determined by considerations of a domestic nature'.[32] He was referring to the tidal wave of anti-Italian and pro-League of Nations sentiment that engulfed Britain that summer and which, even if it came from a vocal minority, the government felt entirely unable to ignore.[33] The flounderings of British policy in the summer of 1935 as the government's foreign policy attentions were virtually monopolised by a subject that it regarded as being without intrinsic importance were such as to cause the French leader, Pierre Laval, to remark that Britain had ceased to exist as a great power.[34]

After the final diplomatic failure of a British–Italian–French conference in Paris in August at which Ethiopia was not represented – an ominous portent of Czechoslovakia and the Munich conference – Italy invaded in October in accordance with little more substantial than the 'raw Social Darwinism' that now came to the surface in

Mussolini's foreign policy.[35] The Anglo-French policy within the League of some economic sanctions, but not oil sanctions that might actually have crippled the Italian war effort, was designed to avoid making a clear choice between Italy and the League. It also nipped in the bud a possible obstacle to British rearmament against Germany because the Cabinet was afraid that if Britain did not impose some sanctions against Italy the government's leftwing critics at home would actively oppose British rearmament for which they already felt great mistrust.[36] The immense importance of articulate public opinion is further underlined by the fact that, immediately after winning a general election in November 1935, the National government felt compelled to repudiate an Anglo-French plan for the partition of Ethiopia between Italy and a rump Ethiopian state, associated with the British and French Foreign Ministers, Samuel Hoare and Pierre Laval, when it was 'leaked' in the French press in December. A version of the plan had been offered to Mussolini by Eden six months earlier and there can have been few in official London or Paris who did not support it. No one was more relieved by its abandonment than Hitler. He had feared that such an offer would propel Mussolini back towards the Anglo-French orbit.[37]

The effects of the Italian conquest of Ethiopia, where organised resistance ended in the spring of 1936, were very adverse for international security. To the Western democracies it made collective security look even more risky and undesirable: it had threatened to involve them in what their leaders would have regarded as the wrong war with the wrong enemy at the wrong time. In addition, it created a widespread popular misconception – not shared by many policymakers with the notable exception of Eden – that the man who really posed a danger to peace was Mussolini, not Hitler. In the words of one historian: 'At least until Munich more people saw Mussolini rather than Hitler as the principal peace disturber.'[38] What could not be appreciated until much later was that Mussolini's ventures in Ethiopia and then in Spain in the civil war were to leave Italy virtually a spent force by 1939. The expenditures involved were literally ruinous for the weak Italian economy and for Italy as a military power. Over 70 per cent of Italian military expenditure between 1935 and 1940 went on these projects, including 'pacification' of a brutal type in Ethiopia. Most of the remaining, less than 30 per cent, had to be spent on the normal, recurrent costs of the armed forces. Unlike Germany and the Western democracies, Italy spent very little on preparing for war with other major powers. Gradually, the German leaders in particular grasped the extent of Italy's enfeeblement and that the best service it could render them would be to keep the Western states convinced that it was still a major player and distract them while Germany expanded in East and Central Europe.[39]

In accordance with this perception and looking forward to the time when the Ethiopian problem would be at an end, Eden, who replaced Hoare as Foreign Secretary in December 1935, wrote soon after taking up his new office that the time had come for 'making some attempt to come to terms with Germany' but only 'upon one indispensable condition ... There must be no concession merely to keep Germany quiet, for that process only stimulates the appetite it is intended to satisfy'.[40] This condition was soon put to the test by the German remilitarisation of the Rhineland in March 1936, an action that the Foreign Office had not expected Hitler to perform for fear of 'throwing away' the chance of a settlement with Britain.[41] The demilitarised status of the zone, which comprised 18 per cent of the territory of Germany and contained 24 per cent of its population, had been in decay for some time. Since 1933 the Nazi regime had sent in large numbers of troops posing as policemen while France was considering offering to accept remilitarisation in 1940 or 1942 when, like Britain, it expected its own defences to be in decisively better shape.[42] Hitler had different ideas and saw compelling reasons for early remilitarisation. These were both domestic, including a desire to boost his own flagging popularity, and international, including a wish to take advantage of the disarray in Anglo-French relations evident from the recriminations that had followed the Hoare–Laval fiasco.[43]

Britain was eager to complement the naval agreement of the previous year with an aerial pact and, a few weeks before remilitarisation, Hitler duly pronounced in favour of an aerial pact for Western Europe.[44] If this should have failed to buy off the Western powers, it is now known that Hitler intended to order resistance, and not a retreat, if France, with or without Britain, embarked on military operations to reimpose demilitarisation. There was actually no risk of having to do that. There was no will to resist in either the French public or the army high command.[45] The British government was willing to accept the broad sincerity of the various offers on means to strengthen peace that Hitler made early in 1936, of which an aerial pact was only one. Substantial elements of the British public were almost ferociously in favour of accepting the German action; in the press only the Communist *Daily Worker* and the rightwing *Daily Telegraph* expressed alarm about remilitarisation. The government itself found extremely unattractive the prospect of a war against Germany (and most probably, it was thought, also Japan) in the company of France, Belgium, Czechoslovakia and possibly Soviet Russia, a country that Eden had recently written of as a 'bear' that had only 'hatred in his heart' for the British Empire.[46] The tendency to put the most favourable possible interpretation upon Germany's Rhineland action stemmed in part also from an extraordinary wave of Francophobia that had afflicted Britain since the leaking of the Hoare–Laval partition plan.[47]

Britain published a White Paper on 20 March in which it offered France talks on security cooperation and, while Eden hoped that something more than merely cosmetic would come out of that, many of his colleagues were determined that something should not. When Anglo-French staff talks were held for two days in London in April Britain responded to the French demand for an alliance with information which, in the case of the Royal Air Force, did not go beyond what was in the *Air Force List*.[48] Thus the Rhineland crisis or 'crisis' in the sense that it never threatened to escalate into confrontation, let alone conflict, between Germany and its neighbours, cost Hitler very little while bringing great benefits. It boosted the dictator's own confidence and that of his military and diplomatic advisers in his judgement. It made France vulnerable to German attack, and revealed Britain as willing to be bought off from resisting or even condemning German forward moves by vague offers, while apparently not being resentful when Germany failed to follow up those offers with concrete proposals. In May 1936 Britain sent Germany a questionnaire about its intentions to which there was no official reply except for a barrage of insults in the German press. Germany offered excuses for not negotiating on security after the West had accepted Rhineland remilitarisation that ranged from preoccupation with the summer Olympic Games in Berlin to the need for France to repudiate its pact with Russia. In fact, the reality was not as dismal as the appearance. Hitler's tactics were fairly transparent by late 1936 and they did cause some in the Western governments to question whether he merited any trust. Both Britain and France increased their defence spending after remilitarisation, the former by a modest extra £20 million and the latter hugely with the announcement in late 1936 that over the next four years £180 million would be spent on the army and £50 million on the air force, while the navy would acquire five new battleships and ten cruisers by 1943.[49] Yet both countries were thinking in terms of safeguarding their own interest in the narrow sense. It is useful to pause to consider the situation as it was in 1936 after Germany had accomplished the one sine qua non before it could commit aggression of Rhineland remilitarisation.

Notes

1 Andrew J. Crozier, *Appeasement and Germany's Last Bid for Colonies* (London, Macmillan, 1988), pp. 120–1, 133, 306–7; Gustav Schmidt, *The Politics and Economics of Appeasement* (Leamington Spa, Berg, 1986), pp. 205–7; A. R. Peters, *Anthony Eden at the Foreign Office 1931–1938* (Aldershot, Gower, 1986), pp. 98–100; Gerhard L. Weinberg, *The Foreign Policy of Hitler's Germany: Starting World War II, 1937–1939* (Chicago, IL, University of Chicago Press, 1980), pp. 131–3.

2 Schmidt, *Politics of Appeasement*, p. 101; Crozier, *Colonies*, pp. 58–63, 102–4, 137–41; Peters, *Eden*, pp. 298–305; Marquess of Londonderry, *Ourselves and Germany* (London, Hale, 1938), pp. 106, 141.

3 Crozier, *Colonies*, traces this in detail, chapters 6–10; see also W. Deist, M. Messerschmidt, H-E. Volkmann and W. Wette, *Germany and the Second World War: Vol. I, The Build-up of German Aggression*, (Oxford, Clarendon Press, 1990), p. 545.

4 Weinberg, *Starting World War II*, pp. 136–40.

5 Schmidt, *Politics of Appeasement*, pp. 85–90, 159–65.

6 Walford Selby, *Diplomatic Twilight 1930–1940* (London, Murray, 1953), pp. 4, 10, 83.

7 Frederick Leith-Ross, *Money Talks* (London, Hutchinson, 1968), pp. 160, 235–41.

8 Schmidt, *Politics of Appeasement*, pp. 186–7, 192–4; Callum MacDonald, 'Economic appeasement and the German "moderates"', *Past and Present* 56 (1972), 103–35.

9 Gaines Post, Jr., *Dilemmas of Appeasement* (Ithaca, NY, Cornell University Press, 1993), pp. 32–4, 343.

10 *Ibid.*, p. 36.

11 For Chamberlain and Churchill see John Charmley, *Chamberlain and the Lost Peace* (London, Hodder, 1989) and R. A. C. Parker, *Churchill and Appeasement* (London, Macmillan, 2000).

12 Post, *Dilemmas*, p. 169.

13 Nicholas Pronay, 'Rearmament and the British public: policy and propaganda' in J. Curran, A. Smith and P. Wingate (eds), *Impacts and*

Influences: Essays on Media Power in the Twentieth Century (London, Methuen, 1987), pp. 57–9.

14 Joseph A. Maiolo, *The Royal Navy and Nazi Germany, 1933–39* (London, Macmillan, 1998), pp. 20, 132.

15 Peters, *Eden*, p. 90.

16 Maiolo, *Royal Navy*, pp. 58–60, 66–7.

17 B. J. C McKercher, *Transition of Power: Britain's Loss of Global Pre-eminence to the United States, 1930–1945* (Cambridge, Cambridge University Press, 1999), p. 211.

18 Maiolo, *Royal Navy*, p. 141; Deist et al., *Germany and the Second World War*, pp. 460–3.

19 Post, *Dilemmas*, pp. 111–14, 188.

20 Schmidt, *Politics of Appeasement*, p. 168

21 Pronay in Curran, Smith and Wingate (eds), *Influences*.

22 G. C. Peden, *British Rearmament and the Treasury: 1932–1939* (Edinburgh, Scottish Academic Press, 1979), pp. 76, 89.

23 Post, *Dilemmas*, pp. 50–4.

24 *Ibid.*, pp. 81, 195.

25 Nicole Jordan, 'The cut price war on the peripheries: the French General Staff, the Rhineland and Czechoslovakia' in Robert Boyce and Esmonde M. Robertson (eds), *Paths to War* (London, Macmillan, 1989), pp. 140–1; Anthony T. Komjathy, *The Crises of France's East Central European Diplomacy 1933–1938* (New York, Columbia University Press, 1976), pp. 80–2, 98–105, 154–5.

26 Post, *Dilemmas*, p. 124.

27 Lawrence R. Pratt, *East of Malta, West of Suez: Britain's Mediterranean Crisis, 1936–1939* (Cambridge, Cambridge University Press, 1975), p. 12.

28 George Scott, *The Rise and Fall of the League of Nations* (London, Hutchinson, 1973), pp. 177–9.

29 K. E. Fischer, 'The Foreign Office and British Foreign Policy during the Abyssinian Crisis 1934–1935' (unpublished M.Phil thesis, University of St Andrews, 1988), pp. 12–22.

30 Richard Lamb, *The Ghosts of Peace 1935–1945* (Salisbury, Russell, 1987), p. 10.

31 Fischer, *Abyssinian Crisis*, pp. 35–41, 198. For summaries of the limitations of the 'Stresa front' see Pierre Renouvin, *Histoire des Relations Internationales: VII, les Crises du XXe Siècle. II. de 1929 à 1945* (Paris, Hachette, 1958), pp. 78–82, and Roy Douglas, *World Crisis and British Decline, 1929–56* (London, Macmillan, 1986), pp. 47–8.

32 Mario Toscano in A. O. Sarkissian (ed.), *Studies in Diplomatic History and Historiography in Honour of G. P. Gooch* (London, Longman, 1961), pp. 137, 146.

33 Fischer, *Abyssinian Crisis,* pp. 67, 148.

34 Nicholas Rostow, *Anglo-French Relations, 1934–36* (London, Macmillan, 1984), pp. 201–2.

35 Alan Cassels, 'Switching partners: Italy in A. J. P. Taylor's *Origins of the Second World War*' in Gordon Martel (ed.), *The Origins of the Second World War Reconsidered* (London, Allen & Unwin, 1986), p. 82.

36 Schmidt, *Politics of Appeasement,* pp. 257–9.

37 Frank Hardie, *The Abyssinian Crisis* (London, Batsford, 1974), pp. 199–200.

38 Neville Thompson, *The Anti-Appeasers: Conservative Opposition to Appeasement in the 1930s* (Oxford, Clarendon Press, 1971), p. 101.

39 For a superb analysis of Italy's declining importance see Brian R. Sullivan, 'More than meets the eye: the Ethiopian war and the origins of the Second World War' in Gordon Martel (ed.), *The Origins of the Second World War Reconsidered: Second Edition* (London, Routledge, 1999), pp. 178–203; see also Mary Habeck 'The Spanish Civil War and the origins of the Second World War' in *ibid.,* p. 218, and Deist et al., *Germany and the Second World War,* pp. 633–5.

40 Peters, *Eden,* p. 173.

41 James Thomas Emmerson, *The Rhineland Crisis 7 March 1936: A Study in Multilateral Diplomacy* (London, Temple Smith, 1977), pp. 64–5.

42 *Ibid.,* pp. 27–30, 33, 43–5.

43 *Ibid.,* pp. 75–9; Ian Kershaw, *The 'Hitler Myth': Image and Reality in the Third Reich* (Oxford, Oxford University Press, 1987), pp. 72–82.

44 Emmerson, *Rhineland,* pp. 90–94.

45 *Ibid.,* pp. 98–118.

46 *Ibid.,* pp. 131–3, 142–7.

47 Lamb, *Ghosts,* pp. 42, 46; see also the contemporary account in Major General A. C. Temperley, *The Whispering Gallery of Europe* (London, Collins, 1938), p. 331.

48 Emmerson, *Rhineland,* pp. 192–200, 217–18; Post, *Dilemmas,* pp. 242, 249.

49 Emmerson, *Rhineland,* pp. 228–33, 237–8, 241; Norton Medlicott 'Britain and Germany: the search for agreement' in David Dilks (ed.), *Retreat from Power* (London, Macmillan, 1981), Vol. One, pp. 99–100.

CHAPTER SIX

PRELUDE TO GERMAN AGGRESSION

From 1936 Hitler felt a new urgency to implement his ambitions while circumstances remained favourable. Britain showed signs of slipping into pure pacifism. In a memorandum for the Cabinet in July 1936 Eden described the aims of British policy as 'first to secure peace in the world, if possible, and, secondly, to keep the country out of war'.[1] In that same summer the chiefs of staff and Hankey joined to demand of the government that for at least the next three years they should make any concessions necessary to prevent war, including a refusal to contemplate military measures in response to adverse developments in the whole of Central and Eastern Europe and in all non-Empire Mediterranean countries except Spanish Morocco with its proximity to Gibraltar.[2] Underlying all this was not only a desire to avoid war while the rearmament programme was carried to completion, but also a high degree of disarray and distrust between the two countries, Britain and France, that most stood in Hitler's way. Some in high positions in Britain wrote off France as almost a cypher. For instance, the powerful civil service head, Warren Fisher, who was a Germanophobe by natural inclination,[3] could write in September 1936 that 'Paris is at present of no great importance whereas Berlin (and Rome) are.'[4] Symptomatic of this were Anglo-French recriminations about events in the relatively distant past that were of no direct contemporary relevance.[5] French leaders, for their part, could feel tempted to have done with Britain and to make their own arrangements with Germany.[6] More seriously, many in France including in their embassy in Berlin,[7] became more convinced than ever that Hitler discounted their country after his Rhineland success and concerned himself only with Britain. This impression of the diminished importance of France is endorsed by perhaps the leading historian of

Second World War diplomatic origins, Gerhard Weinberg, in whose view the Rhineland crisis 'constituted France's abdication from any significant role in European diplomacy. The initiative would pass to Germany, checked if at all by Britain.'[8] Paradoxically, this gradually caused defeatism in France to go into retreat. Once French leaders had identified Britain as being virtually all important, they concluded that they were in a situation in which they could not lose: if appeasement worked it would save France as well as Britain; if it failed and there was war Britain would be on the same side as France without any anti-French recriminations and its industrial and manpower resources would eventually tell against Germany.[9] It was in fact to be the case that the last phase of peace was characterised by the near disappearance of what had been the customary Anglo-French rows about policy to Germany, though quarrels about policy to Italy continued.

Britain was, however, slow to stir. There was, astonishingly, no meeting of the Cabinet's foreign policy committee between 25 August 1936 and 10 March 1937.[10] The danger of Britain tolerating Nazi aggression until it was itself threatened in the most direct way is illustrated by two statements by Eden relating to his foreign secretaryship from 1935 to 1938. Pure fatalism is reflected in his reminiscence in 1957 that, 'It was just an open question then, I thought, whether appeasement might succeed.'[11] In the particular case of Eastern Europe, he expressed an actual conviction that Britain should not act. In July 1936 he informed the cabinet that 'policy ought to be framed on the basis that we could not help Eastern Europe'.[12]

The temptation to be passive was reinforced in the middle and later months of 1936 by two finite blows to any hope of collective security and by two others of a more open-ended nature. The first, and one of the most neglected origins of the war, came in August when King Carol dismissed his anti-Nazi Foreign Minister, Nicolae Titulescu, and effectively made Romania neutral. French military thinking about a war in Central Europe, starting on the Czech–German border, had assumed that Romania would serve as a substantial hinterland. Carol's action raised a question about whether Czechoslovakia was militarily defensible, even in advance of the German annexation of Austria. France was to throw away an opportunity to retrieve the situation in April 1937 when it declined an opportunity not only to rebuild but also to expand a security bulwark in Central Europe when it (and Britain) turned down a suggestion by France's traditional 'Little Entente' friends (Czechoslovakia, Romania and Yugoslavia) to mediate the differences between them and Hungary at a time of poor German–Hungarian relations.[13] Owing to its geographical situation, Hungary was the key to the strategic mastery of central Europe, as Hitler was to show that he understood by his desperate attempts to hang on to it in the last winter of the Second World War. Instead of cultivating Hungary, France, after an initial flirtation in 1920, repeatedly snubbed it.[14] In this way a real opportunity, if not to prevent war, then at least to make Germany's position less favourable, was lost. The form of government in Hungary between the wars was rightwing and authoritarian. The country was heavily dependent on Germany economically,[15] and its regime shared an interest with the Nazis in anti-Semitism. Despite all this, the pre-eminent figure, the Regent, Miklós Horthy, simply did not trust Hitler's judgment and was convinced that he would overreach himself. When he tried to warn the Fuhrer about the danger of eschewing moderation on a state visit to Germany in August 1938, his doubts are unlikely to have been dispelled by Hitler's reply: 'Nonsense, shut up.'[16] Yet, having been itself snubbed by the Western powers and after witnessing the sacrifice of Czechoslovakia by them at Munich, it was inevitable that Hungary should have thrown in its lot with the Third Reich, especially after Hitler allowed it to achieve some of its own ambitions against Czechoslovakia in late 1938 by awarding it some of southern Slovakia.

The second finite event was in Western Europe and can be dealt with more briefly. It occurred in October 1936 when Belgium announced its intention, following the remilitarisation of the Rhineland, to terminate its security links with France and become neutral, placing central reliance on Germany's promise to respect its neutrality. The grateful German General Staff calculated that the virtual elimination of any danger of being attacked from Belgian territory increased their offensive capacity against France by between 20 and 30 per cent.[17]

The most important of the open-ended aids to German aggression also began in October 1936 with Mussolini's celebrated announcement of the Rome–Berlin 'Axis' following German recognition of the Italian annexation of Ethiopia, and his (less well-remembered) pronouncement that the Italian border with France would be militarised. France now had to face uncertainty on the northern border (Belgium) and a potential new enemy on an eastern border (Italy) to add to the prospect that it might no longer be possible to resist German arms in Central Europe. Mussolini's announcement came three months after the start of an episode, the Spanish Civil War, that threatened France with yet another hostile neighbour, on its south western border if the rightwing insurgents won and threw in their lot with Germany and Italy. More immediately this war served, like the one in Ethiopia, to distract attention from Germany, to reinforce conservative fears in both Britain and France of communism as a consequence of Soviet aid to the embattled Spanish Republic,[18] and to add to fears about going to war over an 'irrelevant' country. British and French policy towards the Spanish Civil War centred from the beginning to the end on 'non-intervention' whose purpose was to 'set an example' to other countries that they might follow or might not – as in the cases of Germany, Italy and Russia – but which would ensure that the war stayed localised.[19] In 1938 Chamberlain was to acknowledge with unusual frankness that non-intervention would continue to be British policy even though it was a 'fiction'.[20] Western fears of the war spreading were actually exaggerated; Hitler, also, was determined not to let that happen. In 1936 he gave the Spanish rebels enough aid to ensure that their insurgency did not fail but not enough to bring them speedy victory. A long and localised war in Spain suited his aims as likely to produce problems for his opponents from which he could only profit.[21]

One of the determining factors in British policy was the stability of Portugal which was regarded as vital to the security of the British empire in a way that Spain was not. London shared the view of the Portuguese ruler, Salazar, that a communist Spain would seek to take over his country and was indulgent to his warnings that he would only refrain from total support for Franco if Britain interpreted non-intervention in a way that favoured the latter. This produced the great gain of a Portugal that was likely to be benevolently neutral towards Britain if there was a European war, though Chamberlain, with staggering folly, was willing to throw away this advantage in the winter of 1937–38 by offering Germany some of the very colonies that made Portugal strategically important.[22]

Spain certainly widened the rift between Italy and the democracies. An absurdly named 'Gentlemen's Agreement' between Britain and Italy at the beginning of 1937 was broken by Mussolini within days with the sending of Italian reinforcements to join the 'volunteers' already fighting alongside Franco's forces. At the same time evidence mounted of anti-British Italian intrigues in the Middle East, especially in Egypt and Yemen.[23] In 1938 there was to be a vicious 'radio war' between Britain and Italy with each broadcasting attacks against the other in Arabic.[24] During 1937 and into 1938 most British opinion continued to regard Italy as the greatest menace to peace. In the government only Eden agreed; to him, the Gentlemen's Agreement was simply a way of buying time until British rearmament was so far advanced that Mussolini could be overawed by overwhelming force.[25] However, the government did reclassify Italy first from a friend to a neutral and then to a potential enemy. Much of Britain's small army was now earmarked to defend Egypt and the Suez Canal against a lightning attack from Italian-held Libya, of which there were rumours from time to time.[26] For its part, Italy began to draw up war plans against Britain for the first time in 1937, though the means for such a war had been or were being diminished in Ethiopia and Spain.[27]

In the autumn of 1937 the threat of force was highly successful in causing Mussolini to call off Italian submarine attacks on vessels sailing to Spanish republican ports. After that, however, the Italian factor was to play a major part in prolonging British unwillingness to respond to German forward moves in two ways. The government could not disregard warnings from its military chiefs, especially the Admiralty, that Britain simply could not face three enemies simultaneously, and that Italy was the obvious one to be weaned back to neutrality.[28] Chamberlain did respond to these warnings, and from early 1938 was attracted to winning over Italy as a friendly neutral that might also mediate between Britain and Germany. It was an aspiration that appeared nearer to being realised by the Anglo-Italian agreement of April 1938 on maintaining the status quo in the Mediterranean and Red Sea areas, on withdrawing Italian forces from Spain and on British recognition that Ethiopia belonged to Italy once withdrawal was complete.[29] Chamberlain was not acting alone. Many in British ruling circles yearned for a return to the golden years of Anglo-Italian relations in the early 1930s when a Labour Foreign Secretary had praised fascist foreign policy as being 'as good as gold',[30] and when Mussolini had treated the then British ambassador as a personal friend and the embassy had been a delightful place for a young diplomat to work.[31]

While his most important potential opponent was being distracted in this way, Hitler, in 1936–37, addressed himself to the problem of a timetable for German aggression. The framework within which he would have to operate was becoming clearer to him. Soviet intervention in the Spanish Civil War confirmed, if any confirmation had been needed, that Bolshevism was the ultimate enemy. Of more immediate concern was his recognition that he could not have Britain as an ally and would eventually have to face up to it as a possible enemy. Britain had followed the Anglo-German naval agreement with repeated enquiries about a general political settlement in Europe. It had rejected any idea of dividing part of the world with Germany and such fantasies as Ribbentrop's proposal while he was ambassador in London to join the German–Japanese Anti-Comintern Pact. Hitler relaxed restraints on the publication of expressions of Anglophobia of which he himself had never been a devotee.[32]

Hitler had a sense of urgency stemming partly from fear that he would not live to old age or would lose his faculties and not be able to continue with his 'career'.[33] The German economy was running into problems, some of which were of the Nazis' own making, such as their failure in agriculture as a result of which Germany was having to import essential foodstuffs. Others were outside the Nazi regime's control, including trends in the terms of trade as a result of which German manufactured exports fell in price between 1933 and 1936 by 9 per cent while its imports of raw materials rose in price by the same percentage figure.[34] Relieving economic problems of this kind in a conventional way would have involved taking action to prevent inflation and to boost exports. Instead, as related in chapter 3, a Four Year Plan was initiated under the direction of Goering who shared both Hitler's aims and his view that politics should now assume complete primacy over economics. Germany was to be made as economically self-sufficient as possible with the development of such products as synthetic oil and rubber to make it proof against economic warfare and blockade, and rearmament was to be accelerated with inevitable cuts in living standards for wage-earners and infringements on the rights of owners of private capital, especially industrial.

These policies did not bring about the almost immediate economic collapse that would have occurred in a market economy. Even so, they were not, and were not intended to be, sustainable for more than a few years. Rearmament, intended to make expansion possible, was now also making it an urgent necessity. This raised the danger that time might run out before rearmament was complete. In a somewhat inchoate way the idea of short wars that brought temporary over-whelming force to bear increasingly commended itself.[35] War, conquest and the ruthless exploitation of conquered or merely cowed foreign countries were to be the means of bringing relief to the German economy.[36] War would also provide a convenient pretext for imposing severe economic measures such as food rationing that Hitler would not contemplate in peacetime on a population who were manifestly unresponsive, in the absence of war, to calls for sacrifice and hard work for the sake of the Fuhrer and Reich. In that way could be preserved the 'compartmentalisation of people's consciousness' by which many Germans retained confidence in Hitler but not in many aspects of Nazi rule.[37]

The nature of the warfare that Hitler envisaged remains controversial among historians. There is the view that blitzkrieg wars against weak victims were intended to be the prelude to a large-scale war against other great powers in the mid 1940s. Thus large expansion plans for the army and navy were incomplete or were in their early stages in mid 1939, and Goering's plans for increased steel output were not due for completion till 1944 and for synthetic oil not until 1946.[38] Against this have to be set some of both Hitler's words and his deeds. In September 1935 he told some prominent Nazis that he planned war in four years' time and in October 1936 he told the Italian Foreign Minister, Count Galeazzo Ciano, that he would be ready for war in three years but would prefer to wait for four or five.[39] On the eve of the Munich conference he himself was eager for war with Britain and France if they did not back down and could not be wholly sure that the Soviet Union would not then join in against Germany. After Munich he worked for an early war against the two major Western countries before turning against Poland, if it should be necessary to turn against that country at all. These matters of German policy will be examined in much more detail. At this point it needs only to be argued that the thesis that Hitler was dismayed by the necessity to embark on a big war in 1939 is highly questionable.

Perhaps the key to understanding Hitler's thinking rests in the existence of a streak of fatalism and 'short termism' in his mentality. He would undoubtedly have preferred wars against individual opponents – Poland in 1939, France or Russia in 1941–42 – in which victory would be fairly certain, to be followed by a war with Britain and the United States, or the latter alone after 1943 by which time

Germany would have built up its naval power. On the other hand, he was prepared to wage a war beginning in 1939 in which reliance would have to be placed on blitzkrieg in the absence of German quantitative superiority in arms, provided he was confident of a rapid and cheap victory over one opponent, in the circumstances of 1939, Poland.[40] Hitler's readiness to take this sort of risk was increased by the generally favourable trend of events in the mid to late 1930s. Economically, Germany's industrial output in 1938 was 50 per cent above its peak in the late 1920s, providing vastly for war preparations; exports were only 40 per cent of what they had been ten years earlier.[41] Here was self-sufficiency and growth, no matter how insecure its foundations. In addition the reduced volume of exports was still sufficient to establish predominance for Germany in the foreign trade of the countries of south east Europe with their raw material resources.[42] To set against that, there were looming crises within Germany, not only in agriculture and the near exhaustion of reserves of convertible currency, but also in labour relations and a danger of inflation as the regime printed more and more money to pay its bills. There was, therefore, a 'crisis ridden relationship between domestic affairs and war in 1938–39'.[43] Hitler was aware of the fragility of his regime's achievements, such as they were, and that they could not be sustained by a Reich that remained at peace. In a speech to some of his generals in January 1938 he said that Germany must expand 'by brute force' and that its powerful economic position in central and south east Europe was no more than a starting point: 'One day the entire world must and shall belong to this united block of central Europe.'[44]

Hitler's megalomania was growing. By early 1938 he had abandoned altogether cabinet meetings; admittedly, they had for long been infrequent and perfunctory and cabinet ministers had for some time been officially designated as members of the Fuhrer's 'staff'. He by this time invariably dealt with ministers, as with other leading personalities, individually to give them orders.[45] His concern with maintaining popularity with the German people was still strong in 1936,[46] and was not dead at the time of Munich, but was decreasing. The apparatus of repression and terror in the Nazi state was strengthened between 1936 and 1939 with the specific aim of crushing any manifestations of discontent against Hitler's foreign policy. He felt nothing but hatred for Germans who gave him anything but total support.

Finally, from 1936–37, Hitler had a clearer idea than before of the identity of not only his likely enemies but also of his likely allies. Japan will be discussed in chapter 10. Even as all hopes of an alliance with Britain were ending, a durable pattern of partnership with Italy was taking shape. A de facto German–Italian alliance was in existence as early as March 1936 as League of Nations sanctions estranged Mussolini from the Western powers. A sinister product of this was an agreement on cooperation between the secret police forces of the two states.[47] In late 1936 Mussolini had, as already noted, responded to formal German recognition of the annexation of Ethiopia by announcing the existence of an 'axis' between Rome and Berlin, whatever that meant, and inviting other of what he called peace-loving nations to join. In November 1937 Mussolini was himself persuaded to join the German–Japanese Anti-Comintern pact.[48] What was most gratifying of all to the Germans was that Italy was being acquired as an ally on their terms, as a junior. This stemmed almost inevitably from the growing material strength of the Third Reich and the actually diminishing strength of Italy, whose material base had been a fraction of Germany's even before Mussolini began his interventions in East Africa and Spain. The symbol of the Duce's acceptance of inequality was his yielding to the Nazi aim of the incorporation of Austria into the German Reich. Hitler did offer something in return by sending Goering in early 1937 to inform Mussolini that he was definitively washing his hands of any interest in the ethnic Germans of the South Tyrol whom Italy was free to expel from their homeland if it so wished. Mussolini responded by rejecting an Austrian plea to reaffirm Italy's interest in Austrian independence.[49]

In the same month that Italy joined the Anti-Comintern Pact Hitler summoned a conference of German diplomatic and military chiefs that was recorded by one of the participants, Colonel Hossbach, and that constitutes 'the first ascertainable instance of Hitler expounding long term foreign policy aims to the highest ranking representatives' of government and the armed forces, and that serves, therefore, as 'a sort of "political testament".'[50] Starting from an irrational premise – the familiar proposition that Germany's supposed food problem could only be solved by eastern expansion – Hitler expatiated on the need for such expansion to be embarked upon before 1943–45 for two rational reasons: by then other countries' rearmament would be complete and the leadership of the Nazi movement would be losing its dynamism through old age. He predicted that disarray among the

Western powers in 1938 would make it possible to destroy Czechoslovakia, identified alongside Austria as one of the first victims, without risk from that quarter. Within five weeks the German armed forces adopted Plan Green, a blueprint for a war of conquest against Czechoslovakia.[51] Notably absent from all these plans and preparations was any reference to the well-being of the 'Sudeten German' minority in Czechoslovakia whose wellbeing was to be the Nazis' public pretext for action against that state.[52]

Hitler's forecast of the Western powers' passivity in 1938 received some backing from the recent foreign policy of one of the two countries involved, France. The left of centre Blum government had a typically Marxist belief that Germany's grievances were fundamentally economic, and conducted desultory discussions with the economic technocrat, Hjalmar Schacht, that distracted attention from the real Nazi goals and, in particular, involved France making no attempt to pin Germany down on its aims towards France's ally, Czechoslovakia.[53] The other Western nation, Britain, was more perplexing. Neville Chamberlain had become Prime Minister in May 1937 determined on a more systematic approach to the appeasement of Germany, a country that he defined as posing the only truly serious threat to European peace. Although unduly fixated by colonial appeasement and what might be gained politically by according Germany greater access to tropical raw materials, Chamberlain's thinking in 1937 specifically included the need for a pact by the great powers to protect Czechoslovakia from aggression; while Whitehall minutes dwelt on the impossibility of a war that broke out in Central Europe remaining confined to that area. All this held out little hope for Hitler to pick off his victims one by one.[54] However, opposition to change brought about by force did not mean opposition to change under any circumstances. In November 1937 one of the most senior members of the government, Lord Halifax, visited Germany, in theory unofficially, and was received by Hitler and Goering. He indicated a readiness to agree to German expansion to absorb ethnic German territories in Central Europe into the Reich as part of a settlement for permanent peace, as long as that was all that Germany wanted territorially in Europe.[55]

Notes

1 A. R. Peters, *Anthony Eden at the Foreign Office 1931–1938* (Aldershot, Gower, 1986), p. 222.

2 Gaines Post, Jr., *Dilemmas of Appeasement* (Ithaca, NY, Cornell University Press, 1993), pp. 266–7; Joseph A. Maiolo, *The Royal Navy and Nazi Germany, 1933–39* (London, Macmillan, 1998), pp. 119–20, 137–40.

3 D. C. Watt, *Personalities and Policies: Studies in the Formulation of British Foreign Policy in the Twentieth Century* (London, Longman, 1965), p. 105.

4 Peters, *Eden*, p. 256.

5 George Scott, *The Rise and Fall of the League of Nations* (London, Hutchinson, 1973), p. 343.

6 See for example, Andrew J. Crozier, *Appeasement and Germany's Last Bid for Colonies* (London, Macmillan, 1988), p. 317 n. 136.

7 Armand Bérard, *Au Temps du Danger Allemand: un Ambassadeur se Souvient* (Paris, Plon, 1976), pp. 287–8, 307.

8 Gerhard L. Weinberg, *The Foreign Policy of Hitler's Germany: Diplomatic Revolution in Europe, 1933–36* (Chicago, IL, University of Chicago Press, 1970), pp. 253, 262–3; see also Martin Thomas, *Britain, France and Appeasement* (Oxford, Berg, 1996), pp. 2–3, 19.

9 Thomas, *Britain, France and Appeasement*, pp. 41–2, 55, 69–72, 229–34. For a touching statement about the ultimate fulfilment of this hope see Etienne Mantoux, *The Carthaginian Peace or the Economic Consequences of Mr. Keynes* (London, Oxford University Press, 1946), pp. 200–1.

10 Post, *Dilemmas*, p. 301.

11 Victor Rothwell, *Anthony Eden: a Political Biography 1931–57* (Manchester, Manchester University Press, 1992), p.41.

12 Peters, *Eden*, p. 260.

13 Anthony T. Komjathy, *The Crises of France's East Central European Diplomacy 1933–1938* (New York, Columbia University Press, 1976), pp. 170–9, 195–6, 217; Weinberg, *Diplomatic Revolution*, pp. 321–3.

14 Pierre Renouvin, *Histoire des Relations Internationales: VII, les Crises du XXe Siècle. I, de 1914 à 1929* (Paris, Hachette, 1957), pp. 280–5; *II, de 1929 à 1945* (Paris, Hachette, 1958), pp. 28–9, 71–2.

15 Elizabeth Wiskemann, *Undeclared War* (London, Constable, 1939), pp. 7–46.

16 Gerhard L. Weinberg, *The Foreign Policy of Hitler's Germany: Starting World War II, 1937–39* (Chicago, IL, University of Chicago Press, 1980), pp. 232, 404–9.

17 James Thomas Emmerson, *The Rhineland Crisis 7 March 1936* (London, Temple Smith, 1977), p. 234.

18 Neville Thompson, *The Anti-Appeasers: Conservative Opposition to Appeasement in the 1930s* (Oxford, Clarendon Press, 1971), p. 124; Lawrence R. Pratt, *East of Malta, West of Suez* (Cambridge, Cambridge University Press, 1975), pp. 42–3.

19 Michael Alpert, *A New International History of the Spanish Civil War* (London, Macmillan, 1994); see also Jill Edwards, *The British Government and the Spanish Civil War, 1936–1939* (London, Macmillan, 1979).

20 Renouvin, *Les Crises, II*, p. 107.

21 Weinberg, *Diplomatic Revolution*, pp. 284–99, 359–64.

22 Glyn Stone, *The Oldest Ally: Britain and the Portuguese Connection, 1936–41* (Woodbridge, The Boydell Press for the Royal Historical Society, 1994), pp. 7–14, 23–32, 46, 99–113; see also Frank Roberts, *Dealing with Dictators* (London, Weidenfeld & Nicolson, 1991), pp. 25–6.

23 Pratt, *East*, pp. 63–8, 124–7.

24 W. J. West, *Truth Betrayed* (London, Duckworth, 1987), pp. 103–6.

25 Peters, *Eden*, pp. 232–40.

26 Pratt, *East*, pp. 48, 69–71, 74–8, 80–7, 128–32.

27 Steven Morewood, 'The Chiefs of Staff, the "man on the spot" and the Italo-Abyssinian emergency, 1935–36' in Dick Richardson and Glyn Stone (eds), *Decisions and Diplomacy* (London, Routledge, 1994), p. 99.

28 Pratt, *East,* pp. 103–5, 108–17.

29 *Ibid.,* pp. 135–8.

30 David Carlton, *MacDonald Versus Henderson* (London, Macmillan, 1970), p. 143.

31 Ivone Kirkpatrick, *The Inner Circle: Memoirs* (London, Macmillan, 1959), pp. 45–6.

32 G. T. Waddington, '"Hassgegner": German views of Great Britain in the later 1930s', *History*, 81: 261 (1996), 22–39; W. Deist, M. Messerschmidt, H-E. Volkmann and W. Witte, *Germany and the Second World War: Vol. I, The Build-up of German Aggression* (Oxford, Clarendon Press, 1990), pp. 629–32.

33 See for example, Norman Rich, *Hitler's War Aims: Ideology, the Nazi State and the Course of Expansion* (London, Deutsch, 1973), pp. 81–2.

34 William Carr, *Arms, Autarky and Aggression* (London, Arnold, 1972), pp. 53–4.

35 Wilhelm Deist, *The Wehrmacht and German Rearmament* (London, Macmillan, 1981), pp. 40–3, 100.

36 Timothy Mason, 'Some origins of the Second World War' in Esmonde M. Robertson (ed.), *The Origins of the Second World War* (London, Macmillan, 1971), pp. 103–36; Carr, *Arms*, chapter 3; R. J. Overy,

    Goering: The 'Iron Man' (London, Routledge, 1984), pp. 50–6, 83.

37 Timothy Mason, 'The domestic dilemma of Nazi conquests: a response to critics' in Thomas Childers and Jane Caplan (eds), *Reevaluating the Third Reich* (New York, Holmes & Meier, 1993), pp. 163–8, 171, 173, 186.

38 Overy, *Goering*, pp. 82–7.

39 Weinberg, *Diplomatic Revolution*, p. 355.

40 E. M. Robertson, 'Hitler's planning for war and the response of the Great powers' in H. W. Koch (ed.), *Aspects of the Third Reich* (London, Macmillan, 1985), pp. 206–12; A. Alexandroff and R. Rosecrance, 'Deterrence in 1939', *World Politics*, 29 (1977), 404–24.

41 Maurice Larkin, *Gathering Pace: Continental Europe 1870–1945* (London, Macmillan, 1969), p. 334.

42 See the summary in Pierre Renouvin and Jean-Baptiste Duroselle, *Introduction to the History of International Relations* (London, Pall Mall Press, 1968), pp. 62–4.

43 Mason in Childers and Caplan (eds), *Reevaluating*, pp. 163–4, 167, 175.

44 David Irving, *The War Path: Hitler's Germany 1933–39* (London, Joseph, 1978), p. 67.

45 Martin Broszat, *The Hitler State* (London, Longman, 1981), pp. 280–2.

46 Ian Kershaw, *The Nazi Dictatorship* (London, Arnold, 1985), pp. 78–9.

47 Esmonde M. Robertson, *Mussolini as Empire-Builder: Europe and Africa 1932–36* (London, Macmillan, 1977), pp. 186–8.

48 Elizabeth Wiskemann, *The Rome–Berlin Axis* (London, Fontana revised edn., 1966), chapter 4.

49 Weinberg, *Starting World War II*, pp. 270–4, 286–7, 305–6.

50 Aigner 'Hitler's ultimate aims – a programme of world domination' in Koch (ed.), *Aspects*, p. 264.

51 Carr, *Arms*, pp. 70–80; Robertson in Koch (ed.), *Aspects*, pp. 216–17; Deist et al., *Germany and the Second World War*, pp. 636–9; Gordon A. Craig, *Germany 1866–1945* (Oxford, Clarendon Press, 1978), pp. 698–700.

52 Weinberg, *Starting World War II*, pp. 40–1.

53 *Ibid.*, pp. 89–94.

54 *Ibid.*, pp. 72–6, 96–7, 103–5, 131–3.

55 Andrew Roberts, *'The Holy Fox': A Life of Lord Halifax* (London, Macmillan, 1992), chapter 9, pp. 64–75.

CHAPTER SEVEN

GERMAN EXPANSION IN 1938

Hitler's military chiefs were not optimistic that Czechoslovakia or even Austria could be seized without a general war. Their assessment in late 1937 was that the former could be conquered despite its formidable frontier defences and that if France and Russia joined in under their treaty arrangements with the Czechs the German army would be able to conduct a successful defensive war against them. In this respect they were pleased by Hitler's order in early 1938 for massive acceleration of work on the Westwall fortifications along the Franco-German border.[1] However, the generals were unwilling to accept responsibility for the consequences if Britain entered such a conflict, and still less if both Britain and Poland came in. The army's anxieties were more than matched by those of the navy and air force. The prospect of having to fight the Royal Navy in 1938 instead of at least five or six years later so appalled the naval chief, Erich Raeder, that he waited six months before discussing it with his senior officers who responded that the impossible was being demanded of them, though they might be able to respond if Germany gained control of the coasts of Denmark, the Low Countries and France at least as far as Brittany. Before 1938 the Luftwaffe had hardly considered Britain as a potential enemy. Faced with having to do so, it demanded fantastically increased resources, but had to admit that those would require years, not months, to be forthcoming.[2]

Early in 1938 Hitler decided that the time had come to remove those who doubted his leadership from the military and diplomatic establishments. He had had ample opportunity to sense the pervasive pessimism in the highest levels of the military elite and in particular a tendency to overrate the French army.[3] War minister Werner von Blomberg and army commander Werner von Fritsch were compelled

to resign on morals charges, true in the case of the former, but fabricated in that of the latter. They were replaced by pliable tools of
Hitler's will, Wilhelm Keitel and Walther von Brauchitsch, though
Hitler himself took on the functions of War Minister with Keitel as
merely the head of his staff. Blomberg had advised against the eleva-
tion of Keitel, whom Hitler had never met, on the grounds that his
talents were essentially those of an office boy, to which the Fuhrer
replied that that was precisely what he was looking for.[4] A further
sixty generals were retired or transferred to insignificant positions.
As already noted, von Neurath was replaced as Foreign Minister by
Ribbentrop who was given a brief to nazify the venerable German
Foreign Ministry, the *Wilhelmstrasse*. Even its most senior officials
were now required to have what the new Foreign Minister called a
'blind faith' in the Fuhrer and himself and to understand that their
role was a purely technical one.[5]

After making the changes in military command, Hitler proceeded
to move against Austria. His original intention had been to build up
tension against that country, using concocted provocations that
might have included the assassination of the German minister in Vienna. A puppet Nazi government would then have been installed before annexation or *Anschluss* after an interval. His decision to act
before the winter was over was partly to improve his regime's domestic standing after the sordid Blomberg–Fritsch affair, and was partly
dictated by evidence that the possible opponents of *Anschluss* would
actually do nothing. These included Britain and France but the
Fuhrer, as always in matters Austrian, was most concerned with Italy,
and was conscious from his most recent visit there in the previous
September that Mussolini was ready to lift his veto against annexation, though, with acute sensitivity, he had resisted the urgings of
many of his advisers to seek an explicit undertaking from the Duce.[6]

Without foreign support, the attempts of the Schussnigg government to preserve Austrian independence inevitably collapsed. On 12
March Hitler entered Austria to a tumultuous welcome from part of
the population and the following day, abandoning all caution, he
proclaimed its immediate annexation to the Reich. The reaction of
democratic countries was curiously mixed. On the one hand, there
was complete readiness to accept a fait accompli, symbolised by the
haste with which they converted their legations in Vienna into consu-
late-generals.[7] On the other, enough was known about the brutality
and trickery that had attended the *Anschluss* to cause anger and

dismay, even in the Chamberlain government in Britain, and that made its contribution to the eventual conviction that dealings with Hitler were folly, if only because he was utterly untrustworthy. More immediately, the *Anschluss* provided a temporary lifeline for a German economy that was in a desperate condition because of the reckless concentration of resources on armaments. The gold and foreign currency reserves of Austria, of this small and far from wealthy country were at least fifteen times what the Reichsbank was holding in March 1938. Austria had reserves of oil and iron ore, whose output the Nazis raised to reduce imports of these commodities from outside the enlarged Reich, and it had a pool of unemployed labour, 100,000 of whom – men with skills – were conscripted in 1938 to work in armaments plants in the pre-Anschluss Reich.[8]

Some weeks after the *Anschluss*, Halifax, newly promoted to Foreign Secretary, warned Ribbentrop, who was visiting London, that it would be difficult for Britain to remain passive if Germany again resorted to 'naked force'.[9] This would have been unwelcome to Hitler who was by this time heavily preoccupied with the desire to annex Czechoslovakia without having to fight a general war. Any strategy would, in public terms, have to be based on concern about the Sudeten German minority in that country, though how little Hitler really cared about Germans outside the borders of the Third Reich was demonstrated in May when, during a visit to Italy, he reaffirmed that his interest in whatever might happen to the ethnic Germans of South Tyrol was nil.[10] Relations between Czechs and Sudeten Germans had inevitable strains, but the notion that they were oppressed was exaggerated. Making up one quarter of the total population of Czechoslovakia, they were, in any case, simply too numerous to be an oppressed minority short of the imposition of a full apartheid system. The Nazi lie that the well-being of the Sudeten Germans was of central importance to them was, however, extremely successful with international opinion and not least with the British government.

Britain's entry as a major actor into Central European affairs came with the May crisis of 1938 when British intelligence in London passed to the Czech legation purported information that eleven German divisions were marching towards the Czech border. This was entirely untrue but Prague mobilised its reservists and Europe appeared to teeter on the brink of war. When it became clear that nothing was going to happen the British government publicly rejoiced that Germany had backed down. Hitler appeared to have been outmanoeuvred if not humiliated. He had already decided to eliminate Czechoslovakia and detailed military planning for that purpose had already begun.[11] Even so, the importance of the May episode was great and twofold: Britain was being drawn into Central European affairs and Germany was faced with the prospect of Britain as an enemy and, if so, by definition its most formidable enemy. A meeting of air and naval staffs in Berlin that month agreed that 'Britain is emerging more and more as Germany's principle opponent.'[12] This British interest was the more important in that France was distancing itself from its Czechoslovak ally with warnings that it might not go to war at all if Czechoslovakia were attacked, and that if it did, it would take no military action in Europe but would attack Libya if Italy entered the conflict.[13] No military operation could have brought less succour to Czechoslovakia than that.

British policy has been criticised for becoming involved in a crisis without having any intention of going to war if there was a possibility of backing down. The matter was really more complex. For one thing, the Chamberlain government wanted Czechoslovakia to make a really generous offer on minority rights to force the Berlin government and the Sudeten Nazi leader, the personable, English speaking Konrad Henlein, to show their true colours. Czechosolvakia's failure to do that before September left Britain with little choice but, in effect, to give Germany the benefit of some doubt. A Czech offer would have exposed Nazi intransigence. Henlein enjoyed Olympian support among the Sudeten Germans; in Czech local elections in May his party received 78 per cent of the ethnic German vote. And, as early as 28 March, Hitler had instructed him that Sudeten demands must always be so high that Czechoslovakia would not accept them.[14] The Czechs denied themselves the opportunity to expose this.

At a conference with the French leaders in London in late April the British side stated that war would be inevitable if it became clear that German policy aimed at the complete elimination of Czechoslovakia. About the same time, Chamberlain and senior colleagues spoke freely to acquaintances whom they knew to be likely to pass information on to journalists, that the Czechs might as well surrender their western border areas without war because, even if there was a war and the Western democracies won it, those areas would have to pass to Germany under the doctrine of the democratic self-determination of peoples that should have been applied more consistently in Paris in

1919. Thus, even before the May crisis, British policy was moving towards a position in which Czechoslovakia would be abandoned if it was intransigent while Germany would be fought if its policy was demonstrably one of unbridled aggression. That was, of course, the essence of Nazi policy and, in late May, a date for invading Czechoslovakia was decided upon: 1 October. This was not known in London, or at least not believed, since reliable information about the timetable for German aggression was conveyed to the government by envoys from the anti-Hitler opposition in Germany, who were ignored in this as in all matters.

By contrast, the Czech government's refusal to make sweeping concessions to the Sudeten Germans was only too manifest. This exacerbated the existing absence of goodwill for Czechoslovakia in British policymaking circles. As early as 1933 a War Office document had dismissed Czechoslovakia as a 'ramshackle republic'.[15] The British minister in Prague from 1930 to 1936 was a snob, who despised the Czech political leaders for being bourgeois, and a racist who thought that Slavs were inferior to Germans. He even confessed to finding Czech people physically repulsive. His reports to London reflected these opinions. His successor took only a moderately more balanced view. In 1938 Britain had Germanophil envoys in both Prague and Berlin, the latter the notorious Nevile Henderson.[16] The Czechs themselves were not blameless. Their capacity for alienating British leaders peaked in September, when the Prague government sent really large sums of money into the private account of its minister in London, Jan Masaryk, to spend on buying support for the Czech cause and subsidising such anti-government bodies as Winston Churchill's The Focus organisation. The Germans knew about this from intelligence intercepts that they revealed to the British government. Chamberlain's temper towards the Czechs was not improved by the knowledge that they were subsidising his domestic opponents.[17] He was, not unreasonably, sensitive about such matters. The previous March he had noted that it was impossible to have great confidence in the French government 'which I suspect to be in closish (sic) touch with our Opposition'.[18]

It would be a mistake to exaggerate this factor in the British policy that was to culminate in the Munich agreement of 29 September. In August the government asked a former Liberal 'Cabinet Minister, Lord Runciman, to leave retirement and travel to Czechoslovakia to mediate between the government there and the Sudeten Germans.

This presupposed that the problem was still primarily an internal one within Czechoslovakia. By early September that assumption was starting to look invalid. On 4 September Henlein rejected a belated Czech offer of full autonomy for the Sudeten areas, embodying Runciman's proposal for them to become Swiss-type 'cantons', after which Czechoslovakia as a whole was to be cocooned in Swiss-like neutrality; in particular, it would abandon all links with the Soviet Union, links that British policymakers held to constitute a valid German grievance. Henlein's rupture of negotiations with Prague was a challenge to which the latter rose vigorously. It sent its security forces into the German districts and, with very little bloodshed, restored its authority. Many Nazis fled over the border and more moderate Germans appeared literally overnight, professing readiness to accept Prague's new terms. Faced with losing the initiative, Hitler responded at the annual Nuremburg Nazi Party rally with a vitriolic anti-Czech speech in which he appeared to threaten imminent invasion.

At this point, if consistency had been all-important, Britain should have supported the Czechs, especially as the French Prime Minister, Edouard Daladier, was imposing discipline on the more appeasement-minded members of his government, including his Foreign Minister, Georges Bonnet, in favour of standing by a Czechoslovakia that was now doing everything to be reasonable.[19] Instead, Chamberlain took the view that the stakes were too high for consistency to be the governing factor. The day before Hitler's speech he had written to his sister: 'I am satisfied that we should be wrong to allow the most vital decision that any country could take, the decision as to peace or war, to pass out of our hands into those of the ruler of another country and a lunatic at that.'[20] He was also influenced by an entire battery of domestic and external considerations, one of which, pressure from the dominions of the Commonwealth, took on new and briefly immense importance, though admittedly in the later stages of the crisis rather than in the initial decision that the British Prime Minister should invite himself to Germany.[21] That decision, 'Plan Z', was taken not even by the entire Cabinet but by Chamberlain himself and a small group of 'inner cabinet' colleagues. Hitler was to be informed of the visit, rather than asked whether he would welcome or accept it. He had little choice but to receive Chamberlain and did so at his summer residence at Berchtesgaden on 15 September. The Fuhrer made the apparent concession that he would wait a fortnight to see whether the only solution that he would accept, the outright cession of the Sudeten German areas to the Reich, could be achieved without war. The planned invasion (of the whole of Czechoslovakia) was two weeks away in any case, but Hitler was adopting a mask of reasonableness that it would prove impossible to drop until after the crisis was resolved. Appalled, he ordered the stepping up of plans for fabrication of Czech provocations, and renewed pressure on Poland and Hungary to invade Czechoslovakia simultaneously with Germany, to which the response was equivocation from Poland and an outright refusal from Hungary. Besides this setback, he had to admit to his entourage the existence of 'the danger that the Czechs might accept everything' denying him the war for which he craved.[22]

One thing that his ministers had insisted upon to Chamberlain was the proposition that only areas that were at least 80 per cent ethnic German should be transferred. He had no qualms about reducing that to 50 per cent. The Czech government of President Benes, who effectively made himself dictator of his country during the crisis,[23] accepted this after Britain and France had rejected out of hand his demand that, in return for giving up territory, all Germans in the reduced state should be expelled. Chamberlain flew again to negotiate with Hitler, this time at Godesberg on the Rhine, on 22 September. He was aware of evidence that public opinion in Britain was turning against concessions to a Germany that would concede nothing in return. His own Cabinet and Daladier were insistent on some form of international supervision of the redrawing of the German–Czech border and on the settlement of Polish and Hungarian territorial claims against Czechoslovakia being reserved to a later date. Hitler would concede neither of these points at Godesberg and Chamberlain returned to London in an atmosphere in which everyone, including himself, expected war.

Hitler's decision to back down to the minimal extent necessary to prevent war probably owed most to the 'situation reports' regularly provided by the SD (*Sicherheitsdienst*) police to the Nazi government from all localities in Germany which indicated that the mass of the German people would find a war incomprehensible when the Reich was being offered so much without a fight and that many of them simply did not want war under any circumstances.[24] To that extent, the outcome at Munich vindicated Chamberlain's strategy of appealing to the undoubted anti-war mentality of the majority of Germans. In the parliamentary debate on the agreement Chamberlain questioned whether anyone could doubt that Anglo-German friendship was 'the desire of the two peoples'. He made no assertion that it was Hitler's undoubted desire.[25] Indeed, after their first meeting at Berchtesgaden, Chamberlain had told the Cabinet that Hitler was the 'commonest little dog he had ever seen'.[26] Britain had broadcast what was, in effect, peace propaganda to Germany in the days before Munich, using a continental station (Radio Luxembourg) whose legal status was dubious in the eyes of the government's own broadcasting authorities.[27]

In addition, Hitler was influenced by two of the very few foreign statesmen for whom he had respect and even admiration. One was Mussolini, who not only informed Hitler that Italy would be neutral but who also backed British peace proposals and, in particular, advocated a four power conference to reach a peaceful settlement.[28] The other was King Boris III of Bulgaria who was in London when Chamberlain returned from Godesberg and whom the Prime Minister shrewdly asked to impress upon the Nazi leaders when he would be in Berlin in a few days' time that there was no element of bluff in Britain's threats about going to war if Czechoslovakia was invaded. Boris did so in his talks with Hitler and was not rebuffed. Chamberlain was in no doubt about his debt to the Bulgarian king. After Munich he instructed the British minister in Sofia to 'thank King Boris for what he had done and to tell him that it was felt that he had acted as "a great European"'.[29] The visit of Chamberlain's official envoy, Horace Wilson, also helped to convince Hitler that Britain would not shrink from war.

Hitler agreed to Mussolini's conference idea on 28 September and it met the following day in Munich and quickly reached agreement on German acquisition of all areas that the Reich government considered to be ethnic German, to be followed by the settlement of Polish and Hungarian claims and then the negotiation of an international guarantee of what remained of Czechoslovakia. Germany was to be one of the guarantors. Chamberlain presented an unenthusiastic Fuhrer with an Anglo-German declaration according to which the two countries were to share primary responsibility for preserving peace in Europe, and then returned to London to make an unwise and unplanned boast that he had achieved 'peace in our time'. Meanwhile Hitler was denied his last chance of a war against Czechoslovakia alone by Benes' decision not to fight which was taken against the advice of his army commanders and, easier to ignore, the Czech

Communist Party. He thought that he could keep the army and state intact to participate in the European war against Germany that he was convinced had been only briefly postponed. In fact, his position had become untenable and as early as 5 October he had to resign and go into exile, according to some reports taking £3 million of state funds with him.[30]

The debate about whether the West, led by Britain, should have gone to war in September 1938 goes on. If declarations of war had produced a successful military coup in Germany then resort to it would obviously have been proved right, though Czechoslovakia would have had to make much the same concessions to a post-Hitler Germany as were imposed on it at Munich.[31] There was certainly unease in the *Wehrmacht*, including the curious affair of one hundred officers sponsoring warnings published in the German language press in Switzerland that war would be too risky.[32] Yet it is probable that there would have been no successful coup and that war declarations would have been followed by a stalemate in which Germany would have been unlikely to strike the sort of decisive blow against France that it was to strike in 1940 and in which it would gradually have been weakened as the German economy suffered the consequences of Nazi mismanagement.[33] However, the democracies would have been plagued by doubts about a war in which many would question whether proof of insatiable German aggression had really been provided and, in Britain, in which many would have been embittered by the weakening of the Empire. The most recent scholarship indicates that the two most independent-minded dominions, Canada and South Africa, probably would, very resentfully, have gone to war after Godesberg because they were so locked into the Commonwealth system that they could not have remained neutral, but that they would then have worked to sever their Commonwealth ties as rapidly as possible.[34]

In any case, Chamberlain and his inner circle regarded the balance of military probabilities (though not the attitude of the dominions) as, in a sense, irrelevant. According to one of this select group, they all felt that it would be simply wrong to let the 'very complicated problem of Czechoslovakia' lead to world war.[35] To Chamberlain himself, in his own words: 'Whatever the odds might be in favour of peace or war, it was not money but men with which we were gambling, and he could not lightly enter into a conflict which might mean such frightful results for innumerable families, men, women and children of our own race.'[36] It should be added that, outside the inner group, there were ministers, besides Duff Cooper, the only one who actually resigned, to whom lack of sufficient British strength, about which they had to take the word of the military departments,[37] was the main justification for Munich.[38]

Hitler regarded Munich as a misfortune. He had wanted to destroy Czechoslovakia not only because of craving for a short, victorious war but also because he wanted its industrial capacity and its foreign exchange reserves. He had gained some of the former but none of the latter. He became impatient with a touch of recklessness. In October he remarked that he could not wait for his army to be 'fully prepared for war' because an army was never fully prepared; an army that was less powerful than was theoretically possible would suffice.[39] In the view of one leading scholar, any further backing down would have been a psychological impossibility for Hitler.[40] He was determined to take absolute control of events on the basis of four guiding principles: elimination of rump Czechoslovakia within months; the psychological preparation of the German people for war, coupled with a sharpened apparatus of repression for those who refused to be persuaded; the accommodation of Poland and Hungary to allow a one front war against Britain and France, after which the Soviet Union could be destroyed; and care never again to adopt a public posture that might force him to cancel a military operation that he had ordered. True to the last point, Hitler was never again to reverse a planned aggressive move.[41]

The second of these aims was achieved with surprising success. The Czech crisis had revealed much reluctance among the German public to go to war. After Munich the Nazi regime embarked on a subtle new propaganda line about the regrettable necessity for a country that valued its honour of sometimes resorting to force. After being dripfed with militarist ideas since 1933, many Germans found this convincing. The Nazi propaganda machine attributed war guilt in advance to any countries or peoples with which Germany might go to war, including Hitler's threat in a speech to the Reichstag that the Jews of Europe would be punished with extermination if there was a war.[42] But the most important of the guiding principles was the one under which Germany had to avoid a war on two fronts of the kind that it had fought between 1914 and 1917. It appeared obvious to Hitler after Munich that this must involve a showdown with Britain and France because they would not allow him to pursue his ambitions in the east yet, paradoxically, against a background of peace and tranquillity on Germany's eastern borders. War with France would concern principally the army. War with Britain would most concern the navy and air force. During 1938 the senior leaderships of both began to draw up plans. Realistically, the *Luftwaffe* now devoted nearly one third of its manpower to air defence against British bombing. This was prudent but could do little to win a war. Hitler and the naval leadership, by contrast, ascended into the fantasy world of the Z-plan for a German super navy. The practical requirements for that were hopelessly vast; it would have required oil equivalent to almost the whole of German oil consumption in 1938. In addition, there was no coherent thinking about how such a super navy would be employed even if it could be built.[43] Germany moved towards war with Britain without any rational concept of how it could be defeated.

Hitler had much clearer ideas about ensuring peace in the East while he fought in the West. The two countries that mattered were Hungary and Poland. The former was won over to a policy of benevolent neutrality towards Germany by being allowed to take over and annex part of southern Slovakia in November. In return, Hungary left the League of Nations and joined the Anti-Comintern Pact. Poland, the country barring the way against a Soviet attack on Germany if its forces were engaged in the west, was even more important. Much uncertainty surrounds Hitler's attitude and policy towards Poland. It had been an article of faith to politicians and people in Weimar Germany that Poland must, by one means or another, be forced to give up most, if not all, the German territory that it had acquired under the treaty of Versailles and the return to the Reich of the Free City of Danzig was even more axiomatic.[44] It would have been astonishing if the Nazis had not sought to outbid all other parties in the vehemence of their revisionist demands against Poland during their struggle for power, and, in fact, torrents of anti-Polish vituperation were a feature of Nazi electioneering in the early 1930s. In the summer of 1932 the sentencing to death by a German court of five Nazis for the murder of a Communist Party member who was an ethnic Pole prompted from Hitler the comment that: 'In the National Socialist Reich five German men will never be condemned because of a Pole.'[45] But the propaganda torrent ceased with casual totalitarian ease after Hitler came to office.[46] A very different note was struck towards Poland. In 1933 a Berlin University professor published a book in which he called for German–Polish reconciliation. Problems between the two nations were declared to pale into insignificance beside their thousand-year old 'particularly close political and cultural relationship'.[47] Weimar economic sanctions were ended and Germany suggested to Poland that they conclude a friendship agreement.

The reason for this change was that Hitler regarded Poland, even at this early time, as the possible key to realising his greatest ambitions. If it could be won over France might cease to oppose his ambitions in Eastern Europe and Poland itself would provide a geographical gateway for the invasion of Russia.[48] The Polish strong man, Marshal Pilsudski, was in two minds about how to respond. He allowed his Foreign Minister, Colonel Beck, to conduct secret negotiations with the new German government while simultaneously urging on France a joint preventive war against Germany. France rebuffed him in terms that added insult to injury. France would not go to war with Germany and, if the latter attacked Poland, France would do no more than send it munitions and work for 'the widest possible organisation of world public opinion favourable to Poland'. Pilsudski decided to accept the German offer of a friendship treaty which was signed early in 1934.[49] For years Germany showed every sign of acting within the spirit of such a treaty. It put on a display of elaborate mourning after Pilsudski's death in 1935.[50] With even more exquisite politeness, Poland was not named, though it was the country involved, when it was publicly announced that two female secretaries in the German War Ministry had been beheaded for spying for a foreign power. They had been seduced and lured into espionage by a young diplomat at the Polish embassy.[51] As Hitler prepared more urgently for aggression the goodwill to Poland appeared still to be there. In a speech on 5 November 1937 and again to Jósef Beck the following January he stated that he accepted the existing status of Danzig. However, it was on that same day in November that he had addressed the meeting recorded by Hossbach, and on that occasion he speculated that if Germany went to war Poland would betray the 1934 pact and stab the Reich in the back to seize Silesia, Pomerania and East Prussia – the provinces that Germany was actually to lose to Poland in 1945 as a result of the failure of Hitler's criminal adventures. In this more intimate setting he appeared to be thinking out loud about some 'pre-emptive' attack on Poland.[52]

The form of government in Poland after Pilsudski died was oligarchical and defence and foreign policy were in the hands of an inner oligarchy of five men, including Beck who enjoyed increasing freedom to decide foreign policy.[53] Even so, Beck's authority and durability in office owed much, if not almost everything, to his knowledge of his colleagues' minds and of what would and would not be acceptable to them. Certainly, in the great crisis of 1938 over Czechoslovakia, his policy was a mixture of the parochial and the grandiose characteristic of the Polish political elite. The former revolved around the Teschen district where he was determined to secure parity with whatever Germany gained. If the 'Sudeten' areas became 'German' cantons then Teschen must become a Polish canton. If Germany annexed the Sudetenland then Poland must annex Teschen, as it did after Munich with Hitler's strong support. The latter was enshrined in his vision of a 'Third Europe' of East-Central European states, led naturally by Poland, which no one in London or Paris would take seriously. That was perhaps a mistake because this Third Europe was intended to prevent German expansion, and British and French diplomacy might have tried to make something of it, not least in detaching Hungary from its new and essentially unwanted dependence on Germany.[54]

Shortly after the German conquest of Poland in October 1939 the Nazi government issued a proclamation to the Polish people in which they explained that the extinction of their country's independence had been inevitable because geography had placed the Poles alongside 'the mighty world power of the German Reich'.[55] A year earlier, guided by the same crude Social Darwinist thinking, Hitler had been at first possibly bemused, and later definitely angered, by Poland's refusal to accept that, in the simplest terms of power politics, its importance had lessened after Munich and it should therefore accept the offer that he now made to it of junior ally status so that he could deal with Britain and France. In particular, Poland must accept German annexation of Danzig and must join the Anti-Comintern Pact which had effectively been transformed for the time being into an anti-Anglo-French pact. Beck regarded the former demand as negotiable and the latter as not because it would detract from Poland's sovereign independence. He exaggerated the strength of his negotiating hand with Hitler whose politeness he perhaps misunderstood, though when the German tone became sharper in March 1939, while still offering the same settlement as before, Beck still responded with a sharp refusal.[56]

Notes

1 Gerhard L. Weinberg, *The Foreign Policy of Hitler's Germany: Starting World War II, 1937–39* (Chicago, IL, University of Chicago Press, 1980), pp. 317–19

2 Wilhelm Deist, *The Wehrmacht and German Rearmament* (London, Macmillan, 1981), chapter 4 and pp. 79–81; W. Deist, M. Messerschmidt, H-E. Volkmann and W. Wette, *Germany and the Second World War: Vol. I, The Build-up of German Aggression* (Oxford, Clarendon Press, 1990), pp. 497–8.

3 Donald Cameron Watt, *Too Serious A Business* (London, Temple Smith, 1975), pp. 85–8, 103–9, 116.

4 Robert J. O'Neill, *The German Army and the Nazi Party 1933–39* (London, Corgi edn., 1968), p. 200.

5 Gordon A. Craig and Felix Gilbert (eds), *The Diplomats 1919–1939* (Princeton, NJ, Princeton University Press, 1953), pp. 434–6.

6 Weinberg, *Starting World War II*, pp. 281–9.

7 Karl R. Stadler, *Austria* (London, Benn, 1971), p. 150.

8 Deist et al., *Germany and the Second World War*, pp. 323–7.

9 *Ibid.*, p. 652.

10 Elizabeth Wiskemann, *The Rome–Berlin Axis* (London, Fontana revised edn., 1966), pp. 133–4.

11 Gerhard L. Weinberg, 'Germany, Munich and appeasement' in Melvin Small and Otto Feinstein (eds), *Appeasing Fascism* (Lanham, MD, University Press of America, 1991), pp. 11–12.

12 David Irving, *Churchill's War: The Struggle for Power* (Bullbrook, Australia, Veritas Publishing, 1987), pp. 115–16.

13 Weinberg, *Starting World War II*, pp. 324–8, 341–3, 398–9.

14 Michael Kraus, 'The diplomacy of Edvard Benes: Munich and its aftermath' in Maya Latynski (ed.), *Reappraising the Munich Pact: Continental Perspectives* (Baltimore, MD, The Johns Hopkins University Press, 1992), pp. 62–3.

15 Wesley K. Wark, *The Ultimate Enemy: British Intelligence and Nazi Germany, 1933–1939* (London, Tauris, 1985), p. 102.

16 Peter Neville, 'Nevile Henderson and Basil Newton: two British envoys in the Czech crisis 1938', *Diplomacy and Statecraft,* 10:2&3 (1999), 258–75; also Erik Goldstein 'Neville Chamberlain: the British official mind and the Munich crisis' in *ibid.*, p. 282.

17 Irving, *Churchill's War,* pp. 128–31.

18 Keith Feiling, *The Life of Neville Chamberlain* (London, Macmillan, 1946), p. 347.

19 John E. Dreifort, 'The French role in the least unpleasant solution' in Latynski (ed.), *Reappraising,* pp. 21–46.

20 Keith Middlemas, *Diplomacy of Illusion: The British Government and*

Germany, 1937–39 (London, Weidenfeld & Nicolson, 1972), p. 326.

21 Ritchie Ovendale, *'Appeasement' and the English Speaking World* (Cardiff, University of Wales Press, 1975), p. 161; Alan Watt, *Australian Foreign Policy 1938–1965* (Cambridge, Cambridge University Press, 1967), pp. 1–22.

22 Weinberg, *Starting World War II*, pp. 430–7.

23 Ján Mlynárik in Norman Stone and Eduard Strouhal (eds), *Czechoslovakia: Crossroads and Crises, 1918–88* (London, Macmillan, 1989), p. 114.

24 Ian Kershaw, *The 'Hitler Myth': Image and Reality in the Third Reich* (Oxford, Oxford University Press, 1987) , pp. 133–9.

25 Stuart Hodgson, *The Man Who Made the Peace: The Story of Neville Chamberlain* (London, Christophers, 1938), p. 134.

26 Richard Lamb, *The Ghosts of Peace 1935–1945* (Salisbury, Russell, 1987), p. 80.

27 W. J. West, *Truth Betrayed* (London, Duckworth, 1987), pp. 110–14, 142–3.

28 For a masterly analysis of Italian policy in the Czech crisis see G. Bruce Strang, 'War and peace: Mussolini's road to Munich', *Diplomacy and Statecraft*, 10:2&3 (1999), 160–90.

29 Stephane Groueff, *Crown of Thorns: The Reign of King Boris III of Bulgaria 1918–1943* (Lanham, MD, Madison Books, 1987), pp. 251–2.

30 Michael Kraus in Latynski (ed.), *Reappraising*, pp. 69–73; Ján Mlynárik and Eduard Strouhal in Stone and Strouhal (eds), *Czechoslovakia*, pp. 104–5, 125–6; Irving, *Churchill's War*, pp. 149–50.

31 See for example, Ovendale, *'Appeasement'*, p. 147; Wark, *Ultimate*, p. 211.

32 Donny Gluckstein, *The Nazis, Capitalism and the Working Class* (London, Bookmarks, 1999), pp. 161–2.

33 Williamson Murray, *The Change in the European Balance of Power, 1938–1939: The Path to Ruin* (Princeton, NJ, Princeton University Press, 1984), pp. 363–4.

34 Michael Graham Fry, 'The British Dominions and the Munich crisis', *Diplomacy and Statecraft*, 10:2&3 (1999), 293–341.

35 Viscount Templewood, *Nine Troubled Years* (London, Collins, 1954), p. 289.

36 N. H. Gibbs, *Grand Strategy: Vol. I, Rearmament Policy* (London, HMSO, 1976), p. 645.

37 Wark, *Ultimate*, pp. 105–10, 202–5.

38 R. A. C. Parker, *Chamberlain and Appeasement: British Policy and the Coming of the Second World War* (London, Macmillan, 1993), pp. 138, 172–3.

39 Deist et al., *Germany and the Second World War*, p. 547.
40 Richard Overy 'Germany and the Munich crisis: a mutilated victory?' in *Diplomacy and Statecraft*, 10:2&3 (1999), 210–11.
41 Weinberg in Small and Feinstein (eds), *Appeasing Fascism*, pp. 16–17.
42 Deist et al., *Germany and the Second World War*, pp. 115, 119, 123–4.
43 *Ibid.*, pp. 473–9, 503–4.
44 See the discussion in Michael Laffan (ed.), *The Burden of German History 1919–45* (London, Methuen, 1989), pp. 96–9.
45 Richard J. Evans, *Rituals of Retribution: Capital Punishment in Germany, 1600–1987* (Oxford, Oxford University Press, 1996), p. 617.
46 Lord Kennet in W. F. Reddaway, J. H. Penson, O. Halecki and R. Dyboski (eds), *The Cambridge History of Poland: From Augustus II to Pilsudski (1697–1935)* (Cambridge, Cambridge University Press, 1941), pp. 607–8.
47 Max Weinreich, *Hitler's Professors* (New Haven, CT, Yale University Press, 1999 edn.), p. 69.
48 Deist et al., *Germany and the Second World War*, pp. 577–84, 590–3.
49 Anthony T. Komjathy, *The Crises of France's East Central European Diplomacy 1933–1938* (New York, Columbia University Press, 1976), pp. 42–3, 48–51.
50 Armand Bérard, *Au Temps du Danger Allemand: un Ambassadeur se Souvient* (Paris, Plon, 1976), pp. 270–1.
51 John Whitwell, *British Agent* (London, Kimber, 1966), pp. 211–12.
52 Carl Tighe, *Gdánsk: National Identity in the German–Polish Borderlands* (London, Pluto Press, 1990), pp. 122–3.
53 Antony Polonsky, *Politics in Independent Poland 1921–1939: The Crisis of Constitutional Government* (Oxford, Clarendon Press, 1972), pp. 470, 479–83.
54 Anna M. Cienciala, 'The view from Warsaw' in Latynski (ed.), *Reappraising*, pp. 79–101, discusses some of these matters.
55 The Polish Ministry of Information, *The Black Book of Poland* (New York, G. P. Putnam's Sons, 1942), p. 558.
56 Jan Karski, *The Great Powers and Poland 1919–1945: From Versailles to Yalta* (Lanham, MD, University Press of America, 1985), pp. 241–9; Anita Prazmowska, *Britain, Poland and the Eastern Front, 1939* (Cambridge, Cambridge University Press, 1987), pp. 15–18, 37; Weinberg, *Starting World War II*, pp. 479–90, 497–511.

CHAPTER EIGHT

RESISTANCE TAKES SHAPE

If Germany and Poland were on a collision course the one thing that would have seemed inconceivable in historical perspective was that Britain might, under any circumstances, come to the rescue of Poland. British reluctance to fight over issues in central Europe was usually greatest over Poland whose leaders had an unfortunate propensity to make a poor impression on English statesmen.[1] In 1930 the British ambassador in Berlin, Sir Horace Rumbold, hoped vehemently 'as an Englishman and a parent' that Britain would never fight for Poland.[2] The process by which Britain was to become willing to fight alongside Poland was a byproduct of the decline of the policy of appeasement. In early October, Chamberlain was naturally hopeful that events would vindicate Munich, perhaps even to the Czechs – a touch of guilty conscience? 'And', he wrote to the Archbishop of Canterbury on 2 October, 'I sincerely hope that we have opened the way to that general appeasement which alone can save the world from chaos.'[3] To the King, a fervent admirer of what Chamberlain had done at Munich, he confided his hope that there would be more meetings between himself and Hitler.[4] He seems initially to have been more afraid that there would be a revulsion against Munich among the British public than that the agreement itself would fail.[5] However, by November he felt that he had to strike a more defensive note, telling the Cabinet on 7 November that, 'We were doing our best to drive two horses abreast: conciliation and rearmament.'[6]

What made most Cabinet ministers uncomfortable was the fact that the public face of Nazi policy reflected from the start Hitler's anger about Munich. The dictator himself spoke in hostile terms about Britain in a speech on 9 October, and a propaganda campaign to prepare the German people for even greater rearmament was started before the end of the month, coupled with a fantastic plan for a five-fold increase in the strength of the *Luftwaffe*. In a speech to an audience of journalists on 10 November, Hitler lamented having for too long had to pretend to be a man of peace. There were real men of peace in the audience and one of them made sure that the British Foreign Office had a copy of the speech before the end of the month.[7] By that time the disillusion of the British Cabinet was reflected in their willingness to believe unfounded reports about imminent German aggressive moves such as one about a German plan to invade Holland in early 1939.[8]

If there had to be war with Germany, certain factors were starting to make it look winnable, or at least not suicidal. Intelligence reports on the German economy advised the Cabinet of raw materials, and labour shortages and financial difficulties that made Germany unfit for prolonged war, even if they were coupled with the absurd caveat that the Germans were a uniquely efficient nation and might be able to overcome difficulties that would defeat any other.[9]

In the other great West European democracy, France, there was a similar pattern of increased readiness to resist new aggression, though with the difference from Britain that the Prime Minister, Daladier, was in its vanguard, in contrast with Chamberlain making up the rearguard in his government in this matter; and that France's interests were challenged directly in a way that never happened to Britain when Italy laid claim to two pieces of French territory, Nice and Corsica, and two dependencies, Tunisia and French Somaliland, in late 1938. Almost all French opinion was outraged, and Daladier paid visits to Corsica and Tunis to reaffirm French sovereignty in the first days of 1939.[10] France admittedly had very little to fear from Italy alone. Its position was improving in a situation in which there is much scope for arguing about what was cause and what was effect. Rising national morale coincided with achievements in rearmament and general economic recovery. Although the French government did not reject the idea of eventually acquiescing to more German expansion in Eastern Europe in return for Hitler ruling out aid for Mussolini in his ambitions, their policy essentially veered towards resistance to both dictators if only Britain would offer them support.

By early 1939 Britain was ready to do that, partly because it now feared a German attack on itself from the air or on some vital British interest while France was left alone, and partly because the British

Chiefs of Staff, reversing without apology their consistent argument of the previous several years, now suggested to the government that it was 'difficult to say how the security of the United Kingdom could be maintained if France were forced to capitulate'.[11] Extensive land and air cooperation plans between the British and French staffs were to be drawn up in the months before war started and Britain became ready to send as many troops to France as it could physically muster.

The readiness to do that was given a considerable boost by Hitler's extinction of the independence of what remained of Czechoslovakia in March 1939. Within less than a month of Munich he had ordered the preparation of military plans 'to smash the remainder of the Czech state at any time should it pursue an anti-German policy'. By the next February, growing impatient, he had demanded the formenting of incidents against Germans resident in rump Czechoslovakia to provide a pretext for intervention. There was not much success. One agent reported 'very great difficulty in arousing the Czechs to the necessary state of provocation'.[12] Finally, he bullied the, admittedly not unwilling, autonomous government of Slovakia into proclaiming independence with the threat that if they did not he would authorise Hungarian annexation of their entire territory. He then ordered German troops into the Czech area which was declared to be no longer viable as a state, and acceded to a plea from President Hacha to receive him in Berlin and to accept his government's surrender to avoid bloodshed. Acting very much like the common little dog of Chamberlain's description, he granted the Czech head of state only a few curt words and a few minutes of his time.[13]

Besides huge amounts of gold and hard currency that were invaluable in staving off Germany's foreign exchange crisis, the Reich secured intact major munitions factories and other mining and heavy industrial facilities and a huge weapons haul, including nearly 500 tanks and nearly 1600 military aircraft.[14] Munich, probably, could only have been avoided if Hitler had refused to make a few cosmetic concessions to the West, but a strong argument for regretting that there had not been war in 1938 is that Germany would not then have been able to make such easy gains and would have had to pay a high price for whatever resources it might have captured in Czechoslovakia.

The reaction of public opinion in democratic countries as German troops marched into Prague on 15 March and Germany proclaimed the 'protectorate' of Bohemia and Moravia was generally one of outrage, though less so in the Dominions, which were of such importance to Britain, nor in most of the United States other than the eastern seaboard. An English translation of *Mein Kampf* was at last published in the United States, by a firm no longer worried about Hitler's threat of legal action for breach of copyright, at precisely the time Prague was occupied. It was high on the bestseller lists in New York and Washington but bookstores in Los Angeles reported little demand.[15]

Reaction in Britain and France was naturally most important at government level. In the former, Chamberlain roundly denounced the German action in a speech in his home city of Birmingham on 17 March in which he stressed Nazi perfidy and aggression in terms that he was to duplicate in internal discussions. He talked in Cabinet about the need 'to pull down the bully' and about the aim of British policy as now being 'to check and defeat Germany's attempt at world domination'.[16] The reaction of the French government was along similar lines, though perhaps even more wholehearted than the British. This was somewhat surprising in the light of its earlier contemptuous dismissal of its former Czech ally which one French official had brushed aside after Munich in the following terms: 'It does not represent more than a kind of greater Luxembourg clinging to the flanks of the Reich and has no future except as a German protégé and vassal.'[17] After Munich, France had shown even less interest than Britain in giving form to the international guarantee of rump Czechoslovakia that had been promised at the conference. The fact that there were desultory discussions on this subject until almost the German occupation of Prague, was brought about by Britain. However, Prague tipped the scales further against the appeasement faction in the French government. Daladier was able to bring his government's foreign policy more into line with public opinion, much of which had always been cool towards appeasement. An opinion poll after Munich had shown 70 per cent of respondents opposed to more concessions to Germany and only 17 per cent in favour.[18]

Despite this, the elimination of Czechoslovakia was accepted as an accomplished fact, irreversible unless Hitler committed more aggression, on the grounds that Britain and France could only help countries that resisted aggression. Similar logic was applied to the German seizure of the Memelland area of Lithuania later in the month, and Lithuania received no credit for courageously rejecting a

German guarantee of its remaining territory in return for accepting protectorate status like the new state of Slovakia.[19]

In Britain in the first ten weeks of 1939 before Czechoslovakia was extinguished, there was a paradoxical contrast between military preparations for possible war, which were extensive, and diplomatic preparations which were non-existent, unless the military discussions with France are counted as partly political. In January every citizen received a copy of a forty-eight page booklet, *The National Service Handbook,* and in a broadcast the Prime Minister called it 'a scheme to make us ready for war'. It dwelt on such subjects as air raid precautions.[20] From this it was logical enough to proceed to the introduction of a scheme for military conscription in April, to appoint a Minister of Supply to direct all necessary resources to the needs of the armed forces and to double the state budget from the figure of the previous year to finance defence preparations, though it must have been almost unbearable for politicians like those who ruled in 1939 to increase the deficit between expenditure and revenue from £13 million in 1938 to a planned £768 million in 1939.[21] Against this, little was done diplomatically before Prague to fight on the most advantageous terms if war came. Moves to strengthen British links with Balkan countries and Turkey through increased trade did not amount to much[22] and, in comparison with similar German efforts, were of the too-little-and-too-late variety. Germany admittedly had a stronger hand to play. In Romania, for instance, the army was dependent on munitions works in former Czechoslovakia for spare parts and ammunition, and the Germans threatened to halt all such supplies unless Bucharest accepted a trade treaty that, if fully implemented, would have made it a German economic satellite, as it did on 23 March.[23] Any chance of building up a collective security system in circumstances which were not ones of almost desperate crisis was thus forfeited. Logically, such an effort would have started with countries directly threatened with German or Italian aggression and would have moved on to the big prizes, Russia (especially desired by France) and Turkey (of special interest to Britain).

Frantically and belatedly, in the wake of the occupation of Prague, the two large West European powers embarked on diplomatic moves, as a minimum to reassure their own public opinion but also, they hoped, to make Hitler pause and moderate his ambitions. Much academic effort has been expended on the supersession of appeasement by deterrence, albeit in a somewhat incoherent manner, as the main response to the now much better perceived danger from Nazism.[24] After a brief post-Prague phase of concern that Romania might be the next country to be attacked by Germany, the British government discussed their next policy move effectively in terms of a choice between an arrangement with Poland or with the Soviet Union. The former insisted that Britain could not chose both, and Chamberlain and Halifax railroaded a decision in favour of Poland through the Cabinet. Chamberlain elevated Poland to the status of one of 'the big three powers' alongside Britain and France.[25] His grandiose description accorded ill with the advice of the Chiefs of Staff about the military contributions that Poland and Russia could be expected to make. They had enormous reservations, both military and political, about the latter,[26] but were quite dismissive about the former. They saw Poland as certain to fall to German attack without Soviet assistance, but granted it minor value in distracting large German forces from the West for a short time while it was being overrun and much greater value in that Germany would have to keep most of those forces in the East indefinitely to defend its new border with Russia.[27] This naturally assumed the absence of an accord between Moscow and Berlin. The validity of their point was acknowledged by Hitler himself to Beck to whom he remarked in January 1939 that he wanted a strong Poland because every Polish division along the eastern border 'saved Germany just as much military expenditure'.[28]

This does not necessarily leave Chamberlain's policy without justification. The most cynical possible interpretation would be that he took to heart what the Chiefs had said about Poland's military situation. He was to resist implacably any idea of adding a military dimension to the new Anglo-Polish relationship. Theoretically Chamberlain might actually have looked forward to a German conquest of Poland and then to Russia, still neutral, tying down far larger German forces than Poland ever could, in much the same way as Japan was to tie down huge and inactive Soviet forces in southeast Siberia between 1941 and 1945. Against that must be set the wartime testimony of the Cabinet Secretary, Edward Bridges, that the choice between Russia and Poland was made in favour of the latter on 27 March as the only certain way of guaranteeing that if war came there would actually be warfare on two fronts and, even more to the point, that if only Hitler could be convinced that Britain would no longer allow countries to be 'sapped, undermined and finally suffer the fate of Czechoslovakia', he could be deterred from future aggression: 'After all, hitherto, Hitler had got his way by threats of war. There was always the chance that when he saw quite definitely that we were not to be deterred by threats, he might climb down, provided always that we so conducted affairs as to give him a possible way of escape.'[29]

In addition, the Polish policy of rejecting Russia as any sort of ally, though they did favour pinning it down to promises of strict neutrality, was intransigent and therefore a choice had to be made. (It is worth nothing that the United Kingdom faced a similar situation on its own sole land border with what is now the Irish Republic, then Eire. In July 1940, at a time when a German invasion of southern Ireland was widely expected, its Prime Minister, Eamon De Valera, sent a message that, if it were to happen, his government would not accept the entry of British troops; Canadians or Australians perhaps, but British were a different matter.)[30] Secondly, though Chamberlain cannot have had much understanding of this, official Polish distrust and even sheer dislike of Britain was intense and was not coupled with any realisation that German attitudes against their country were hardening. Poland might well have rejected any offer from Britain that was in any way conditional.[31] Britain could still, of course, have declared war on a Germany that had attacked a Poland which had spurned Britain, but that would have been a spectacularly unsatisfactory and almost quixotic step to take.

At the very end of March the government was panicked into acting immediately to guarantee Poland against aggression by completely false reports, which they nevertheless believed, that a German attack or ultimatum to Poland was imminent. Just how little British Cabinet ministers understood about Poland – the key to whose policy was that it was a country still intoxicated with joy at being independent after more than a century of partition and servitude[32] – glares forth from their belief that without the guarantee it would have yielded to German demands without a fight.[33] Chamberlain had to set aside any idea of confining the guarantee to Poland's independence and not also its territorial integrity. He would probably not have got such a limitation through the Cabinet in any case. Within a week Beck, as complacent as ever about German–Polish relations and much preoccupied with thoughts of dumping Polish Jews in the British Empire, visited London. The guarantee was made mutual and, it was agreed in principle, into a full treaty of alliance for mutual defence against Germany. Giving possibly even greater satisfaction to

Poland, France, not wishing to be outdone by the British, gave Poland for the first time ever a wholly unconditional pledge of support against aggression, 'direct or indirect'.[34] However, Beck warned that Poland would almost certainly be neutral if any other East European country were attacked, not excluding its traditional friend, Romania. Later in April Romania returned the compliment by stating that it would be neutral if Poland were attacked.[35] Shambles prevailed among Germany's potential eastern victims in the spring of 1939. Well might the Romanian Foreign Minister of that date have referred in his memoirs to 'a profound tragedy of mutual incomprehension' at that time.[36]

It is not difficult to detect second thoughts among British policymakers about their involvement in Eastern Europe. The British attitude to Romania was hardly different from Beck's, despite Romania's position as the only important oil producer in non-Soviet Europe. Urgent Romanian pleas for a guarantee fell on deaf ears in London, and only a unilateral French decision to give one to the Balkan kingdom forced Britain to act in the same way on 13 April to avoid the 'evils of divergence between France and Great Britain' as Halifax described the situation.[37] This had been immediately preceded by a British guarantee of Greece which stood in no imminent danger from Germany but rather from Italy which had occupied Albania during the recent Easter weekend. Chamberlain even equated this step with Prague, writing that the occupation of Albania had blocked 'any chance of further rapprochement with Italy ... just as Hitler has blocked any German rapprochement'.[38] Britain accepted that it had no choice but to treat an Italian attack on Greece from Albania as an attack on Britain itself, and could not object when Greece said that if Mussolini confined aggression to seizing the island of Corfu, as he had done in 1923, it would not this time turn the other cheek but would declare war on Italy.

Mussolini was to commit no such aggression until 1940 but was in a boorish mood towards the Western democracies in the middle months of 1939, for instance responding to a statement from the British ambassador in Rome that it might be possible for Germany to acquire Danzig if the Fuhrer were polite and used peaceful means, that Germany was entitled to take it by any means.[39] In May, Germany and Italy concluded a formal alliance, the so-called Pact of Steel, but Hitler did not now take his supposedly closer ally into his confidence about his plans to invade Poland. On the contrary,

Ribbentrop assured Ciano that there would be no war in 1939.[40] The Pact of Steel was, in the words of its historian, 'born of the Germans' duplicity and the Italians' failure to clarify and stipulate the common objectives'.[41]

Hitler's almost farcical dealings with Italy in 1939 illustrated the change in his tactics. Until 1938 he had waited for events to provide opportunities. From late 1938 he sought to perform the much more difficult task of manipulating events including the forging of alliances with Italy, Japan and Poland.[42] Apparent success could only be achieved with the first of these countries, though with such a complete mutual lack of candour as to make their pact a nullity. No success was achieved with Japan because the Japanese were only interested in an exclusively anti-Soviet arrangement whereas Hitler wished to offer no threat to Russia; he was, even so, slow to think of making an actual arrangement with that country. Poland would not agree to an alliance at all. If the Poles thought that possibly Italy and very probably Japan could preserve the essentials of independence in alliance with Germany while they could not, they would have been right. In April 1939 a German official wrote that 'Poland's real crime was refusal to give up its independence.'[43]

There is uncertainty about whether Hitler's decision to order his generals to prepare plans to invade Poland – the actual order was issued on 3 April, four days after the British guarantee – preceded or followed that guarantee, but it would be a mistake to labour the point. Once Poland had rejected Hitler's overtures of the winter its fate was sealed. Instead of an early war against Britain and France in which Polish benevolent neutrality would be guaranteed, the dictator turned to a war against Poland in which the neutrality of the Western powers would be desirable but was not essential. As he was to reminisce in November 1939, 'Under pressure the decision came to fight with Poland first.'[44]

Given the shakiness of his alliance with Italy and the disappointing relationship with Japan, Hitler's foreign policy from April to the end of August revolved to a considerable extent around attempts to lure Britain back to neutrality (thereby automatically ensuring that France also would be neutral) or, if that could not be done, keeping in reserve the option to seek from Russia the sort of friendly neutrality that Poland had declined. Conscious of the extreme difficulty of defeating Britain in a war, Hitler convinced himself that its neutrality was attainable. This illusion was facilitated by bad advice about

British 'decadence' from Ribbentrop, based on his perceptions from when he had been ambassador in London, and by the British press, summaries of whose editorial content were sent to him daily by his press office; many newspapers continued to peddle a pro-appeasement line that was out of step with both government policy and public opinion.[45] He also simply did not understand the depth of Western revulsion against his violation of a pact, Munich, that he himself had never taken seriously. It is remarkable that he was not to issue his military commanders with guidelines for war with Britain and France until 31 August, only hours before Poland was invaded.[46]

On the specific matter of enticing Britain away from its new Polish commitment, Germany resorted to two arguments, one of which fell flat while the other struck an almost semi-responsive chord. The first was propaganda about ill-treatment of the German minority in Poland. There was a little truth in that, though in any moral sense it was vitiated by Weimar and Nazi discrimination against the large Polish minority in eastern Germany. In 1938 there were two Polish language secondary schools in Germany and twenty-six German language secondary schools in Poland. Poland actually made a major, though almost wholly unsuccessful, attempt to conciliate its German minority during the 1930s.[47] What is more to the point is that the propaganda about ill-treatment was greeted with complete derision in Britain after the revelation in March 1939 that Germany's interest in the Sudeten Germans had only been an excuse to destroy Czechoslovakia. The propaganda still served a useful purpose in Germany itself where many were delighted, after six years of enforced abstinence, to be able to give vent to their pent up hatred of Poland. Anti-Polish propaganda, which was carefully modulated by Goebbels to rise to a crescendo as the date for invasion approached, was highly successful in persuading many Germans to give Hitler their wholehearted support when he started the war.[48] The people who paid the price for it were the ethnic Germans of Poland. After German troops crossed the border on 1 September nearly 60,000 of them were to be massacred by furious Poles.[49] The first victims of large scale massacres in the Second World War were Germans.

Less unsuccessful in relation to Britain was the Nazi harping on whether it really wanted to go to war over Danzig. This self-governing and ethnically nine tenths German 'Free City' at the mouth of Poland's great river, the Vistula, had been one of the most remarkable creations of the Paris peace settlement of 1919. It was also a British creation because France and the United States would have given the city outright to Poland. Yet the British never really believed in it. David Lloyd George, Prime Minister and father of the Free City if there was one, asked in 1919: 'France would tomorrow fight for Alsace if her right to it were contested. But would we make war for Danzig?'[50] He was obviously doubtful, but in 1939 it seemed that it might be time to answer the question.

The still pro-appeasement British press (Beaverbrook's *Express* group newspapers and *The Times*) had tried to answer the question negatively in the wake of the British guarantee by stating that it referred only to Poland's independence and not to all its territory, still less to Danzig which was not part of Poland. The government had made no such stipulation and on 3 April the Foreign Office issued a denunciation of such interpretations, partly in response to Polish protests.[51] After that Britain could not easily deny that it was committed to maintaining the status quo in the Free City if that was what Poland wanted. Ruling circles agonised about what they should actually do in the event of a German aggression confined to Danzig. Border incidents in the summer, some of them almost amusing such as the arrest and mild punishment of some Polish boy scouts who crossed into the territory of the Free City, fuelled the concern, and the Cabinet rejoiced in the later summer when border tensions appeared to abate.[52] Whether Britain would have declared war on Germany in response to a Nazi coup in Danzig is open to some doubt, though in a Gallup poll in early August 76 per cent of respondents did favour going to war over the city and only 13 per cent were definitely opposed.[53] This may be compared with the view of Ribbentrop, who greatly influenced Hitler in 1939, that ninety-nine 'Englishmen' out of every hundred would be overjoyed to concede the 'natural German demand' to annex Danzig.[54] The Danzigers themselves had been voting for Nazi administrations since the Third Reich had begun, though the Nazi leader there and future gauleiter, Albrecht Forster, had a curious tendency to act decently at times, as the Poles were to acknowledge after the war by sparing his life.[55] Hitler was actually absolutely determined not to limit himself to Danzig or even to Danzig and the neighbouring 'Corridor' that separated East Prussia from the rest of Germany.

False hopes about the other abounded in both of the countries that most mattered in Europe in 1939. Hitler's would certainly have been raised even higher if he had known about the refusal of Britain to add a military dimension to its relationship with Poland and about Britain's extreme unwillingness to meet any of Poland's requests for finance and material aid. The Treasury did not want to part with money and the Committee of Imperial Defence placed Poland ninth in order of preference on a list of countries that might receive aid in the form of military supplies; Egypt was first. Nor was there any political will to make these august bodies think again.[56] Even this compares favourably with the French, who lied to Poland that they would attack Germany if it invaded Poland while having no intention of doing so.[57] The Dominions were as resentful about the thought of going to war over Poland as they had been over Czechoslovakia the previous year, though with the difference that they now accepted that it might be necessary. Their policy could still not be taken entirely for granted. As late as 26 August New Zealand was to inform Britain that it would be willing to return Western Samoa to Germany if that would help to keep the peace.[58] In 1943, on learning about the discovery of mass graves of Polish officers murdered on Stalin's order at Katyn, the long-serving Canadian Prime Minister, Mackenzie King, was to write spitefully in his diary that the Poles had only themselves to blame for not yielding to Hitler's demands in 1939.[59]

The virtual lack of substance, other than purely political, to Anglo-Polish relations after the guarantee of 31 March 1939 is one of a number of factors that have fuelled debate on whether Britain was really serious about going to war against any new Nazi aggression whatever. Hitler himself threw down the most unmistakable of gauntlets by denouncing the Anglo-German naval agreement, as well as Germany's 1934 treaty with Poland, in a speech to the Reichstag on 28 April. Disposal of the former was an urgent necessity in any case because of recent decisions on increasing the size of the German navy that would violate the agreement and which could not possibly be concealed. If there was any unwillingness to pick up the gauntlet in Britain, the place to look for it would be in the actions of Chamberlain, not only because he was Prime Minister and a somewhat 'presidential' one at that, but also because he was 'the man who was prepared to go furthest in giving credit to German declarations' (clearly referring to ones of peaceful intent) as his colleague, John Simon, pointedly called him in a parliamentary debate in April.[60] He certainly was not prepared to endanger any remaining hope for peace by encouraging overtures from German opposition elements whose proposals included indignant demands that Poland must give up Danzig and the Corridor and that Munich was sacrosanct, though some rump Czech state might be restored.[61] Chamberlain would only listen to the German government, and was no more interested in German oppositionists than he was in his domestic critics who urged in vain the admission of Churchill into the Cabinet.[62]

As spring gave way to summer in 1939 without war Chamberlain thought that the new emphasis on deterrence might be working and this gave rise to the idea that Germany's remaining aims might be limited and negotiable after all, entailing demands for sacrifice on Poland. When he wrote to his sister in the late spring that he could not imagine Hitler 'starting a world war for Danzig',[63] he clearly imagined that the Free City really was of central importance in German policy and lacked any inkling that the dictator was willing to start a war not for Danzig but to destroy Poland. At the end of July he speculated that Germany had become convinced that war would be too costly. If so, and as a 'corollary', it must be offered 'fair and reasonable consideration and treatment from us and others'.[64] The 'others' would undoubtedly have included Poland and its position in Danzig and possibly the Corridor. He and his aide, Horace Wilson, encouraged contacts between Hitler and Ribbentrop and British figures sympathetic to Nazi Germany, including E. D. Tennant, a businessman, and Lord Kemsley, a newspaper proprietor, who was granted an hour of the Fuhrer's time on 27 July when they were both at Bayreuth for the annual Wagner festival, and who reported enthusiastically on what he had heard to an interested Chamberlain. The Prime Minister was looking for evidence that Hitler now eschewed military aggression. So were all but a very few even of the most devoted admirers of the old policy of appeasement in British public life.[65] Only greater patience and diplomatic skill than Hitler was capable of might, in conjunction with complete crassness in Polish policy, have led to an Anglo-Polish breach.

Notes

1   See for example, Charles Petrie, *Life and Letters of the Rt. Hon. Sir Austen Chamberlain, Vol. II* (London, Cassell, 1940), p. 320; Earl of Avon, *The Eden Memoirs I: Facing the Dictators* (London, Cassell, 1962), pp. 168–71.
2   Martin Gilbert, *Sir Horace Rumbold* (London, Heinemann, 1973),

p. 351.

3 John W. Wheeler-Bennett, *King George VI: His Life and Reign* (London, Macmillan, 1958), p. 355.

4 Sarah Bradford, *George VI* (London, Fontana edn., 1991), p. 369.

5 R. A. C. Parker, *Chamberlain and Appeasement* (London, Macmillan, 1993), p. 181.

6 Ritchie Ovendale, *'Appeasement' and the English Speaking World* (Cardiff, University of Wales Press, 1975), p. 182.

7 E. M. Robertson, 'Hitler's planning for war and the response of the Great Powers' in H. W. Koch (ed.), *Aspects of the Third Reich* (London, Macmillan, 1985), p. 230.

8 Sidney Aster, *1939: The Making of the Second World War* (London, Deutsch, 1973), pp. 45–9.

9 Wesley K. Wark, *The Ultimate Enemy: British Intelligence and Nazi Germany, 1933–39* (London, Tauris, 1985), pp. 172–4, 239.

10 See the contemporary witness in Alexander Werth, *France and Munich: Before and After the Surrender* (London, Hamish Hamilton, 1939), pp. 394–413.

11 N. H. Gibbs, *Grand Strategy: Vol. I, Rearmament Policy* (London, HMSO, 1976), pp. 666–7.

12 Norman Rich, *Hitler's War Aims: Ideology, the Nazi State, and the Course of Expansion* (London, Deutsch, 1973), pp. 11–15.

13 John Weitz, *Joachim von Ribbentrop: Hitler's Diplomat* (London, Weidenfeld & Nicolson, 1992), pp. 188–9.

14 Rich, *Hitler's Aims,* p. 118.

15 Ovendale, *'Appeasement',* p. 234.

16 Keith Middlemas, *Diplomacy of Illusion* (London, Weidenfeld & Nicolson, 1972), p. 440; Christopher Hill, *Cabinet Decisions on Foreign Policy: the British Experience October 1938–June 1941* (Cambridge, Cambridge University Press, 1991), pp. 20–3, for the Birmingham speech.

17 René Girault, 'The Impact of the economic situation on the foreign policy of France, 1936–9' in Wolfgang J. Mommsen and Lothar Kettenacker (eds.), *The Fascist Challenge and the Policy of Appeasement* (London, Allen & Unwin, 1983), p. 222.

18 Anthony Adamthwaite, 'France and the coming of war' in *ibid.,* p. 253.

19 Gerhard L. Weinberg, *The Foreign Policy of Hitler's Germany: Starting World War II, 1937–39* (Chicago, IL, University of Chicago Press, 1980), pp. 484–6, 539–45.

20 Asa Briggs, 'First shots of the phoney peace', *The Times*, 31 December 1988.

21 G. C. Peden, *British Rearmament and the Treasury: 1932–1939* (Edin-

burgh, Scottish Academic Press, 1979), p. 207.

22 Donald Cameron Watt, *How War Came: The Immediate Origins of the Second World War, 1938–1939* (London, Heinemann, 1989), pp. 82–3.

23 Elizabeth Wiskemann, *Undeclared War* (London, Constable, 1939), pp. 65–6.

24 To which A. Alexandroff and R. Rosecrance, 'Deterrence in 1939', *World Politics,* 29 (1977), 404–24, remains a good introduction.

25 Hill, *Cabinet Decisions,* p. 29.

26 James S. Herndon, 'British perceptions of Soviet military capability, 1935–9' in Mommsen and Kettenacker (eds), *Fascist Challenge,* pp. 297–318.

27 Gibbs, *Grand Strategy,* p. 700.

28 Jan Karski, *The Great Powers and Poland 1919–1945* (Lanham, MD, University Press of America, 1985), pp. 244–5.

29 Letter by Edward Bridges to Alexander Cadogan, 19 March 1943, Public Record Office, FO 371/34482/3138.

30 Robert Fisk, *In Time of War: Ireland, Ulster and the Price of Neutrality 1939–45* (London, Paladin Books, 1985), p. 244.

31 Anita Prazmowska, *Britain, Poland and the Eastern Front, 1939* (Cambridge, Cambridge University Press, 1987), pp. 47–9.

32 Józef Garlinski, 'The Polish view' in Roy Douglas (ed.), *1939: A Retrospect Forty Years After* (London, Macmillan, 1983), pp. 64–73.

33 Parker, *Chamberlain,* pp. 213–14.

34 Karski, *Great Powers and Poland,* pp. 271–2.

35 Prazmowska, *Britain, Poland,* pp. 59–64.

36 Grigore Gafencu, *Prelude to the Russian Campaign* (London, Muller, 1945), p. 17.

37 Aster, *1939,* pp. 137–41.

38 Gibbs, *Grand Strategy,* p. 711.

39 Gordon Waterfield, *Professional Diplomat: Sir Percy Loraine* (London, Murray, 1973), pp. 234–5.

40 Watt, *How War Came,* pp. 240–1.

41 Mario Toscano, *The Origins of the Pact of Steel* (Baltimore, MD, The Johns Hopkins Press, 1967), p. 376.

42 Watt, *How War Came,* pp. 41–2.

43 Weinberg, *Starting World War II,* pp. 560.

44 *Ibid.,* p. 558.

45 Watt, *How War Came,* pp. 34–7.

46 W. Deist, M. Messerschmidt, H-E. Volkman and W. Wette, *Germany and the Second World War: The Build-up of German Aggression* (Oxford, Clarendon Press, 1990), pp. 534–7.

47 Wiskemann, *Undeclared War,* p. 191; Antony Polonsky, *Politics in*

Independent Poland 1921–1939 (Oxford, Clarendon Press, 1972), pp. 464–5.

48 Deist et al., *Germany and the Second World War*, p. 118; Fritz Redlich M. D., *Hitler: Diagnosis of a Destructive Prophet* (New York, Oxford University Press, 1998), p. 147.

49 Martin K. Sorge, *The Other Price of Hitler's War: German Military and Civilian Losses from World War II* (Westport, CT, Greenwood Press, 1986), p. 89.

50 Alan Sharp, *The Versailles Settlement: Peacemaking in Paris, 1919* (London, Macmillan, 1991), p. 123.

51 Watt, *How War Came,* pp. 186–7.

52 Prazmowska, *Britain, Poland,* p. 153.

53 Weinberg, *Starting World War II,* pp. 555–6.

54 Karski, *Great Powers and Poland,* p. 245.

55 Watt, *How War Came,* p. 536, states incorrectly that they executed him.

56 Prazmowska, *Britain, Poland,* pp. 94–6, 115–17, chapter 6.

57 Weinberg, *Starting World War II,* pp. 624–6.

58 Ovendale, *'Appeasement',* pp. 286–7.

59 Lawrence Aronsen and Martin Kitchen, *The Origins of the Cold War in Comparative Perspective: American, British and Canadian Relations with the Soviet Union, 1941–48* (London, Macmillan, 1988), p. 159.

60 Parker, *Chamberlain,* p. 205.

61 Richard Lamb, *The Ghosts of Peace 1935–1945* (Salisbury, Russell, 1987), pp. 105–7.

62 Aster, *1939,* pp. 234–6.

63 Parker, *Chamberlain,* pp. 260–1.

64 Aster, *1939,* p. 250.

65 Richard Griffiths, *Fellow Travellers of the Right* (London, Constable, 1980) pp. 363–7.

CHAPTER NINE

THE SOVIET UNION

The most damaging feature of what was essentially the non-phenomenon of post-Prague British appeasement was the Wohltat affair in July 1939 when Helmut Wohltat, an adviser to Goering, visited London, ostensibly for a conference on the regulation of whaling, and held talks with Chamberlain's civil servant adviser, Horace Wilson, and with Robert Hudson, a junior minister and notorious busybody. Those with Wilson did not leak out and were innocuous; Wilson said that economic appeasement could resume if Germany definitively renounced the use of force. Those with Hudson were also about economic panaceas to world problems and were leaked to the press in an exaggerated form. Hudson had acted independently and what he had to say was, in any case, soon dismissed by Hitler on the grounds that 'Germany was not after money'.[1] In Britain the storm caused by the leak was soon almost forgotten, but the affair made a more permanent impression in Moscow. In Soviet historiography it was a matter of 'documentary precision' that the British guarantee to Poland and later negotiations with the Soviet Union were 'only the small change with which it intended to pay Nazi Germany for ensuring the interests of imperialism.'[2]

In 1939 it is unlikely that the Soviet government were so certain about British perfidy, but it is probable that they had the strongest suspicions about whether appeasement had really been abandoned. These would have been strengthened by the tardiness with which Britain and France, but especially Britain, turned to trying to forge security arrangements with Russia. Many at the time regarded these as the only effective deterrent to Nazi aggression and they would, undoubtedly, at least have made Hitler pause. There were, however, obstacles in the way, even in addition to Anglo-French caution and

Poland's intransigent refusal to consider Russia as an ally. Stalin had good intelligence sources about Germany and Japan in 1939 and they all informed him that Russia was now low on the list of possible targets for German aggression. In particular, he was aware of German rebuffs to Japanese overtures for an anti-Soviet combination. This gave him a sense of having alternatives to collective security and going to war if that failed that Britain no longer felt that it had.[3]

Before returning to the events of 1939, the failure to bring about a common front of the Western powers and Soviet Russia can only be understood against the background of not only these immediate factors but also the entire chequered relationship of the Soviets with Germany and with the Western democracies in the 1930s. The Soviet regime had shown every sign of incapacity to understand Nazism from the time that it became too important to ignore in the early 1930s. E. H. Carr, historian of Soviet Russia and of the Communist International, referred to Communist 'inability to analyse and understand a conflict of two ideologies resting on conceptions of the historical and political process so alien to each other as to preclude meaningful argument between them'. Attempts to explain the rise of Hitler in Marxist terms of class struggle 'led to endless embarrassment'.[4] In 1931 Moscow welcomed the rise in support for the Nazis. Its faithful German servant, the Communist leader Ernst Thalmann, explained that this 'brought confusion into the camp of the bourgeoisie'. By the next year a few doubts were creeping in but they were weakened by the dying Weimar Republic's hostile attitude to Russia, expressed for instance in Germany's rejection in the autumn of 1932 of the Soviet proposal that the tenth anniversary of the German–Soviet Rapallo treaty should be celebrated.[5]

Once the Nazis were in power Stalin entertained the hope that Hitler might be at heart an orthodox German conservative politician with an anti-Western bias and a Bismarckian desire for good Russo-German relations, and the fear that the Western powers might be intent on turning German expansionist appetites eastwards. By contrast, he seems to have been consistent in not suspecting the West of egging on Japan to attack the Soviet Far East despite chronic Soviet–Japanese tensions.[6] In Europe, Western leaders, while not necessarily averse to Germany and Russia fighting one another without outside instigation, almost always rejected as shortsighted actual encouragement of such a conflict. They feared that that would make Germany too powerful and a mortal danger to the West in the expected event of its victory. As the former Foreign Secretary, Simon, wrote in his diary in 1936: 'The Cyclops paid Odysseus the compliment of promising to eat him last.'[7] One of the few really ideological rightwingers in British politics in the 1930s, though never a figure of much importance, Lord Londonderry, deplored his countrymen's lack of appreciation for Nazi anti-communism and unwillingness to see it as a natural bridge between Britain and Germany.[8] Occasionally, Hitler was informed explicitly of British lack of interest in joining an ideologically based combination against Soviet Russia. In late 1937, for instance, Foreign Secretary Eden told the British ambassador in Berlin to make that clear to the German head of state.[9]

Stalin's perceptions were, however, such that he consistently saw merit in being ready to consider settling differences with the Third Reich. In late 1933 his Foreign Minister, Litvinov, declared that, though Russia deplored Nazi persecution of the German Communists, it was irrelevant to relations between the two states. At the Soviet Communist Party congress in 1934 Stalin himself gave an explicit indication that a change in German foreign policy would open the door to better relations with Russia.[10] This evoked no response. The German embassy in Moscow in the 1930s was a solitary surviving bastion on the German side of the desire for German–Russian friendship even after Hitler sacked ambassador Nadolny in 1934 for being a Russophil. The German diplomats would have been delighted to make discreet enquiries to their Soviet colleagues about a German–Soviet entente if Berlin had so ordered them to do but, frustratingly for the diplomats, no such instruction was received from one year to the next.[11]

And yet, when Russia looked west for security the response was hardly more encouraging. The seventh congress of the Communist International in Moscow in 1935 set aside proletarian revolution as a practical objective for the time being and urged communists everywhere to abandon the 'sectarian narrowness' of the past and unite with anti-fascists. Communist advocacy of colonial liberation, which had struck at a particularly raw nerve in the West European colonial powers, was played down and, in a gesture to Britain, no delegates from India were invited.[12] As the starting point for an anti-Nazi coalition of states this failed. Any Western observer would have found it strange that this somersault in the aims of international Communism produced no word of criticism at the congress.[13] It would have been naive not to doubt both the sincerity and the durability of the change.

Neither would it have been convenient to give up the need for vigilance against communism in general and Soviet Russia in particular as an alibi for doing nothing against Hitler. Britain had used this ploy to justify not helping Austria when its independence was threatened in 1934 and only Italy had saved it.[14]

All the old fears about Soviet intentions were to be strengthened by Russian aid to the Spanish republic in the Civil War that began in mid-1936, though Stalin had mixed feelings about intervening in a situation in which Soviet credentials to be the embodiment of socialist orthodoxy were challenged by Anarchists and the dissident Marxists of the POUM.[15] In limiting Soviet aid to the Republic Stalin also seemed to have had a particular concern with conciliating Mussolini at least as much as the Western democracies.[16] If that indicated that he despaired of the latter, his view would not have been unjustified. The British government had decided in the winter of 1935–36 that any sort of accord with Russia was incompatible with the appeasement of Germany and that the latter goal was the one to pursue.[17] Perhaps sensing that his regime had been snubbed, the future Soviet Foreign Minister, Molotov, responding to German remilitarisation of the Rhineland toward the end of that winter, gave an interview to a French journalist in which he declared that the 'chief tendency' in Soviet policy 'thinks an improvement in Soviet–German relations possible'.[18] As before, this produced no positive response from Berlin. Molotov's implicit overture to Germany was based on illusion, rather than delusion, about Nazi Germany. The Soviets perceived the depth of Hitler's hostility to them but thought that a combination of moderates in the ruling elite and Germany's economic difficulties might force him to become more amenable to them.[19] This rested on premises not greatly different from those of Western appeasement of Germany. There was also a readiness to treat Nazi references to *Lebensraum* in Russia, in any case almost totally absent from public discourse in Germany after 1933, and to Slav racial inferiority as verbiage that sophisticated men of the world could safely disregard.

Ideological prejudice and an adverse, even contemptuous, assessment of Russian military capabilities interacted with one another to continue to cause the Western powers to keep Soviet Russia at arm's length in the late 1930s. The most important element in the ideological factor was a profound suspicion that the Soviet regime would feel no obligation in difficult circumstances to keep its word to those whom its ideology characterised as the bourgeois class enemy. In

1935 France signed a pact with the Soviets after the latter had threatened to sever all relations unless it was signed. The French general staff ensured that nothing serious came of it, and insisted that, in military terms, France needed Italy much more than it needed Russia.[20] After the dashing of their Italian hopes, the French turned more and more to Britain and told the Soviets bluntly that they could not develop military ties because Britain would object and Britain was more important to them than the Soviet Union.[21] The British military chiefs were actually less doctrinaire than their French counterparts, but a Soviet decision in 1936 to invite them to send observers to the Red Army's annual summer manoeuvres backfired. The British officers were unimpressed by what they saw of the Red Army at first hand.[22] The infamous purge of the officer corps over the next two years was inevitably and rightly perceived as making matters worse, but the British service chiefs never wholly discounted Russia as a military factor. In an appreciation of the overall strategic situation in the spring of 1937, in discussing why they thought it unlikely that Germany would resort to war in the near future, they noted that the threat of Russian intervention in such a war constituted 'a powerful moral (sic) deterrent against Germany going to war'.[23]

Russian support, 'moral' or otherwise, was not sought by Britain in the crisis leading up to Munich, despite highly ambiguous signals from the Soviet government that it might be available for war if various conditions were met. During September 1938 Stalin devoted much time to the project of purchasing a battleship from the United States as part of a long-term policy of restoring the Soviet Union as a naval power. This hardly showed preoccupation with an immediate crisis in Central Europe. Three times between January and September 1938 Foreign Minister Litvinov warned the director general of the Czech foreign ministry that Russia would be neutral if the Western powers went to war on the side of Czechoslovakia.[24] A recent study concludes that it is certain that Stalin did not intend to come to Czechoslovakia's military assistance under any circumstances in September 1938.[25] Although unable to be sure of this, the Germans discounted the risk of Soviet intervention and had a realistic conception that the Soviet Union was not in a position, in the absence of a Czech–Soviet border, to offer more than limited aerial support that would not seriously impede German military operations. The British chiefs of staff made much the same lowly assessment of what Russia could offer in aid to Czechoslovakia.[26] However, as the Munich deal showed signs of unravelling there was regret, shared by Foreign Secretary Halifax though not by Chamberlain, that the Soviets had been ignored. The former noted in November that Russia 'for good or evil is part of Europe and we cannot ignore her existence'.[27]

Unfortunately for peace, Hitler too was beginning to think that he could not ignore Russia. He was encouraged by Ribbentrop who was agnostic about a *Lebensraum* empire in the east, and who had been interested in a Russo-German combination (including also Italy and Japan) to create an anti-British bloc spanning two continents since the failure of his ambassadorship in London in 1937.[28] Stalin had no intention of playing easy to woo. As has already been noted, he had a strong sense of various options being open to him: alignment with the Western powers, with Germany, or neutrality while the other large powers fought and weakened one another, making Russia relatively stronger without it having to make any actual effort. Even a study sympathetic to the problems facing Soviet policymakers can say no more than that there were 'attitudinal dualisms' in which collective security was the preferred policy but not the only one.[29] After Munich the Soviet media referred frequently to the inevitability of a new war, but they called it the Second Imperialist War, a designation that appeared to preclude Soviet participation.[30]

Then, in March 1939, Hitler removed what would otherwise have been an insuperable obstacle to a German–Russian entente by allowing Hungary, in the wake of the final downfall of Czechoslovakia, to annex Sub-Carpathian Ruthenia, a small and, even by East European standards, poor and backward region that had been included in Czechoslovakia in 1919 but whose affairs are so profoundly obscure that linguistic and folklore specialists can still not agree on whether the arcane dialect spoken by most of its rustic inhabitants is a derivative of Russian or of Ukrainian. To Ukrainian nationalists it was an article of faith that it was the latter. If there was one subject on which Stalin was paranoid, before he became obsessed by anti-Semitism towards the end of his life, it was Ukrainian nationalism and the threat that it posed to the unity of the Soviet Union. In November 1938 Hitler had allowed Hungary to annex part of southern Slovakia but not much of Sub-Carpathian Ruthenia as well; the Hungarian rulers wanted all of it. The province became nominally self-governing under the continuing aegis of Prague but Nazi German officials largely usurped Czech authority and encouraged Ukrainian nationalism.[31] German motives remain obscure, though they must have included a desire to punish Hungary for being a somewhat uncooperative vassal. To the Soviets they smacked of a favourite technique of their own: the establishment of a small puppet state to which a much larger neighbouring entity with real or fabricated ethnic links with the puppet entity could be added by various military and political means from 'Karelia', bordering on Finland, in the north west to Tajikistan, bordering on Iran, in the far south.[32] To the Soviets Hitler's gift of Ruthenia to Hungary meant that he was no longer toying with Ukrainian nationalism. Whether Hitler himself realised it, and he probably did not, he had performed a masterstroke in the service of German–Soviet relations.

Chamberlain's gesture in overcoming his scruples and becoming the first prime minister to accept an invitation to a reception at the Soviet embassy in London on 1 March (whose purpose was to celebrate the overthrow of the last tsar) hardly compared with what Hitler had done, but Stalin was not to be won over by one German action, no matter how important. In fact, Russia made proposals to Britain and France for collective security both before and after the British guarantee to Poland on 31 March over which the British themselves were conscious that, at least in the short term, they were choosing between Russia and Poland. Soviet proposals in mid April endorsed a French plan for the three big powers to guarantee Poland, Romania and the small Baltic states against a German attack, and went on to propose an actual alliance of those three powers, plus several other items including that all three should supply military materials to Turkey, which may have been a gesture to Britain's preoccupation with that country in 1939.[33] Chamberlain was unreceptive. He had been delighted, not dismayed, by Beck's anti-Russian outpourings during his visit to London, he found the Labour and Liberal oppositions' clamour for Soviet links extremely offputting, and he was ill-advised by the Foreign Office permanent head, Alexander Cadogan, that the one thing that had to compel a rethinking of British security policy, an actual link-up between Germany and Russia, was utterly unlikely. By this time wiser voices within the Office, including that of Cadogan's predecessor, Vansittart, saw such a link-up as a very real possibility.[34] It was, however, left to the French to deliver what Litvinov called a 'mockery' of a reply to Soviet security proposals with counter-proposals under which Soviet aid to Britain and France would have been automatic while Anglo-French aid to Russia would have been voluntary.[35]

This contributed to Stalin's decision in early May to replace Litvinov with Vyacheslav Molotov. This was important. Litvinov had been a sincere exponent of collective security. Molotov was an opinionated and rather stupid man who had formed a conviction, from which he could not be budged, that Soviet–German cooperation was both possible and desirable. During his first two years in office Stalin was willing to be influenced by him, though after the German invasion in 1941 his status was to sink to little more than that of a clerk.[36] Even in 1939 the change at the foreign ministry did not mean that the Soviet Union ceased to have any interest in a coalition against Hitler. Litvinov's deputy remained in office and did not cancel a planned visit to capitals of East European countries that still remained independent of Germany, including Warsaw. The Deputy Foreign Minister, Vladimir Potemkin, argued energetically the case for collective security in these capitals.[37]

Ironically, the danger of alienating these countries was a main argument in Chamberlain's political armoury as he fought a rearguard action against mounting pressures in Britain to seek an alliance with the Soviets. One backbench Conservative MP remarked: 'I know they have shot a lot of people but there are about 170 million of them left.'[38] On 24 May Chamberlain finally had to yield and agree that Britain should seek a treaty arrangement with Russia. The pressure inside and outside the Cabinet had finally become irresistible.[39] Two institutions that did not like this decision, the Commonwealth in the form of the governments of the dominions, and the monarchy in the person of the King, were given assurances that the government's quest for arrangements with Russia was not central or essential to its foreign policy.[40] To Chamberlain at least, it remained an optional and distasteful extra.

The considerations militating against a British attempt at almost any cost to bring about an alliance with Russia included continuing deep – and in Chamberlain's case ineradicable – doubts about whether the Soviet regime could be trusted and (diminishing) concern about the reactions of Japan and a Spain that was now firmly under Franco's rule. Against that, the British had to set mounting fears of a Soviet–German accord. The interaction between Stalin's increasing interest in such an accord and the problems involved in actually agreeing the terms of an alliance between Soviet Russia and Britain and France was to prove fatal to the enterprise. Through press articles and remarks to diplomats from various countries who could be expected to pass the message on, the Soviets made it very clear that they did not trust the 'English government' and would therefore only be satisfied with an agreement that left any commitments it might make 'without loopholes'.[41] It was, therefore, deplorable that Chamberlain initiated the negotiations with a piece of transparent trickery by attempting to link a treaty with the Covenant of the League of Nations. Molotov fulminated against Hitler being allowed to commit aggression because of a 'Bolivian veto' and Britain and France then abandoned the idea of a link with the League and set a pattern of retreating in the face of Soviet demands. This process continued with Britain conceding that there should be a full alliance between the three countries. It had wanted a three power pact that would only have come into force if one of the three were directly attacked, thus meeting the Polish wish to avoid involvement with Russia. Neither Russia nor France would agree to that. Then Britain abandoned its opposition to a provision in the alliance against any signatory making a separate peace. This was against Britain's better judgement because it thought that such an undertaking would only be truly binding on the Western democracies and would be disregarded by a regime like the Soviet if it was convenient to do so. Any favourable impression produced by this stream of concessions was weakened when Britain and France sent two relatively junior professional diplomats to negotiate with Molotov in Moscow. There was an odd contrast between this and the later despatch of military missions with middle ranking heads and the intense Cabinet interest in the negotiations.[42]

The political negotiations reached stalemate, though not breakdown, over the question of countries that did not wish to be guaranteed, in particular the small Baltic republics of Latvia and Estonia which had rejected a Soviet offer to guarantee them in March and which, scarcely without reason, feared the threat to their independence from their old master, Russia, at least as much as from Germany.[43] Britain and France could stomach an unwanted guarantee against an unprovoked German attack. Indeed Britain wanted to guarantee the Netherlands in disregard of Dutch protests that they did not want to be guaranteed. But they baulked at Molotov's new demand, on 3 July, that the Soviet Union must have the right to intervene against 'internal aggression' in either of these states. This meant, in effect, a right to intervene, with the possible consequence of a European war, if Estonia or Latvia was deemed by Russia to have made a voluntary choice in favour of Germany. With safeguards the demand was not inherently unreasonable and Soviet anxieties appear to have been genuine. In the summer of 1939 Stalin seems to have been in a highly nervous state about the security of Leningrad. A formula could almost certainly have been found that would have protected legitimate Soviet security interests without giving them the right to occupy two small countries that had committed no real offence.[44] However, a formula there had to be. Vansittart was a long time advocate of alliance with Russia, but in July he wrote to the distinguished historian of that country, Bernard Pares, that Soviet demands regarding the Baltic states were, as they stood, simply unacceptable as being grossly unjust to the states themselves, and because they amounted to a demand to Britain 'that we should virtually give them a warrant to interfere in the internal affairs of these states and go to war if this leads to trouble'.[45] In October Halifax was to reminisce that the government feared that Stalin would have abused a free hand for him in the East Baltic 'on which we, suspecting motives, were sticky'.[46]

With the political talks statemated, on 23 July the Soviet side made a new demand for an agreement on military cooperation to be negotiated and signed simultaneously with the political alliance. Once again, Britain and France agreed and sent over military missions. The British mission was led by the magnificently named Admiral Sir Reginald Plunkett-Ernle-Erle-Drax who was later to turn to authorship with a book on *World War Three: Pros and Cons*. (Not to be outdone, the German navy of the 1930s had an Admiral Albrecht Freiherr von Freyberg-Eisenberg-Allmendingen. Both men were competent naval strategists with a gift for diplomacy as well.) These negotiations took place against a background of Molotov writing about 'swindlers and cheats, such as negotiators on the Anglo-French side have shown themselves to be all the time'. The Soviet ambassador in London contributed the thought that appeasement again reigned supreme in the British government while his counterpart in France doubted whether the military missions had any purpose other than espionage.[47] The actual negotiations were conducted in a civil way but the Soviets wanted extremely detailed military commitments that the Western side regarded as neither possible nor desirable. The British Admiral justifiably condemned as 'quite childish' a Soviet proposal that if Germany attacked in the West Russia should engage German forces equivalent to 70 per cent of the number of that country's troops in the West, while Britain and France would pin down seven out of every seventeen troops in the German army if Hitler attacked in the East.[48] But, above all, the Soviet government wanted the right to send troops into Poland or Romania if either was attacked but could offer no help on how those countries might be induced to accept such assistance.[49] By mid August the British Chiefs of Staff were urging the government to put whatever pressure was required on Warsaw and Bucharest to agree to admit the Red Army.[50] By then Stalin had decided to break off the talks and accept a deal with Hitler.

Hitler began making overtures to Russia in late May by proposing a trade agreement. The Soviets agreed on the explicit condition that it was to be the precursor to a political arrangement and not an end in itself.[51] Exactly two months later they had grown impatient, and Molotov instructed the Soviet chargé in Berlin to inform the Germans that they must say 'in concrete terms' what they would be willing to offer. The Germans were still in no great hurry, but on 12 August he was able to reply that the answer was 'the Baltic, Bessarabia [north-eastern Romania, formerly Tsarist Russian], Eastern Poland' as what 'the Germans would give up (sic) in order to secure a promise from us not to intervene in their conflict with Poland'.[52] To lubricate the process of policymaking the Soviets leaked information about the progress of their negotiations with the Western powers. Perhaps the greatest tragedy of 1939 is that between late July and the signature of the Nazi–Soviet pact on 23 August Britain received almost no intelligence of any value about the now fast-developing Soviet–German relationship.[53] If it had done, Britain – and France would undoubtedly have raised no objection – could have agreed to every Soviet demand, forcing Stalin either to sign with the Western powers or to reveal that he would no longer do so under any circumstances.

It has often been speculated that Stalin thought that the Western powers would desert Poland if he made a pact with Germany with the result that there would be no general war, but, in one of the most interesting revelations to come out of the dying Soviet Union, a Russian historian called Vladimir Rezun, who writes under the pseudonym Victor Suvorov, has reproduced an address by the Soviet dictator to his Politburo on 19 August in which he said that he both wanted and expected a war between Britain and France and Germany so that Russia could intervene and expand when they were

exhausted.[54] By then matters were moving fast between Moscow and
Berlin. Although Hitler had threatened as long ago as April to con-
coct a 'diabolical beverage' for the British to punish them for guaranteeing Poland, it was not until 14 August that the German
ambassador in Moscow was told to ask the Soviet government for a
speedy and comprehensive agreement between the two countries.
Hitler had overcome his residual repugnance against seeking a pact
with Stalin after his generals had presented him with the dismaying
advice that they could no longer guarantee the success of their
planned pincer movement to encircle and eliminate the bulk of the
Polish army in western Poland at the start of the impending campaign. That created the possibility that most of the Polish forces
might escape east and link up with the Red Army to form a formidable combination if the Anglo-French–Soviet negotiations succeeded
and if Poland changed its policy towards Russia following an actual
German invasion.[55] Finally, Hitler was dismayed by the patching up
of Anglo-Japanese relations in July and the definitive failure of attempts at a German–Japanese alliance with Japan breaking off negotiations on 12 August.[56] This was as bad a blow to Hitler as was the
impending failure of the Anglo-French–Soviet project to London and
Paris. He had hoped that the threat of a war on two fronts – in Europe and the Far East – would be as much a nightmare to Stalin as it
was to himself and would force him to remain neutral when Poland
was attacked. With that hope gone, he turned to the repugnant last
alternative of a deal with Stalin.

Stalin, having been offered much and probably mistrusting Hitler
marginally less than he mistrusted Chamberlain,[57] accepted. Germany and Russia signed their pact on 23 August in the form of a ten
year non-aggression treaty under which each country promised
friendly neutrality if the other were at war. There was no provision,
as in previous such treaties, that this undertaking would be void if the
country at war was in that state owing to aggression that it had itself
committed. A secret protocol, discovered in Nazi archives soon after
1945 but denounced by the Soviet regime as a forgery until the late
1980s, placed the Baltic states of Finland, Estonia and Latvia (but
not Lithuania) and the Romanian province of Bessarabia at the
Soviet Union's disposal, and divided Poland into German and Soviet
spheres 'in the event' of military operations on Polish territory.
Reflecting the German concern for speed, the agreement was to come
into force immediately without any ratification procedures.

Members of the German negotiating team in Moscow recorded the impression that Stalin made on them as solemn but happy and over-flowing with goodwill for them. Members of his entourage recalled that in the private celebrations that followed the pact he was beside himself with joy and very definitely not a man who was conscious of having had to make a choice between two difficult, almost evenly balanced, alternatives.[58] However the blame is apportioned for the failure of the Anglo-French–Soviet negotiations and the subsequent Nazi–Soviet pact, there can be no doubt that these were an unmiti-gated catastrophe for all humanity and for the peoples of the Soviet Union in particular. There is considerable evidence that if an Anglo-French–Soviet alliance had been formed Hitler would have called off the invasion of Poland and would have tried to salvage something politically by claiming that he had disproved the slanders of his en-emies who accused him of being a warmonger.[59] After that it is diffi-cult to visualise how he could have found an alternative strategy for committing successful aggression.

And yet it would be a mistake to suppose that the failed alliance negotiations with the West had no useful results at all. In April 1941 Orme Sargent, one of the highest of the Foreign Office grandees, was to write in an internal document that in 1939 Britain and France had been too highminded in defending the legitimate interests of the small Baltic states and that it was 'probable' that Stalin would have allied with them if they had sacrificed those states. He concluded that it would be unwise to be 'equally uncompromising' with the Soviets in the future.[60] Sargent exaggerated; there was, at best, only a possi-bility that an action of the type about which he retrospectively specu-lated might have succeeded. In 1942 Molotov was to remark to the British negotiator of 1939, William Strang, 'We did our best in 1939, but we failed: both were at fault.'[61] That might seem mild, but it was extremely rare for the Soviet regime under Stalin to admit to any degree of error. From the debris of the failed negotiations of 1939 the British drew the conclusion that they had been insufficiently cynical, while the Soviets appeared to concede that they had been too cynical in their deal with the man whom they had for so long denounced as 'the hangman of the working classes'. That was not a bad starting point for a working relationship between the two countries when they actually became allies between 1941 and 1945.

Notes

1   Sidney Aster, *1939: The Making of the Second World War* (London, Deutsch, 1973), pp. 344–57; Donald Cameron Watt, *How War Came* (London, Heinemann, 1989), pp. 390–400; Martin Gilbert, 'Horace Wilson: Man of Munich?', *History Today*, 32 (October 1982), 3–9.

2   A. A. Gromyko and B. N. Ponomarev (eds), *Soviet Foreign Policy: Vol. I 1945–1970* (Moscow, Progress Publishers, 1981), p. 371.

3   Gerhard L. Weinberg, *The Foreign Policy of Hitler's Germany: Starting World War II, 1937–39* (Chicago, IL, University of Chicago Press, 1980), pp. 530–4, 549–52; Watt, *How War Came*, pp. 115–18.

4   E. H. Carr, *Twilight of the Comintern, 1930–1935* (New York, Pantheon Books, 1982), pp. 104–5.

5   *Ibid.*, pp. 41–3; Lionel Kochan, *The Struggle for Germany 1914:45* (Edinburgh, Edinburgh University Press, 1963), p. 59; John Hiden, *German and Europe 1919–1939* (London, Longman, 1977), p. 97.

6   Carr, *Twilight,* pp. 387–8.

7   James S. Herndon, 'British perceptions of Soviet military capability, 1935–9' in Wolfgang Mommsen and Lothar Kettenacker (eds), *The Fascist Challenge and the Policy of Appeasement* (London, Allen & Unwin, 1983), p. 313.

8   Marquess of Londonderry, *Ourselves and Germany* (London, Hale, 1938), pp. 129–30.

9   Andrew J. Crozier, *Appeasement and Germany's Last Bid for Colonies* (London, Macmillan, 1988), pp. 220–2.

10 Carr, *Twilight*, pp. 117–18; Gerhard L. Weinberg, *The Foreign Policy of Hitler's Germany: Diplomatic Revolution in Europe, 1933–36* (Chicago, IL, University of Chicago Press, 1970), pp. 220–3, 310–12; W. Deist, M. Messerschmidt, H-E. Volkmann and W. Wette, *Germany and the Second World War: Vol. I, The Build-up of German Aggression,* (Oxford, Clarendon Press, 1990), pp. 612–14.

11 Johnnie von Herwarth, *Against Two Evils* (London, Collins, 1981), pp. 54, 88–9, 112–15.

12 Carr, *Twilight,* chapter 18.

13 Julius Braunthal, *History of the International 1914–1943* (Edinburgh, Nelson, 1967), p. 470.

14 A. R. Peters, *Anthony Eden at the Foreign Office 1931–1938* (Aldershot, Gower, 1986), pp. 75–6; Gaines Post, Jr., *Dilemmas of Appeasement* (Ithaca, NY, Cornell University Press, 1993), p. 106.

15 Michael Alpert, *A New International History of the Spanish Civil War* (London, Macmillan, 1994), pp. 48–52.

16 Anthony T. Komjathy, *The Crises of France's East Central European Diplomacy 1933–1938* (New York, Columbia University Press, 1976), p. 167.

17 Victor Rothwell, *Anthony Eden: A Political Biography 1931–57* (Manchester, Manchester University Press, 1992), pp. 15–16; Robert Manne, 'The Foreign Office and the failure of Anglo-Soviet rapprochement', *Journal of Contemporary History*, 16:4 (1981), 725–55.

18 Kochan, *Struggle*, pp. 68–9.

19 Geoffrey Roberts, *The Unholy Alliance: Stalin's Pact with Hitler* (London, Tauris, 1989), chapter 5.

20 Nicole Jordan, *The Popular Front and Central Europe: The Dilemmas of French Impotence, 1918–1940* (Cambridge, Cambridge University Press, 1992), pp. 29–31, 105–7, 308–14.

21 Michael Jabara Carley, *1939: The Alliance That Never Was and the Coming of World War II* (Chicago, IL, Dee, 1999), pp. 24–6.

22 W. P. and Zelda K. Coates, *A History of Anglo-Soviet Relations* (London, Lawrence and Wishart, 1943), p. 557.

23 Post, *Dilemmas of Appeasement*, p. 285.

24 Nicolai Tolstoy, *Stalin's Secret War* (London, Cape, 1981), pp. 75–6.

25 Igor Lukes, 'Stalin and Czechoslovakia in 1938–39: an autopsy of a myth', *Diplomacy and Statecraft*, 19:2&3 (1999), 13–47.

26 Weinberg, *Starting World War II*, pp. 352–4, 414–18.

27 Watt, *How War Came*, pp. 83–4.

28 Geoffrey T. Waddington, 'Ribbentrop and the Soviet Union, 1937–1941' in John Erickson and David Dilks (eds), *Barbarossa: The Axis and the Allies* (Edinburgh, Edinburgh University Press, 1994), pp. 7–12.

29 Roberts, *Unholy*, p. 48; see also the same author's *The Soviet Union and the Origins of the Second World War: Russo-German Relations, 1933–1941* (London, Macmillan, 1995), chapter 6.

30 Gerhard L. Weinberg, *Germany and the Soviet Union 1939–1941* (Leiden, Brill, 1954), p. 7.

31 Elizabeth Wiskemann, *Undeclared War* (London, Constable, 1939), pp. 224–41.

32 See Walter Kolarz, *Russia and Her Colonies* (London, Philip, 1952).

33 N. H. Gibbs, *Grand Strategy: Vol. I, Rearmament Policy* (London, HMSO, 1976), pp. 721–2.

34 R. A. C. Parker, *Chamberlain and Appeasement* (London, Macmillan, 1993), pp. 219, 223–9; Waddington in Erickson and Dilks (eds), *Barbarossa*, pp. 12–14; Lloyd C. Gardner, *Spheres of Influence: The Partition of Europe, from Munich to Yalta* (London, Murray, 1993), pp. 47–81.

35 Roberts, *Unholy*, pp. 128–31.

36 Jonathan Haslam, 'Soviet–German relations and the origins of the Second World War: the jury is still out', *Journal of Modern History*, 69:4 (1997), 785–97.

37 Weinberg, *Germany and the Soviet Union*, pp. 16–20.

38 Neville Thompson, *The Anti-Appeasers* (Oxford, Clarendon Press, 1971), p. 203.

39 Christopher Hill, *Cabinet Decisions on Foreign Policy: The British Experience, October 1938–June 1941* (Cambridge, Cambridge University Press, 1991), pp. 55–70; Robert Manne, 'The British decision for alliance with Russia, May 1939', *Journal of Contemporary History*, 9:3 (1974), 3–26.

40 Ritchie Ovendale, *'Appeasement' and the English Speaking World* (Cardiff, University of Wales Press, 1975), p. 229; Sarah Bradford, *George VI* (London, Fontana edn., 1991), p. 394.

41 Lord Strang, *Home and Abroad* (London, Deutsch, 1956), pp. 176–7; Roberts, *Unholy*, p. 149.

42 Analysed in Hill, *Cabinet Decisions*, pp. 70–84.

43 Watt, *How War Came*, pp. 223–4.

44 *Ibid.*, pp. 365–7; Strang, *Home and Abroad*, pp. 177–90.

45 Gardner, *Spheres*, p. 57.

46 Andrew Roberts, *'The Holy Fox': A Life of Lord Halifax* (London, Macmillan, 1992), p. 159.

47 'Soviet–British–French talks in Moscow, 1939: A documentary survey', *International Affairs* (Moscow, July–November 1969), October issue, pp. 64–5; November issue, p. 78.

48 Gibbs, *Grand Strategy*, p. 756.

49 Roberts, *Unholy*, pp. 154, 262.

50 Herndon in Mommsen and Kettenacker (eds), *Fascist Challenge*, p. 311.

51 Weinberg, *Germany and the Soviet Union*, pp. 24–32; Weinberg, *Starting World War II*, pp. 602–10.

52 Roberts, *Unholy*, p. xiv.

53 Aster, *1939*, pp. 314–18.

54 V. Suvorov (aka V. Rezun), *Icebreaker: Who Started the Second World War* (London, Hamish Hamilton, 1989), pp. 42–6.

55 Esmonde M. Robertson, 'German mobilization preparations and the treaties between Germany and the Soviet Union of August and September 1939' in Robert Boyce and Esmonde M. Robertson (eds.), *Paths to War* (London, Macmillan, 1989), pp. 335–40.

56 William Carr, *Poland to Pearl Harbor: The Making of the Second World War* (London, Arnold, 1985), p. 62.

57 Gabriel Gorodetsky, *Grand Delusion: Stalin and the German Invasion of Russia* (New Haven, CT, Yale University Press, 1999), pp. 6–7.

58 Robert C. Tucker, *Stalin in Power: The Revolution from Above, 1928–1941* (New York, Norton, 1990), pp. 592–8.

59 Deist et al., *Germany and the Second World War*, pp. 703–6.
60 Victor Rothwell, *Britain and the Cold War 1941–1947* (London, Cape, 1982), p. 77.
61 Strang, *Home and Abroad*, p. 159.

CHAPTER TEN

THE FAR EAST

The Second World War was to be fought mostly in two great geo-graphical areas, Europe and the Far East. The latter was of secondary importance. Without the severe disturbances to the established order that occurred in Europe in the 1930s, conflict in the Far East, if any, would almost certainly have remained in the region, confined to Ja-pan, China and the Soviet Union. The Far East did, even so, play a fundamental part in shaping the world war that was taking place by the end of 1941. The country most obviously responsible for the Sec-ond World War in the Far East was, of course, Japan, but, as the historian Ian Nish noted, it was responsible by a process that was 'haphazard and disordered',[1] and which contrasted starkly with the deliberate quest to create a situation in which it could commit suc-cessful aggression by Germany. Another German–Japanese contrast is that between a country that had been central to a continental civi-lisation for a millennium and one that had been in insular isolation for centuries until only fifty years before the start of the post-1914–18 war era. The Japanese as a people in the 1920s and 1930s were still labouring under an inability to adequately comprehend the rest of the world.[2] The contrast is reflected in the circumstances in which Germany and Japan went to war in 1939 and 1941 respectively. Hit-ler would only go to war when the forces ranged against Germany were, at most, evenly matched with those at his disposal. In 1941 Japan took a much wilder gamble in going to war with a gross na-tional product of 9 billion dollars against the United States with its 90 billion dollars gross national product.[3] It should be added that, in some respects, Japan was all too ready to fall in with global trends. It attuned itself to the concerns for justice and humanity that were widespread in the late nineteenth century, and showed that it could practise what it preached by its favourable treatment of prisoners in the Russo-Japanese war of 1904–05.[4] If the pacesetters for the decline of those concerns in the 1930s were Hitler's Germany and Stalin's Soviet Union, Japan did not lag far behind, beginning with its massacre of the population of the Chinese capital city of Nanking early in the Sino-Japanese war that began in 1937.

The Far East was much less affected by the 1914–18 war than Europe had been, and by 1922 appeared to have achieved a durable peace that still eluded Europe. The most important players in the region as the post-war era opened were Britain, the United States and Japan. China, with a population greater than all three of these combined, was regarded explicitly as existing on a lower level. At the Washington conference in 1921–22 China was told by the United States, supposedly its friend, that it would be informed about decisions concerning its fate but not consulted.[5] Divided between warlords, most of whom were little better than barbarians, and a nationalist movement whose most prominent figure, Sun Yat-sen, was widely regarded in the great powers as an utter poltroon,[6] China cut a sorry figure. One of its main aims was to throw off the humiliating as well as financially damaging indemnity that had been imposed on it after the Boxer rebellion in 1900, and – the sign of a weak country – was only able to do that by cunning and trickery. The Soviet Union and China colluded to claim that the former had given up all rights to the Russian share of the indemnity. The Soviets gained a propaganda advantage and China was able to use this (false) claim to pressure other countries into agreeing that their indemnity money should be spent inside China on such purposes as railway building and the development of civil aviation.[7] And yet, from this low point, China was to achieve an improvement in its fortunes that was to compel its detractors to consider whether to welcome it on its journey to international equality or to try to make it even more subordinate than before. The Japanese response to this dilemma was to bring about war between the two states.

If Sino-Japanese conflict was one root cause of the Second World War in the Far East, another was American–Japanese confrontation. Britain was still a major power in the Far East after the First World War. Indeed, Britain was to make a serious attempt to re-establish itself as a major player in Chinese affairs even after the Second World War.[8] In their more realistic moments, however, the British realised the inevitability of some waning of their position in the region and were ready to accommodate both China and Japan, while hoping that most of what they lost would pass to the United States. Although there were important people there and in Japan who saw no irreconcilable differences between the two nations, there were also a great many who felt the opposite, often racially motivated. In February 1917 President Woodrow Wilson told his cabinet that the United States would make its final decision on whether to enter the war according to what was best 'to keep the white race or part of it strong to meet the yellow race – Japan, for instance, in alliance with Russia, dominating China'.[9] Wilson neatly united a liberal distrust of Russia with a racist distrust of Japan. The American 1924 immigration law, which sought to end literally all immigration from the Orient, caused great resentment in Japan.

The immigration law was one of the more clearly valid of Japanese grievances. Japan also had a tendency to regard agreements that objectively were fair compromises as giving away too much. This applied most obviously to the Washington agreement of December 1921 on naval levels in which Japan agreed to limit its fleet to 60 per cent of the size of the British or American navies. The two latter countries had an overwhelming case for claiming larger fleets for their defensive needs than Japan, but many in Japan, and not only in naval circles, took a different view, especially after Britain, in response to American and Canadian pressures, had just declined to renew the Anglo-Japanese alliance. Japan had an army, the Kwantung army, in southern Manchuria, the north-eastern region of China, dating from the time of its victory in the Russo-Japanese war of 1904–05. This force did not like the second Washington treaty of February 1922 in which Japan joined seven other countries (plus China itself) in undertaking to respect the independence and integrity of China. Again, what seemed manifestly fair in the West did not seem just to many in Japan who took the view that their country had a moral and economic right to special privileges in China. Even so, the most important figure in Japanese politics in the 1920s was Shidehara Kikujo who believed in cooperation with the other three powers that really mattered to Japan: Britain, China and the United States. (The new Soviet Union certainly also mattered but was in a separate, unique category.) He did not feel threatened, but rather was inclined to follow suit, when Britain, under successive Conservative and Labour foreign secretaries, embarked on placing Anglo-Chinese relations on a more modern and equal footing.[10] The United States, interestingly, was content for Britain to be the pacesetter in this process and was ready to make concessions to China comparable with whatever Britain and China agreed upon.[11] Yet even Shidehara would have agreed that Japan had a vital stake in China that contrasted with Britain for whom China was, in the last resort, expendable. Thus British capital invested in China in 1931 was greater than Japanese although it was only 6 per cent of total British overseas investments compared with China's 82 per cent share of Japanese overseas investments. Even Shidehara would not have ruled out resort to force as China developed ports and railways other than ones in which Japan had interests.[12]

Then came the Wall Street crash in October 1929. In no country did this do more damage to the cause of free market capitalism that America had championed than in Japan. This applied both in a general sense and in a particular one in that Japan's main export to America, silk and silk goods, was severely damaged. Both American and British imperial markets were increasingly closed off to Japan by high tariffs and other measures. Extremists in Japan, and especially in the Kwantung army, used this as an excuse to take firm control of Manchuria. A fabricated incident of Chinese aggression at the city of Mukden in September 1931 was used as the excuse to take full control not only of southern Manchuria but also of the north in which the Soviets retained interests, including ownership of a major railway, the Chinese Eastern, that they had inherited from the tsarist regime and which they had refused to hand over to China. China appealed to the League of Nations which appointed a commission of enquiry under the chairmanship of Lord Lytton, a former governor of Bengal, while, outside the League, the United States proclaimed a doctrine of non-recognition of Japanese conquests early in 1932. Both the League and the United States were taking evasive action to avoid any serious steps against Japan. However, non-recognition did take the United States partly along a road towards all-out confrontation with Japan over China. Secretary of State Henry Stimson, admittedly by inclination an opponent of isolationism, referred to America's 'foothold in the minds of the Chinese people, which is pregnant with possibilities for good, provided we do not forfeit it'.[13]

Britain, for its part, had always regarded Japanese ambitions in Manchuria with some equanimity,[14] but was alarmed when Sino-Japanese fighting spread to Shanghai, China's commercial capital and the centre of British trade and investment, from late January to early March 1932, even though it was essentially the work of a Japanese admiral who chafed at the army having all the glory. From this time on, there were suspicions that Japan harboured the widest imperialist ambitions. For instance, in mid 1934 *The Economist* newspaper commented on a new Japanese law under which foreign petroleum companies had to build up huge reserve stocks, with the Japanese government taking price-fixing powers, that it conjured up the spectacle of Western oil companies paying through the nose to help the Japanese navy to invade south-east Asia.[15] A British publisher, sensing a commercial opportunity, commissioned a translation of a potboiling book by a failed Japanese naval officer and published it under the title *Japan Must Fight Britain.*[16]

In the Foreign Office some lingering sympathy for Japan coexisted uneasily with what may have been the first enunciation of what later became the celebrated Asian domino thesis: if Japan was allowed to squeeze Western interests out of China it would proceed to do the same in south-east Asia, then in India and finally in the Middle East.[17] In Washington the consensus was a combination of anti-Japanese feeling and impotence: a conviction that the United States was unprepared to confront Japan either militarily or psychologically and that that would remain the case for the foreseeable future. American Far Eastern policy fell back on attaching a fantastically exaggerated degree of importance to the moral condemnation of aggression, to which the non-recognition doctrine was central. In the summer of 1932 the United States combined a diplomatic campaign to drum up support for non-recognition of the state that Japan had proclaimed in Manchuria, under the name of Manchukuo, with refusal of Chinese pleas to buy surplus American arms and for the United States to send an aviation mission to China; Britain was willing to send such a mission.[18] To set against such hypocrisy, it should be noted that this crisis put paid to the movement in the United States to reduce still further its pitifully low level of defence spending; in particular, there was no longer serious pressure to reduce the size of the navy. Finally, there is some evidence that by 1940 and 1941 the proven futility of diplomatic non-recognition to achieve change played a part in causing the United States to take more material measures to oppose Japan.[19]

On the ground, the Lytton commission conducted its work with maximum courtesy not only to Japanese officials but also to those of the 'puppet state' of Manchukuo even when they spoke about the state having been created by the spontaneous uprising of the

'Manchurian masses' with some altruistic Japanese assistance. Before leaving, Lytton himself warmly shook the hand of the former child emperor of China, Pu Yi, who had been appointed by Japan as 'chief executive' of the state – only later, after serving his apprenticeship as a puppet, was he promoted to 'emperor' – and said, 'I wish the new state of Manchukuo a healthy development.'[20] Lytton's only reward for this arguably excessive display of goodwill was to be snubbed when he arrived in Tokyo. Even that did not prevent his commission from producing a report that was as favourable to Japan as possible without sinking into manifest dishonesty. In Japan a prime minister, Tsuyoshi Inukai, was assassinated in May 1932, partly because he hesitated to bestow formal recognition on Manchukuo. The combination of economic and Manchurian crises had brought about a decisive, though not total, shift in power from civilian politicians to the army and navy. Until a late stage Western diplomats in Tokyo found relations at the personal level with the Japanese foreign ministry pleasant,[21] but the decline in its importance and that of the civilian politicians was unmistakable. As early as 1931, the British ambassador lamented being 'in the unpleasant position of seeking assurances from a government which had not the power to make them good'.[22]

This was the situation when the League Assembly debated the Lytton report early in 1933 with delegate after delegate dwelling on the favourable points that it made about Japan and ignoring or explaining away the adverse ones. The Canadian delegate doubted whether China, not Japan, qualified for League membership. None of this prevented Japan from walking out of the League in February 1933 after the Assembly voted to endorse the report. There were no dissenting votes and only one abstention. That came from Thailand and not from the new Nazi regime in Germany. Nothing could have been more uncertain, even unlikely, in 1933 than that there would ever be a link-up between Germany and Japan that would bring about a true world war.

Although Britain was by 1935 taking seriously the possibility of war with a German–Japanese alliance,[23] its fears were exaggerated. The racial factor was a real one in keeping the two regimes apart. The Japanese were deeply offended by Nazi exaltation of the white, 'Aryan' race.[24] Goebbels had to admit that the racial factor in relations with Japan was 'ticklish and delicate'.[25] His solution in Nazi propaganda of depicting the Japanese as an exception to the inferiority of non-white peoples ran the risk of adding insult to injury.[26] In practice, the old-fashioned skills of German diplomats, which the Nazis despised, did much to smooth the path of relations between the Third Reich and both Japan and China, the latter very much Germany's traditional friend in east Asia. Yet the influence of these diplomats, still important in this backwater of German foreign policy, would also naturally be exercised to preserve that traditional friendship. The apparent exception was the Anti-Comintern Pact that Ribbentrop, as head of the Nazi Party foreign policy office, negotiated with Japan in late 1936. The pact was a theatrical gesture in which Germany and Japan made literally no commitments to one another. Also, since China and Japan were at peace then, it was hardly anti-Chinese.

The key to Japan's role in Second World War origins lies not in its relations with Germany but with China and their repercussions in Japanese relations with the United States. Also involved is one of the might-have-beens of twentieth century history, a great war between Japan and the Soviet Union before a war between Germany and the Soviets became a practical possibility. Japan wanted to dominate China to provide itself with an economic sphere of influence and to consolidate its credentials as a great power. It also intended to drive the Soviets out of eastern Siberia – not precisely defined – with the aim of removing a military and ideological threat and to acquire raw material resources and territory on which Japanese could settle.

The realisation of these objectives would fall largely to the Japanese army which left the navy disgruntled. In 1936 Japan took what had for long been the inevitable step of refusing to renew its agreement with Britain and the United States to limit the size of its navy in relation to theirs. This did not mean that there was going to be a huge surge in naval construction: Japan was still a poor country and simply could not afford to spend heavily on the army and navy simultaneously. In the circumstances of the mid 1930s the army was in a position to lay claim to the greater share of resources. The war in China from 1937 meant that naval spending would continue to be restrained. It is true that by 1936 the navy was drawing up war plans for expansion into south east Asia (excluding the American colony of the Philippines) which would have meant war with Britain, 'utilising the complicated political situation in Europe and taking advantage of British defence vulnerability in the Far East', as the naval planners expressed it.[27] In reality, Britain's situation in Europe would have to be much more precarious than it was in 1936 for the Japanese elite as a whole to be willing to take on Britain alone, and, influenced by both their own racism and their awareness of 'Anglo Saxon' racism, they thought that Britain and the United States would probably make common cause in a real crisis.

The issue before Japan therefore became whether to strike at Russia or China first in a context of the near irrelevance of the Third Reich. One of the few services that Germany could have rendered Japan would have been the withdrawal of the German advisory mission to the Chinese army – China having decided in 1930 that Germany should be its sole source of technical military advice – but Hitler was reluctant to do that and the military mission was only to leave in July 1938. As late as 1936 Germany and China signed a major new barter agreement (German armaments in return for Chinese raw materials), raised their diplomatic relations from legation to embassy level and agreed on an academic exchange programme with German university staff visiting China and Chinese visiting Germany.[28]

The reason why the 'Attack Russia' faction in the Japanese elite had to yield to those who favoured first dealing with China resulted from the contrast between a Soviet Union whose policies were flexible and a China that was increasingly unwilling to compromise its independence. In a mirror image of British appeasement policy towards Germany, the Soviets in the 1930s reinforced their army in the Russian Far East (just as Britain was rearming) while making appeasement-like concessions to Japan. Most notably, they sold the Chinese Eastern Railway and their interests in northern Manchuria to Japan after the establishment of Manchukuo. This completed the process of their expulsion from Manchuria that had begun when Russia lost the war with Japan in 1905. Echoing the distinction that they drew between platonic concern for German communists under Nazi rule and Soviet–German state-to-state relations, they proclaimed, in relation to Japanese policy in China, a combination of sympathy for 'the struggle of the Chinese workers and peasants for freedom' and their policy on Sino-Japanese relations which was an 'unshakeable line of strict non-intervention'.[29] This sounded remarkably like an invitation to Japan to do what it wished in China if only it would leave the Soviet Union alone.

If the origins of the Sino-Japanese war owed something to this Russian washing of hands, they also owed something to signs of the

United States moving in the opposite direction. Franklin Roosevelt began his presidency in 1933 with a flurry of foreign policy activism for which the phrase 'more apparent than real' might have been specially invented. One feature was his diplomatic recognition of the Soviet Union which, the world soon realised, signalled very little of any importance.[30] Another was a show of interest in the independence of China which caused the Japanese army to decide that imposing its will on that country brooked little delay. It, in effect, gave the Japanese foreign ministry one last chance to bring China to heel by diplomatic means.[31] As if to emphasise its point, the army occupied a province of China adjoining Manchuria in early 1933 and incorporated it into Manchukuo. This brought it within easy striking distance of the two major cities of north China, Beijing and Tientsin. In April 1934 the Japanese foreign ministry served notice on China of the minimum that was demanded of it with the Amau declaration, named after the head of information in the ministry, which, though much concerned with technical issues of foreign loans to China, was rightly interpreted as an 'Asiatic Monroe Doctrine',[32] in which Japan claimed exclusive rights of tutelage over China.

Faced with this challenge, Chinese policy appeared inconsistent. In June 1935 it issued the 'Goodwill Mandate', a blanket promise to suppress anti-Japanese activities. Even before that it had bowed to Japanese demands to restore rail and other economic links between Manchukuo and China. The other links included a particularly bitter pill for the Chinese to swallow: the restoration of postal communications which involved the Chinese post office having to process and deliver letters with Manchukuoan stamps on them. Then, in July 1937, China responded to a border incident by going to all-out war with Japan, though officially the war was described as an 'incident' until 1941. One reason for the earlier appeasement was simplicity itself, a desire to buy time. That dictated actions of an appeasement nature, but the differences between Chinese appeasement and British appeasement were several and fundamental. First, British appeasement had the optimum goal of achieving permanent peace. China was solely concerned with purchasing time. The Chinese doubted whether Japan would desist from its designs against them without full-scale war and they were convinced that only war would dislodge it from Manchuria, which they were determined to recover. Secondly, some of the pressures for British appeasement came from below. The rulers were convinced that they could never lead a public inclined towards pacifism into war unless every reasonable means of preserving peace was seen to have been exhausted. In China all the pressures from below were for immediate resistance and they eventually became irresistible. Thirdly, and most important of all, Britain knew that if war came it would itself have to shoulder the heaviest load in resisting the enemy. Almost all politically conscious Chinese knew that their country could not do that, and waited for other countries to turn against Japan so that China would only be one component of a mighty anti-Japanese coalition, consisting at its maximum conceivable extent of China, the United States, the Soviet Union and Britain. In the absence of such a coalition it became a question of which would give way first, the patience of the Chinese masses as their government played its waiting game, or the credulity of the Japanese before they realised that China would never give them what they wanted from it unless they resorted to force.

One interesting feature is that many Chinese recognised that a war in Europe would probably be necessary to trigger the anti-Japanese coalition war that they desired. As early as 1932 one Chinese writer proclaimed, 'We need a second world war.'[33] Guessing the date for such a war to start became a favourite game of Chinese intellectuals with many in the early 1930s plumping for 1936. The leader of the Chinese government, Chiang Kai-shek, was a particularly convinced devotee of the 'inevitability of war' thesis. His most important rival, Wang Ching-wei, who was prime minister from 1932 to 1935, doubted whether any country would come to China's aid and feared that Chiang's policy would only lead to Japanese occupation of the wealth-producing areas of China along the coast and in the lower Yangtse valley. Even Chiang could hardly not be disappointed by the weak British and American responses to the Amau declaration which consisted of advice to China and Japan to settle their differences peacefully and bilaterally.[34] He felt compelled to issue the Goodwill Mandate and to accept Japanese demands for Chinese government troops to be withdrawn from the state's five northernmost provinces, which reduced the authority of the central government in that area to a precarious level. The Japanese army wasted little time in fostering an 'autonomy movement' in these provinces.

This was the point at which the patience of the Chinese public began to snap. The 9 December Movement, named after student demonstrations in Beijing on that date in 1935, demanded no more concessions and the formation of a united front, including the

Chinese communists, against whom Chiang's policy had been one of simple extermination. The communists themselves professed readiness to join such a front, increasing still further the pressure on Chiang. A choice in favour of armed resistance was made inevitable by the curious affair of the Sian incident in which Chiang was kidnapped by a warlord of patriotic inclinations and released to resume the leadership of China on the clear understanding that his life was being spared because he was looked upon as the only man who could lead the Chinese nation in resistance to any further Japanese encroachments. This ironically coincided with a Japanese policy of drawing back from conflict with China. This was expressed in a Japanese approach to Britain for the two countries to resume a cooperative relationship in China and elsewhere. Japan expressed interest in access to the London capital market and in export opportunities to British colonial markets.[35]

It is probably unlikely that anything would have come of this. If there was a hope it vanished with the Marco Polo Bridge incident near Beijing in July 1937. This was a Sino-Japanese clash that the Japanese would have been content to settle in return for a few localised concessions. It was Chiang who raised the stakes by sending in his own troops to reinforce those of the local warlord and by rejecting any compromise. Japan quickly occupied Beijing and Tientsin but Chiang was unworried; he serenely expected the United States, the Soviet Union or both to declare war on Japan. When that did not happen he raised the stakes further by extending the war to the commercial capital of Shanghai which had thousands of Western residents. Three months of fighting, colossal Chinese casualties and the loss of territory that provided the Chinese government with 85 per cent of its revenues still (inevitably) failed to bring any other country into the war. An international conference on China in Brussels, boycotted by Japan, only served to confirm China's isolation. In late 1937 and 1938 Chiang, by then in despair, intimated peace to Japan, but opinion there was divided between those who were prepared to extend to China peace terms that were extremely harsh, and others who would only offer terms that were completely crushing under which China would have become a puppet state like Manchukuo. China had no choice but to fight on, despite the appalling double blow in October 1938, as the world digested the Munich agreement, of losing its last port, Canton, and its last industrial centre, Wuhan.

At this desperate point China did start to receive some help from outside, although it was meagre. In December 1938 the United States made the first of a series of loans to China. Before Pearl Harbor these were all small. The Chinese hopefully attached to one of them the epithet 'small money, big meaning'. (Britain also made some loans which, unlike America, it could ill afford.) The loans from the United States had rather meanspirited conditions attached on the grounds that the American taxpayer had to be protected; one, for instance, was guaranteed against tin exports from the southern province of Yunnan. They were dwarfed by Soviet loans which, by early 1940, totalled $250 million against an American total of $45 million. Aware of Japan's extreme hostility to his regime, Stalin had a clear interest in helping to prolong Chinese resistance, facilitated by threats from Chiang to make peace if the aid did not flow.[36] His policy nearly backfired. It was one reason why Japanese–Soviet relations deteriorated to the point where two localised border wars were fought between them at Changkufeng and Nomonhan in 1938 and 1939. And yet the United States, not Russia, was to be China's essential saviour. Stalin had no desire for all out war with Japan and the latter's army drew back from the brink, not least because the Red Army won in the border conflicts. Its victory at Nomonhan under Zhukov's command was decisive. Japan knew that it needed an ally for war against the Soviet Union and the only possible ally ruled itself out with the signing of the Nazi–Soviet pact on 23 August 1939.

The circumstances in which war started in Europe in September 1939 were such as to ensure that it would have the opposite effect from the one in the Chinese dream of the 1930s of sparking off a general conflict in which the democratic and communist worlds would combine to come to China's rescue. Ribbentrop's failure in his aim after he became Foreign Minister in early 1938 of negotiating an alliance between Germany and Japan was a subject of immense relief to Britain and France and a tragedy in the view of the Chinese. The Nazi–Soviet pact was to them another tragedy with its consequence of ending any chance, at least for a time, of Japan diverting resources into a war with Russia.

In September 1939 the prospect was one of two separate wars, one in Western Europe between Britain and France and Germany, and a continuing one in the Far East between China and Japan. This obviously fell far short of a world war. Two questions need to be addressed at this point: firstly whether there would even have been this war in Europe if Britain and France had thought that they would have to fight on another front against Japan; and secondly whether, or rather how, the situation in the Far East before September 1939 was forcing the United States towards reconsidering isolationism, in relation to that region and the Pacific at least. The first question can, with some confidence, be answered in the affirmative. Britain was never ready to allow fear of Japan to dictate its overall foreign policy, whatever Japan's capacity to increase the dangers that Britain faced in Europe. The existence of such dangers was acutely appreciated. In October 1937 Chamberlain told the Cabinet that: 'If this country were to become involved in the Far East the temptation to the dictator states to take action whether in Eastern Europe or in Spain would be irresistible.'[37] Yet Chamberlain, after the dashing of earlier hopes for an equitable settlement of Anglo-Japanese differences, joined a consensus that there should be no active appeasement of Japan of the kind that he was practising towards Germany.[38] Given American aloofness, to be discussed later, the British could not actively oppose the Japanese army's expansion in China, especially as it coincided with a dramatic increase in tensions in Europe. However, their sympathies were with the strongly pro-Chinese British ambassador to the country, Archibald Clark Kerr, and his counterpart in Tokyo, Robert Craigie, was slapped down when in late 1938 he advocated what, in effect, would have been a Far Eastern equivalent of Munich.[39] Beyond China the British, as already noted, enunciated a 'domino theory' about the likely consequences of Japanese aggression that they were loathe to apply to Germany in 1938. They were convinced that if Britain was serious about remaining an imperial power, then all colonies, even one as vulnerable as Hong Kong, had to be defended to the last.[40] And, during the 1930s, they were intransigent about the need to protect Australia and New Zealand from Japanese encroachments despite annoyance about the low levels of these dominions' own defence expenditures.

Within this framework, British policy towards Japan resolved itself into a matter of naval deployments and not doing anything unnecessarily provocative. The Royal Navy's agonisings between 1936 and 1939 over the distribution of its resources, other than those needed for home waters and the Atlantic, between the Mediterranean and the Far East are a subject in themselves. Under pressure from France, there was a tendency to keep forces in the Mediterranean, but there was never any question of abandoning, even temporarily, the Far Eastern empire, Australia and New Zealand.[41] As for avoiding unnecessary provocations, there was no inclination to respond strongly when British owners of Chinese railway bonds ceased to receive interest payments and British shipping was harassed after the Japanese occupation of the economically valuable areas of China. A more sensitive issue arose in 1939 when the Japanese blockaded the British 'concession' in Tientsin, making a number of demands of which the most difficult to accept was for the handing over of some Chinese resistance fighters who had sought refuge. This crisis was resolved by the middle of August, though at the cost of surrendering the Chinese fugitives to certain execution.[42] During the last fortnight of peace in Europe the Japanese rulers were in a mood of some slight goodwill towards Britain, anger towards Germany because of the pact with Russia and grudging respect for the Red Army as well as being heavily committed in China. This was a near perfect combination of factors to keep Japan neutral unless circumstances changed drastically.

If there was no excessive complexity about British Far Eastern policy in the 1930s, the same would not appear to be true about American policy when viewed in the light of the transition from the futility of non-recognition to the hard and unyielding line that was to be adopted towards Japan in 1941, though in this chapter the concern is only with the period up to the start of the European war in September 1939. In the middle 1930s, if China had a Western friend it was Britain. In 1935–36 Britain gave China real help with its finances and showed real concern about Japanese encroachments in north China. Realising that the only hope of inducing Japan to moderate those activities lay in an Anglo-American joint front, Britain proposed that a number of times, but was always rebuffed by Washington.[43] The start of the Sino-Japanese war was followed by the United States recalling nineteen military aircraft that were being transported on the high seas to China which had paid for them. This was to avoid breaching the neutrality laws and also to keep in step with public opinion which did not quickly warm to the Chinese cause. In opinion polls in late 1937 and 1938, 55 per cent of respondents described themselves as neutral between China and Japan and 64 per cent opposed arms sales to China.[44] American opinion was later to become more favourable to China as evidence accumulated of Japanese war crimes and as the Chiang regime mounted an effective propaganda campaign in the United States, including the masterstroke of appointing the respected philosopher, Hu Shih, as ambassador in Washington.[45]

Before that, however, came the pattern to which reference has been made of British proposals for a joint approach on China and American rejection, including the notorious turning of the other cheek in late 1937 when Japanese planes damaged a British vessel, *Ladybird*, and sank an American ship, USS *Panay*, on the Yangtse with loss of American lives. Washington rejected the British proposal for a joint protest and a joint show of naval strength in Far Eastern waters and sought satisfaction from Japan within the narrowest possible parameters of an apology and financial compensation.

What caused the beginnings of a change in policy was the revelation in 1938 of the possibility that Japan had aims so sweeping that isolationism might not be a sustainable policy in relation to the Far East. The year started with the Foreign Minister, Hirota Koki, using for the first time what was to become a notorious phrase, that Japan favoured a 'new order' in east Asia. There were more and more references to this, culminating in its endorsement by the Prime Minister, Prince Konoe, in November.[46] Not only did this 'new order' appear more and more to preclude allowing China any real independence at all, but also it explicitly, if vaguely, extended beyond the borders of China. Leading figures in Washington took alarm. It frightened them in a way that the prospect of the expansion of Nazi German power in Europe did not. The first results were, as has been noted, some rather niggardly loans to China. The new concern also resulted in two intentionally contrasting actions by President Roosevelt in 1939. In the first in February he responded to the death of the Japanese ambassador in Washington by ordering an American warship to return the body in state to its homeland – a rare honour. In the second in July he ordered that Japan be given the necessary six months' notice of the termination by the United States of the commercial treaty between the two countries. The implication was obvious: after six months America would be free to impose economic sanctions on Japan. The President was serving notice to Japan that he wanted its friendship but was now ready to go beyond non-recognition if Japan spurned him.

However, as soon as American strategists began to draw up contingency plans for a conflict with Japan, even before war began in Europe, they became convinced that they had been dealt a poor hand by the international situation and by their own past actions (or inaction). As to the former, they had no doubt from the first that war with Japan alone would not be possible; it was axiomatic that Germany and probably Italy would enter on Japan's side. This led on to the self-inflicted wound of the extent to which the navy had been neglected and was consequently unfit for a major war against more than one enemy. It was assumed that any war that America fought would be primarily naval in character, and most of a navy that might just have been adequate against Japan alone would be needed for anti-German work in the Atlantic–Caribbean area. This, combined with the non-fortification provisions in the 1922 Washington treaty, dictated the conclusion that at the start of any war America would have to abandon the western Pacific to Japan. Hawaii would become the furthest extension of American power until a super navy could be built. Finally, American planners could not carry the hypothetical failure of isolationism to the point of embracing Britain as an ally. They thought that unless Britain was kept at arm's length it would do nothing but try to manipulate them into diverting precious resources towards the defence of British interests such as Singapore. Their contacts with British naval strategists, who waxed lyrical about Singapore and its 'fundamental importance to the Empire', did nothing to dispel this impression. The conclusion was that even if Britain and America were pitted against the same enemies they should fight 'parallel' wars with little cooperation.[47]

This pessimistic analysis must be viewed against the fact of a United States in 1939 that still desperately wanted to make a success of isolationism. Yet it did mark the beginning of the consideration of an alternative. That would not have happened without China's willingness to continue its war with Japan against all the odds. It was China's war, not anything that happened in Europe, that began to chip away with some effect at the edifice of American isolationism. China's importance in the origins of the 'real' Second World War cannot easily be exaggerated. It is time, in the next chapter, to consider more generally the part played by the United States.

Notes

1 Ian Nish, *Japanese Foreign Policy 1869–1942* (London, Routledge, 1977), p. 264.
2 Akira Iriye, 'Culture in Japanese foreign affairs', in T. G. Fraser and Peter Lowe (eds), *Conflict and Amity in East Asia* (London, Macmillan,

1992), pp. 47–58.

3 *Ibid.*, p. 52.

4 Olive Checkland, *Humanitarianism and the Emperor's Japan, 1877–1977* (London, Macmillan, 1994) includes a chapter on 'Japan, humanitarian world leader, 1894–1905'.

5 Walter LaFeber, *The Clash: US–Japanese Relations throughout History* (New York, Norton, 1997), p. 141.

6 On British contempt for Sun see Wm. Roger Louis, *British Strategy in the Far East 1919–1939* (Oxford, Clarendon Press, 1971), pp. 111–17.

7 Bruce A. Elleman, *Diplomacy and Deception: The Secret History of Sino-Soviet Diplomatic Relations, 1917–1927* (London, Sharpe, 1997), pp. 143–58.

8 Lanxin Xiang, *Recasting the Imperial Far East: Britain and America in China, 1945–1950* (London, Sharpe, 1995).

9 LaFeber, *Clash*, p. 113.

10 Richard S. Grayson, *Austen Chamberlain and the Commitment to Europe: British Foreign Policy 1924–29* (Ilford, Cass, 1997), chapter 7; David Carlton, *MacDonald versus Henderson: The Foreign Policy of the Second Labour Government* (London, Macmillan, 1970), chapter 9; for a summary of British concessions to China at this time see Irving S. Friedman, *British Relations with China, 1931–1939* (New York, Institute of Pacific Relations, 1940), pp. 14–17.

11 Christopher Thorne, *The Limits of Foreign Policy: The West, the League and the Far Eastern Crisis of 1931–1933* (London, Macmillan, 1972), pp. 51–2.

12 *Ibid.*, pp. 32, 37–8.

13 *Ibid.*, p. 195.

14 Louis, *British Strategy*, pp. 200–1.

15 Friedman, *British Relations*, p. 49.

16 Tota Ishimaru, *Japan Must Fight Britain*, (London, Hurst & Blackett, 1936).

17 Thorne, *Limits*, p. 238.

18 *Ibid.*, pp. 298–301.

19 *Ibid.*, pp. 414–15.

20 *From Emperor to Citizen: The Autobiography of Aisin-Gioro Pu Yi* (Beijing, Foreign Languages Press, 1965), Vol. II, pp. 269–70.

21 Paul Gore-Booth, *With Great Truth and Respect* (London, Constable, 1974), pp. 79–81.

22 Nish, *Japanese Foreign Policy*, p. 264.

23 Gaines Post, Jr., *Dilemmas of Appeasement: British Deterrence and Defense, 1934–1937* (Ithaca, NY, Cornell University Press, 1993), pp. 108–9.

24 E. M. Robertson, 'Hitler's planning for war and the response of the

Great powers' in H. W. Koch (ed.), *Aspects of the Third Reich* (London, Macmillan, 1985), pp. 212–14.

25 Robert Edwin Herzstein, *When Nazi Dreams Come True* (London, Abacus, 1982), p. 136.

26 Gerhard L. Weinberg, *The Foreign Policy of Hitler's Germany: Diplomatic Revolution in Europe, 1933–36* (Chicago, IL, University of Chicago Press, 1970), pp. 120–1.

27 Ikeda Kiyoshi, 'The road to Singapore: Japan's view of Britain, 1922–41' in Fraser and Lowe (eds), *Conflict*, p. 37.

28 Hsi-Huey Liang, 'China, the Sino-Japanese conflict and the Munich crisis', *Diplomacy and Statecraft*, 10:2&3 (1999), 342–69; for a full treatment see John P. Fox, *Germany and the Far Eastern Crisis 1931–1938* (Oxford, Clarendon Press, 1982).

29 George Alexander Lensen, *The Damned Inheritance: The Soviet Union and the Manchurian Crises 1924–1935* (Tallahassee, FL, The Diplomatic Press, 1974), p. 365.

30 Edward M. Bennett, *Recognition of Russia: An American Foreign Policy Dilemma* (Waltham, MA, Blairside Publishing Company, 1970), especially chapter 5.

31 Dorothy Borg, *The United States and the Far Eastern Crisis of 1935–1938* (Cambridge, MA, Harvard University Press, 1964), pp. 139–41; LaFeber, *Clash*, pp. 176–7.

32 The Royal Institute of International Affairs, *China and Japan: Information Department Papers*, No. 21 (London, 1938), p. 56.

33 Youli Sun, *China and the Origins of the Pacific War, 1931–1941* (London, Macmillan, 1993), p. 153; what follows about the Sino-Japanese conflict draws heavily on Sun's book.

34 *Ibid.*, p. 49.

35 Kiyoshi in Fraser and Lowe (eds), *Conflict*, p. 35; Ian Nish, 'Anglo-Japanese alienation revisited' in Saki Dockrill (ed.), *From Pearl Harbor to Hiroshima* (London, Macmillan, 1994), pp. 11–25; Friedman, *British Relations*, pp. 89–91.

36 Michael M. Sheng, *Battling Western Imperialism: Mao, Stalin and the United States* (Princeton, NJ, Princeton University Press, 1997), p. 45.

37 B. J. C. McKercher, *Transition of Power: Britain's Loss of Global Pre-eminence to the United States, 1930–1945* (Cambridge, Cambridge University Press, 1999), p. 245.

38 G. C. Peden, *British Rearmament and the Treasury: 1932–1939* (Edinburgh, Scottish Academic Press, 1979), pp. 110–11.

39 Donald Gillies, *Radical Diplomat: The Life of Archibald Clark Kerr, Lord Inverchapel, 1882–1951* (London, I. B. Tauris, 1999), chapter 6 for his ambassadorship to China; Louis, *British Strategy*, pp. 254–62.

40 On the defence of Hong King see Ian Cowman, *Dominion or Decline:*

Anglo-American Naval Relations in the Pacific, 1937–1941 (Oxford, Berg, 1996), pp. 43–6, 281–2.

41 Lawrence R. Pratt, *East of Malta, West of Suez: Britain's Mediterranean Crisis, 1936–1939* (Cambridge, Cambridge University Press, 1975), chapters 4–7; Martin Thomas, *Britain, France and Appeasement: Anglo-French Relations in the Popular Front Era* (Oxford, Berg, 1996), pp. 162–3; Cowman, *Dominion*, pp. 37, 141–5; Joseph A. Maiolo, *The Royal Navy and Nazi Germany, 1933–39* (London, Macmillan, 1998), pp. 174–6.

42 Nicholas R. Clifford, *Retreat from China: British Policy in the Far East 1937–1941* (London, Longmans, 1967), pp. 62–3 and chapter 11.

43 Borg, *United States*, pp. 147–9, 155–6, 165, 179–80.

44 Christopher Thorne, *The Far Eastern War: States and Societies 1941–45* (London, Unwin/Counterpoint, 1986), p. 117.

45 Sun, *China*, pp. 137–46.

46 Clifford, *Retreat*, pp. 52, 95–6.

47 Cowman, *Dominion*, pp. 86, 91–8, 128–39, 148–53, 194–5.

CHAPTER ELEVEN

THE UNITED STATES

The United States' potential for influencing international affairs between the wars was great. Its population in the late 1930s was not far short of those of Germany and Japan combined and was nearly treble that of Britain. Even more important was its economic potential for war. In 1938 the United States produced 26 million tons of steel compared with Germany's 20 million tons, but the German steel industry was operating at full stretch whereas two thirds of US steel making capacity was dormant as the American economy struggled with only limited success to lift itself from the depression that had followed the Wall Street crash in 1929. In 1937 the United States spent 1.5 per cent of its national income on defence compared with the British figure of 6 per cent and the German of 23.5 per cent, leaving vast scope for military expansion with little economic or social strain. Japan's rulers were acutely aware that they would become hopelessly inferior as the United States belatedly embarked on rearmament. They calculated that in late 1941 their naval strength would be 70 per cent that of the United States, falling to 30 per cent in 1944.[1]

War between America and Japan was, however, never likely without a catastrophic decline of the situation in Europe such as actually occurred at the end of the 1930s. American–European relations during most of the inter-war years were dominated by economic and financial quarrels with Britain and, to a lesser extent, France, and relatively harmonious economic relations with Germany under the Weimar Republic. Following rejection of League membership and the proposed security pact with France and Britain in 1919, the United States in the 1920s, under Republican administrations that maintained close links with big business, regarded economic matters as virtually all-important in America's foreign relations, and there were particularly acrimonious quarrels with Britain over war debts and such economic matters as oil concessions, producing mutual bitterness and astonishing scares about possible war between the two countries in 1920–21 and 1927–29. During the latter even Winston Churchill, then Chancellor of the Exchequer and normally a passionate supporter of Anglo-American amity, remarked that everyone knew that war with America was possible; it was 'in fact, the only basis upon which the naval discussions at Geneva are proceeding'.[2] After the American economy suffered catastrophic damage in the world depression of the early 1930s, it is not surprising that the preoccupation with economic matters in foreign relations continued after Franklin D. Roosevelt won the presidential election of 1932 for the Democratic Party. He inherited, and did little or nothing to ameliorate, quarrels over finance with Britain and France that distracted attention in all three countries, but particularly in the United States, from possible dangers from the new Nazi regime in Germany. Anglo-American relations fell to their twentieth century nadir during his first two years as president.[3] The British government was appalled when Roosevelt ruined an international economic conference in London in July 1933, on which it had pinned many hopes, by sending a message demanding that the conference should agree on nothing.[4] This followed on evidence that the United States was completely opting out of power politics. It had a puny army but had had a significant navy, yet it carried out no new naval construction at all in 1930–32.

This is not to suggest that American grievances against Britain and France were imaginary or utterly unreasonable. Most Americans in official or influential positions believed that the US economy could not really recover without trading and investment opportunities on a global scale and were, therefore, dismayed at the British construction of an Empire–Commonwealth economic bloc which began in earnest with a conference at Ottawa in 1932, and at France's evident aim of a gold bloc in East and Central Europe. The United States objected to these developments while bringing in the astronomically high Smoot-Harley tariffs which were justified by the argument that they did not discriminate between different foreign countries. It is also important to note that the dominant liberal element in the Roosevelt administration feared that these blocs, if they succeeded, would be damaging to the United States not only economically but socially and politically as well. They would cause the country to turn in on itself and probably give success to those who, in Secretary of State Cordell Hull's words, regarded 'national planning, self-containment and eventually socialism' as the solutions to America's problems.[5]

The economic preoccupation not only embittered America's relations with the other great democracies, but also helped to perpetuate an anachronistic attitude to Britain as a sort of big brother in international security matters which it should handle alone or at least without seeking to involve the United States. The failure of Woodrow Wilson's vision of a Pax Americana in 1919–20 was widely seen as confirming the validity of this thesis.[6] In his voluminous memoirs Roosevelt's Secretary of State, Cordell Hull, noted crisply that Hitler's remilitarisation of the Rhineland in 1936 was 'a European development in which we were not involved'.[7] British perceptions of the United States in the 1930s were steeped in equally exotic misunderstandings,[8] though these probably had much less impact on actual British foreign policy than United States' perceptions of Europe.

By 1933 Germany had gone far towards superseding France as the United States' special friend among the European great powers. Condemnation of the Versailles treaty was almost as total in the United States as in Germany, and German (and also Italian but not Japanese) ambitions were regarded with indulgence as those of 'have-not' states that were entitled to considerable favourable consideration, especially from Britain which was supposedly the supreme 'have' country. Above all, the Germans were looked upon as a cultured people who were central to Western civilisation. This was, of course, correct, but it was followed by a less fortunate corollary that the United States needed to distinguish between the Nazi regime, which was widely criticised, and the true Germany that could not really be in eclipse.[9] In any case, Nazism was vastly preferable to what might be its only real alternative in Europe, Soviet-type Communism. In 1935 the American ambassador to Italy remarked that Nazism was an 'intensification(sic) of a culture which is more akin to ours' than Russia's.[10]

These attitudes of Anglophobia, goodwill to Germany and the primacy of trade and economics dominated the State Department in the 1930s. Hull was not a particularly effective Secretary of State and, with reason, often felt humiliated. Roosevelt was almost the de facto holder of the office[11] but, with vast domestic responsibilities, could often exercise only loose supervision of the machinery for foreign policy. Real power in this way devolved to the leading figures in the department who were nominally under Hull. These included Adolf Berle, Jay Pierrepoint Moffat and Sumner Welles who took full advantage of opportunities to give expression to their highly opinionated convictions. Berle carried Anglophobia to obsessive and absurd lengths, but none of this dominant clique could rid their minds of the notion that German Nazism rested on the same moral plane as British imperialism. On a visit to Britain and France in March 1940 Moffat was to note in his diary his admiration for the clarity of vision of Joseph Kennedy, the ambassador to Britain, whose dismissive encapsulation of British pretensions to moral superiority over Nazi Germany Moffat summarised as: 'For Christ's sake stop trying to make this a holy war, because no one will believe you; you're fighting for your life as an Empire and that's good enough.'[12] Given such entrenched attitudes it is possible to exaggerate the impact that Nazi policies that were specifically hostile to, or contemptuous of, the United States had on majority American public opinion or on foreign policy.[13] Even the anti-Jewish Crystal Night enormity in Germany in November 1938 produced a wave of *anti-British* feeling in the United States, or so Kennedy informed Halifax.[14] Britain was evidently to blame for not having alone provided German Jews with the means of salvation. There were actually dismayingly high levels of anti-Semitism in the United States at this time. An opinion poll in April 1938 found that 58 per cent of respondents believed that the Jews in Germany were wholly or partly to blame for their misfortunes.[15] Repugnance against anti-Semitism could not be a key factor in taking the United States out of isolationism.

There were, of course, important persons in Washington in the 1930s who had a good understanding of the international situation. One was Harold Ickes, but he was Secretary of the Interior and therefore poorly placed to influence foreign policy. Given this, it says much for Roosevelt that he was not the slave of the conventional wisdom about the United States' international interests, but rather had an open mind that led to a certain proneness to mental confusion. He approved the plethora of Neutrality (with a capital N) legislation that poured out of Congress during his early years as President, and yet from an early stage toyed with ideas about America supplying other democracies with the materials of war if that should start in Europe, and even, in the last resort, involving the country in a limited form of undeclared war that would be strictly confined to the sea and the air to keep down casualties. (Much British strategic thinking before 1939 ran along the same lines, though Britain rejected the undeclared war idea that was to become the norm after 1945.)

An early instance of a presidential interest in preserving peace came with Roosevelt's proposal to Chamberlain early in 1938 for an international conference. The British Prime Minister was unenthusiastic but not wholly dismissive. Roosevelt chose to back down from the idea for pragmatic reasons. Japanese aggression in China showed no sign of abating and the disconcerting Ribbentrop had just been appointed Foreign Minister of Germany. The President perceived that if Japan and Germany agreed to participate in his conference it would be a mockery.[16] By then the prevalent official British attitude to the United States had changed from the undiluted scorn of the mid 1930s to a belief that it might be marginally helpful in international security, coupled with doubts about whether it actually wanted the United States to be more than marginally helpful. This was because of the likely price of full scale aid, including 'the loss of Britain's major overseas markets in Latin America, the break-up of the sterling area, the dismantlement of the Commonwealth trade preference system, the loss of Canada and Australia to American leadership in the Americas and the Pacific, the wholesale admission of American oil business into the British controlled Middle East, and much else besides'.[17] It is unsurprising that ambassador Kennedy should have written to a senator in 1938 that Chamberlain and Halifax respected his commitment to isolationism and that all their policies were drawn up 'without counting on the United States to be either for or against them. They have never given me the slightest impression that they want or expect anything special from us.'[18]

As the pace of events quickened in the summer of 1938, and very speedy decisions about war and peace had to be made, the United States was an irrelevance. Roosevelt's main public contribution was a speech at a Canadian university on 18 August in which he expatiated on United States' interest in distant events and its intention to become involved if there was any threat to the security of the country that he was visiting. That Canada was the only country that the United States would help if it was attacked seemed to be the clear presidential message. Although he summoned the British ambassador to a meeting on 19 September what he said was of so little interest that Chamberlain and Halifax justifiably did not consider it worth mentioning to the Cabinet.[19] Roosevelt approved of Munich but it would not have differed in the slightest if he had not. Perhaps

chastened by awareness of his insignificance while Europe had tee-
tered on the brink of war, he started to come round to the view that
words alone would leave the United States in world affairs at best a
nullity, at worst a laughing stock. He seems to have concluded that
Germany was an undoubted menace to American security because its
ambitions were global and extended in particular to Latin America
where it had no intention of respecting the Monroe Doctrine. With
his penchant for conspiracy theories it was axiomatic to him that
Germany and Japan were working in the closest collaboration, rather
than the pathetically ramshackle arrangement that they really had.
Never entirely free from a patrician disdain for economics and trade
deals, he now lost interest in them completely as instruments of
peace, telling a colleague that 'the world is marching too fast'.[20] In
November the United States signed a commercial treaty with Britain
over which both countries felt that they had made excessive concessions. Both, in effect, agreed to suspend their economic disagree-
ments while peace was under global threat.[21] Roosevelt still thought
that the primary responsibility for resisting Hitler was Britain's and
that it and France could perform the task if only they recovered their
'nerve'.[22] Until literally the moment that Britain declared war he had
at most only an open mind about whether the Chamberlain government would cave in to a (completely mythological) 'City group' of
top London financiers that he imagined to be pulling every string to
give Hitler a free hand against Poland.[23]

The material contribution that he envisaged the United States
making was a massive drive to produce military aircraft, some of
them from factories in Canada whose output could go to France
without violating the letter of the Neutrality laws. This would preclude the need not only for a large American army but even for large
numbers of airmen. The planes would be made without any corre-
sponding drive to recruit and train air crews or build bases and other
facilities because, he explained to his military chiefs at the end of
1938, Hitler would not be impressed by 'barracks, runways and
schools for mechanics'. Fortunately, the chiefs convinced him of the
senselessness of that, and the greater part of the increased air power
spending that Congress was asked to approve was to go on personnel
and bases.[24] By then the President was in danger of outstepping public, or at least Congressional, opinion. In the middle of 1939 the Sen-
ate blocked his proposal that the blanket embargo on arms exports to
countries at war should be modified to allow them to buy such arms

for cash and then 'carry' them home on their own ships. This would obviously have been useless to Germany and could only have benefited Britain and France with their naval supremacy in the Atlantic. The administration was at least giving the nation a lead in thinking that it could not ignore the war danger in Europe or that war could necessarily be confined to that continent. The victory of Franco in the Spanish Civil War in March 1939 produced fears of the duplication of his supposedly pro-German regime in Latin America, especially in Brazil, though it was not clear why a Portuguese speaking country should be deeply influenced by events in Spain. The sudden and simultaneous appearance of a German threat to Poland also produced alarm in Washington, not least because Poland was many Americans' favourite among the non-great power European states. Again, there was a contradiction: the United States had repudiated the Paris peace settlement and had refused to ratify the treaty of Versailles and yet the German–Polish border was wholly their creation.

To their credit the Chamberlain government from late 1938 ceased to be indifferent to the United States, despite all the contradictions and hesitations in American policy and despite the increasingly fantastic accusations against Britain emanating from Adolf Berle and other State Department Anglophobes. Little was still expected from the United States in a European war but there now seemed to be a chance of American cover for the British Empire's Far Eastern flank. The transfer of much of the US fleet from the Atlantic to the Pacific in April 1939 was regarded as a magnificent action to deter Japan from joining in aggression initiated by Germany. Roosevelt's main concern in making this move was actually to steady France in its readiness to resist Nazi aggression by ensuring that Britain had no reason or excuse to withdraw its fleet from the Mediterranean if there should be war with Germany, Italy and Japan. He also demanded a quid pro quo from Britain in the form of the introduction of conscription.[25] Conversations between senior British and American naval officers gave relations between the two countries an intimacy previously almost unknown, though it is remarkable that the post of naval attaché at the American embassy in London remained vacant from January to June 1939.[26]

And what, finally, of the United States in German calculations about war? From the time of coming to power Hitler had shown no interest in cultivating American goodwill and lost nothing from not doing so until after Munich. Economically, nothing German seemed

too provocative for America to swallow. It accepted the Nazi preference for trading by barter, and direct United States investment in
Germany rose by a third between 1936 and 1940, by which time it
was not far short of investment in Britain ($206 and $275 million
respectively). Such Nazi tricks as repudiating Austria's debt to the
United States after the *Anschluss* while continuing to pay that former
country's debts to countries that Germany was cultivating evoked no
serious protest.[27] Politically, Hitler concluded that Roosevelt was a
fool, or was served by fools, when he issued a message in April calling on Germany to respect the sovereign rights of thirty-one listed
countries. Not only did these include several countries such as Belgium and Lithuania that were trumpeting their belief that Germany
already respected their rights, but it also included territories that
were not independent states, including Syria (under French administration) and Palestine (under British). Hitler regarded United States
policy as a positive inducement to go to war; the transfer of part of
the fleet to the Pacific that so encouraged Britain also encouraged
Hitler as meaning that the United States was turning its back on Europe. He reposed great hopes in Anglo-American rivalry, not realising that he had caused it to be temporarily set aside to a major extent,
and his offer to guarantee the British Empire after postponing the
attack on Poland on 25 August was a guarantee against United States
depredations and not German, the danger of which the British were
invited to regard as non-existent.

Publicly, Roosevelt continued to the very end to indulge in gesture
politics with an appeal at the end of August to Hitler, the King of
Italy and the President of Poland to preserve peace. Hitler reasoned
that if that was all he had to fear from America it was very little.[28] No
doubt Roosevelt wanted to discredit Hitler if he could not deter him,
but it coincided with the Fuhrer remarking all too truly to his
courtiers that all that mattered was success in the forthcoming campaign.

Notes

1 Paul Kennedy, *The Rise and Fall of the Great Powers: Economic Change
   and Military Conflict from 1500 to 2000* (London, Unwin Hyman,
   1988), pp. 331–3.
2 D. Cameron Watt, *Succeeding John Bull: America in Britain's Place
   1900–1975* (Cambridge, Cambridge University Press, 1984), p. 59.

3 *Ibid.*, pp. 65–8; Robert Boyce, 'World war, world depression: some economic origins of the Second World War' in Robert Boyce and Esmonde M. Robertson, (eds), *Paths to War* (London, Macmillan, 1989), chapter 2.

4 B. J. C. McKercher, *Transition of Power: Britain's Loss of Global Pre-eminence to the United States, 1930–1945* (Cambridge, Cambridge University Press, 1999), pp. 171–2.

5 Lloyd C. Gardner, *Spheres of Influence: The partition of Europe, from Munich to Yalta* (London, Murray, 1993), p. 64.

6 Watt, *Succeeding*, pp. 17, 22, 72.

7 *The Memoirs of Cordell Hull: Volume One* (London, Hodder & Stoughton, 1948), p. 453.

8 See for example, David Reynolds, *The Creation of the Anglo-American Alliance, 1937–1941. A Study in Competitive Co-operation* (London, Europa Publications, 1981), pp. 11–13.

9 Arnold A. Offner, 'The United States and National Socialist Germany' in Wolfgang Mommsen and Lothar Kettenacker (eds), *The Fascist Challenge and the Policy of Appeasement* (London, Allen & Unwin, 1983), pp. 414–15.

10 Arnold A. Offner, 'Influence without responsibility: American statecraft and the Munich conference' in Melvin Small and Otto Feinstein (eds), *Appeasing Fascism* (Lanham, Maryland, University Press of America, 1991), p. 54.

11 Cecil V. Crabb, Jr., and Kevin V. Mulcahy, *Presidents and Foreign Policy Making: From FDR to Reagan* (Baton Rouge, LA, Louisiana State University Press, 1986), pp. 83–4; McKercher, *Transition*, pp. 158–9.

12 Nancy Harrison Hooker (ed.), *The Moffat Papers: Selections from the Diplomatic Journals of Jay Pierrepoint Moffat 1919–1943* (Cambridge, MA, Harvard University Press, 1956), p. 298.

13 As the usually sound Gerhard L. Weinberg does: *The Foreign Policy of Hitler's Germany: Diplomatic Revolution in Europe, 1933–36* (Chicago, IL, University of Chicago Press, 1970), pp. 133–45; and *The Foreign Policy of Hitler's Germany: Starting World War II, 1937–1939* (Chicago, IL, University of Chicago Press, 1980), pp. 35, 249–55.

14 Ritchie Ovendale, *'Appeasement' and the English Speaking World* (Cardiff, University of Wales Press, 1975), p. 195.

15 Alexander J. Groth, *Democracies against Hitler: Myth, Reality and Prologue* (Aldershot, Ashgate, 1999), p. 170.

16 Reynolds, *Creation*, pp. 16–20; Offner in Small and Feinstein (eds), *Appeasing*, p. 57.

17 D. C. Watt, review of Reynolds, *Creation*, in *History Today*, 32 (May 1982), pp. 52–3; see also Watt, *Succeeding*, pp. 73, 83–6.

18 Groth, *Democracies*, p. 177.

19 David Reynolds, *Britannia Overruled: British Policy and World Power in the Twentieth Century* (London, Longman, 1991), pp. 35–6; Offner in Small and Feinstein (eds), *Appeasing*, pp. 63–4.

20 Gardner, *Spheres*, pp. 25–6.

21 Hans-Jürgen Schröder, 'The ambiguities of appeasement: Great Britain, the United States and Germany, 1937–9' in Mommsen and Kettenacker (eds), *Fascist Challenge*, pp. 390–9; McKercher, *Transition*, p. 260.

22 Reynolds, *Creation*, pp. 40–4.

23 Callum A. MacDonald, 'The United States, appeasement and the open door' in Mommsen and Kettenacker (eds), *Fascist Challenge*, pp. 408–9.

24 Robert Dallek, *Franklin D. Roosevelt and American Foreign Policy, 1932–1945* (New York, Oxford University Press, 1979), pp. 172–3.

25 Callum A. MacDonald, 'Deterrent diplomacy: Roosevelt and the containment of Germany, 1938–1940' in Boyce and Robertson (eds), *Paths*, pp. 317–18, 332; Ian Cowman, *Dominion or Decline: Anglo-American Naval Relations in the Pacific, 1937–1941* (Oxford, Berg, 1996), pp. 146–8.

26 Reynolds, *Creation*, pp. 44–69; Cowman, *Dominion*, p. 154; Donald Cameron Watt, *How War Came* (London, Heinemann, 1989), pp. 260–70.

27 Watt, *How War Came*, pp. 256–8; Offner, 'The United States' in Mommsen and Kettenacker (eds), *Fascist Challenge*, p. 416; Weinberg, *Starting World War II*, p. 251.

28 Watt, *How War Came*, pp. 553–6.

CHAPTER TWELVE

THE EUROPEAN WAR

Many did not see a major European war as following inevitably from the Nazi–Soviet pact, though few were as sanguine as the Polish ambassador in Moscow who reported to his government that it 'considerably improved Poland's situation'.[1] If Stalin really did understand that the pact made war inevitable then he showed more foresight than Hitler who expected it to strengthen what he thought was the real possibility of Britain deserting Poland. As Halifax had said to the Cabinet after the destruction of Czechoslovakia: 'We were the only country who could organise such resistance' against 'Germany's attempt to obtain world domination', and if Britain did not, 'we might see one country after another absorbed by Germany'.[2] Halifax was effectively Chamberlain's equal in directing British foreign policy between Prague and the outbreak of war and entertained few of the Prime Minister's lingering thoughts about whether appeasement in its old meaning of both parties accommodating one another could be resumed.[3]

The conviction that any further German aggression must be resisted was very strong in Britain by the spring of 1939. The only developments that might have forced it into reverse gear would have been compelling evidence that war with Germany would be suicidal and that therefore the Nazi challenge should be yielded to, either permanently or until conditions were more favourable for Britain and its allies. The contrary view gained ground: that circumstances would never be more favourable for victory than they were in 1939. One factor in this was that intelligence estimates to the government continued to breathe optimism and, in their comparisons of allied and German economic and military resources, now conveyed the message that a war would be winnable in stark contrast with their defeatism of the previous year.[4] There was a similar metamorphosis in what French intelligence reported to its government.[5]

Growing British confidence stemmed primarily from the by now massive sacrifices that were being made for rearmament. In February a £580 million defence budget was announced and this was raised in July to £750 million. That was 22 per cent of national income, a percentage not greatly below Germany's, and compared with 3 per cent defence spending in 1933 and still only 8 per cent in 1938. In April a limited system of military conscription was nervously announced, despite the protests of the Labour Party leader, Clement Attlee, that it would 'weaken and divide'. The government tried to make it palatable to the public, and especially the working classes, with the argument that it was essential to provide manpower for defences against air attack, an objective that few would question. In reality, they had already decided that the army should cease to be starved of funds, the navy and air force having been previously heavily favoured, and that Britain should send ten divisions to France within six months of war starting instead of the originally planned two.[6] There was an uneasy awareness that this level of preparation could not be sustained in peace conditions for any long period of time. This generated an actual wish that if Germany was determined to be aggressive it should make its move in the near future.

This last consideration was given added strength by the fact that the British economy was experiencing difficulties in 1938 and 1939 owing to the combination of depressed international economic conditions and the cost of rearmament. In the fifteen months from April 1938 Britain's gold reserves fell by £300 million, leaving £500 million, plus £200 million of foreign securities. The escalating bill for rearmament in 1939 threatened to wipe out the reserves completely within a few months, and, unlike the situation between 1914 and 1917, Britain was now barred by United States legislation from borrowing on the American money markets. Here again, the only conclusion possible was that if there had to be a showdown, it had best be in 1939 while there was still a modicum of financial strength left. In February the limit on government borrowing was raised from £400 million to £800 million. In the middle of the year taxes were increased. Borrowing was disliked because it carried with it the danger of inflation while taxes were certain to make worse an already depressed economy.[7] More palatable than increased borrowing or taxation would have been the devaluation of sterling to make British exports more competitive, but that was ruled out in 1939 because of President Roosevelt's vehement protests that it would be unfair to the United States' export trade. Britain deferred to Washington for political reasons as the two countries warily edged a little closer towards one another.

It was encouraging that two other countries, Japan and Italy, were edging not towards Britain and France but away from Germany. Japan's position has already been considered. The pasteboard nature of the 'Pact of Steel' between Italy and Germany has, again, already been noted. It is unsurprising that Hitler did not inform Mussolini (through his Foreign Minister, Ciano) of his intention to invade Poland until as late as 12 August. The Duce reluctantly had to accept the material impossibility for Italy of entering a major war then or soon afterwards. The Germanophobe Ciano gleefully informed Britain of Italy's likely neutrality. To most members of the Cabinet the benefits of Italian neutrality outweighed the adverse consequences of the failure that was by then looming in the alliance negotiations with the Soviet Union.

Such was the situation by August, the last month of peace, during which Hitler was both deceiver and deceived. He laid false trails, particularly to give the impression that Poland was not in danger. The Poles were invited to post-August events, including a despicable invitation from Goering to the Polish ambassador in Berlin to join him for hunting in October or November. Elaborate preparations went on for the annual Nuremberg rally due in September, though that event was cancelled in the middle of August.[8] At the same time there was anxiety that Poland might offer concessions over Danzig, which would have weakened Germany's main propaganda justification for war. In the middle of the month it seemed that Poland might yield in a dispute about management of the Danzig customs. The Nazi government in the Free City reassured Berlin that, 'Gauleiter Forster intends to extend claims ... Should Poles yield again it is intended to increase the claims further in order to make accord impossible.' This was approved by Berlin with the proviso that, 'Discussions will have to be conducted and pressure exerted against Poland in such a way that responsibility for failure to come to an agreement and the consequences rest with Poland.'[9] This exchange, on 19 August, set the pattern for the public relations side of Nazi war preparations, culminating in the drawing-up of a list of demands that were actually considerably less sweeping in scope than those that

Czechoslovakia had been obliged to accept at Munich. It was, however, presented in garbled form and without giving Poland time to answer before the German army crossed its borders. There was also a faked Polish attack on a German radio station. What stands out about all this is the crassness of Hitler's belief that Britain (followed by France) would eagerly seize on any spurious justification for a German attack to abandon Poland. He had no understanding of their view that if they allowed Poland to fall their own vital interests in Europe, Africa and Asia would be at risk. Nor did he have any knowledge of their conviction that the summer of 1939 was the time when their ability to resist German aggression would be at its peak.

Instead, Hitler continued to seek evidence of Western defeatism and found it in a number of places. German intelligence intercepted some British and French communications with Poland in which the Poles were urged not to be intransigent over Danzig and were refused material aid. In the high summer of 1939 there was a flurry of Anglo-German contacts between self-appointed peacemakers such as the newspaper magnate, Lord Kemsley, on the British side and Goering's friend, the Swedish millionaire businessman, Birger Dahlerus, on the German. Hitler also relied on his assessment of the character of the British ruling class which was not very different from Ciano's celebrated description of them as 'the tired sons of a long line of rich men'.[10] In the summer of 1938 Hitler had told a Nazi whom he had sent to Britain to investigate whether the country would fight and who had reported that it would, that he was simply wrong.[11] Such prescience in the recent past reinforced his confidence in his judgement. On 22 August, with the pact with the Soviets due to be signed the next day, Hitler reaffirmed to a meeting of his military chiefs his determination to begin the invasion of Poland in four days' time and his conviction that there would be no significant response from the Western powers, though a war with them within a few years was inevitable.

The German dictator suffered a rude awakening on 25 August when Britain and Poland signed a formal treaty of alliance. This had to be taken seriously and played its part in his decision, with only hours to spare, to postpone the attack on Poland until 1 or 2 September. He accepted military advice that 2 September was the latest date to launch a campaign that could be concluded before the autumn rains made advance difficult. Of at least equal importance in forcing this decision on Hitler was the news received later on the same day that Italy would be neutral if there was a war. The Fuhrer and his generals had been relying on Italian belligerency to force France to keep fifteen divisions along its border with Italy. Italian neutrality created the possibility that most of those troops could be moved north, giving France sufficient strength to strike through Belgium and possibly also Holland and into Germany's industrial heartland in the Ruhr while most of the German army was fighting in the east. German military planners feared a short period of only about a week between the time when French mobilisation was effective and when they were able to switch large forces to the west after breaking the back of Polish resistance. The French general staff wished to take advantage of this opportunity, but on 28 August their government announced that Belgian neutrality would be respected. Any possibility that there might not be war in 1939 disappeared at this point.[12] Belgian policy was in the baleful hands of King Leopold III, a royal person of wretchedly unsound judgement who was convinced that Hitler would respect his kingdom's neutrality if only it was constantly reaffirmed in word and deed. Belgium had given the clearest indication that it would declare war on France if French troops crossed its borders.[13]

Against this background, only limited importance attaches to the diplomatic moves, mostly between Britain and Germany, of the last few days of peace. Their essence consisted of an effort by Hitler, finally abandoned on 30 August, to cause Britain to break with Poland by making the 'reasonable' demands referred to above in the hope that Britain would endorse them and Poland reject them.[14] As the admiring Goebbels wrote on 29 August after a talk with his Fuhrer: 'His hope is to de-couple Warsaw from London and still find an excuse to attack.'[15] Hitler was determined on war. He had engineered its timing in a way that the German rulers of 1914 had not (or, at least, Hitler believed that they had not). He had ensured that it would not be a two front war, a respect in which his superiority to his predecessors was clear. He acted when Germany's armaments position was relatively strong, although in that matter any comparison with 1914, when the Imperial German government felt the same confidence, would have been uncomfortable. He feared the possibility of his own early demise from illness or assassination or, less rationally, that his powers of 'genius' might soon decline, though he was only fifty. His psychological need not to be 'cheated' out of war as he had been in 1938 was great.

In Britain the Chamberlain government was willing to put pressure on Poland to abandon its rights in Danzig and to allow Germany extraterritorial transport rights across the Corridor to East Prussia if they could be convinced that Germany sought no more from Poland and was ready for change to be gradual in a way that the implementation of the Munich agreement had not been. A similar tendency prevailed in French policy.[16] There was scope for destroying the Anglo-French alliance if Hitler had been willing to proceed in relatively leisurely stages. Polish policy at this time, at least with Beck as its exponent, was not only intransigent but also bordered on the megalomaniac. His old fears of British trickery reawakened, he had circulated a message to all Polish diplomatic missions on 15 August in which he declared: 'I have warned that in the case of any attempt to trade our interests I shall take decisive action against Germany, against the League of Nations, and finally against any allied power which would associate itself with these moves.'[17] Hitler was not willing to follow that route, though he did not rule out the continued existence of a rump Polish state, especially if Stalin chose not to invade eastern Poland, even after the German invasion began on 1 September. Stalin did invade later in the month, and shrill Soviet demands that Poland must disappear from the map, anger at Polish atrocities against ethnic Germans and murdered war prisoners,[18] even though he was their ultimate progenitor, and the entire twisted logic of the Nazi ideology of racism and conquest, soon led to the abandonment of that idea.

The notion that sinister motives can be read into the delay between the German invasion of Poland and the British and French declarations of war more than forty-eight hours later on 3 September, with a six hour gap between the British and French declarations, is incorrect. In the absence of a formal German declaration of war on Poland, several hours were needed for London and Paris to learn beyond all doubt that there was a full scale war in Central Europe and not border incidents. After that their commitment to a Poland that was the victim of unprovoked aggression left no room for more than minimal delay during which Hitler could be given a chance to relent and withdraw from Polish territory and, of particular importance to France as a result of having a border with Germany, defensive measures could be carried out. Even Chamberlain was not rueful about the prospect of war in the way that he had been after the failure of his Godesberg talks with Hitler nearly a year earlier. One of his partners in appeasement at the time, Cadogan, saw no reason to cancel his attendance as a guest at a wedding on Saturday 2 September. The two Western governments offered to refrain from declaring war if Hitler would withdraw all German troops to where they had been on 31 August after which there might be negotiations on Danzig and extraterritorial rights for Germany in the Corridor. They were only prepared to support a plan of Mussolini's on 2 September for a major international conference to revise the provisions in the Versailles treaty of 1919 that were 'causing the present grave trouble in the life of Europe' (that is, presumably, the German–Polish border since very little else survived from Versailles to which the fascist dictator states professed to take exception) if the troops were withdrawn first. The most enthusiastic supporter of the Mussolini plan was Bonnet who was willing to leave German soldiers on Polish soil. The eclipse of the plan within hours was to enable Bonnet to keep his job, but only for a further twelve days until Daladier sacked him as Foreign Minister on 14 September.[19]

The war that started in September 1939 was, of course, a war in Europe only. It can be narrowed down even further, as in Donald Cameron Watt's judgement: 'The war which was to break Europe into two, into the eastward and westward-looking parts of today, was in the beginning fundamentally a war between the British and German peoples.'[20] Professor Watt wrote, it almost goes without saying, on the eve of the beginning of the end of that division. The eclipse of France, *the* European great power of the 1920s, was, by the late 1930s, truly remarkable, no matter how much one may admire the loyalty of Francophile historians in trying to present a rather different picture.[21] The superpowers of the future, the United States and the Soviet Union, were unwilling to oppose a Nazi Germany whose expansionist appetite did not appear immediately to threaten them. By contrast, an Anglo-German clash was virtually inevitable because of Hitler's rejection of the British concept of appeasement as a process of satisfying legitimate grievances through compromise. For long the British baulked at accepting that *any* territorial changes would represent the satisfaction of a legitimate grievance. In February 1936 Ramsay MacDonald, until the previous year Prime Minister and still a member of the Cabinet, a long-term friend of Germany, could write: 'The greatest potential danger of the whole situation is the new Nazi doctrine that the existence of a German population in a foreign country was sufficient to justify an extension of German territorial sovereignty in that direction. If this line were persisted in, negotiations would be impossible.'[22]

In 1938 Britain set aside that reservation and became a party to the partial dismemberment of Czechoslovakia on ethnic or pseudo-ethnic lines. (Austria earlier in the year was a different case, given its almost wholly German character and longstanding doubts about the legitimacy of forcing independence on it in 1919.)[23] After those precedents, Britain would almost certainly have been willing to tolerate German annexation of Danzig – on the analogy of Austria: an overwhelmingly German entity – and the Polish Corridor – on the analogy of Munich: part of the population was German. That would, however, have required great finesse from Hitler. By early 1939 the governing conviction in London was, in the words of the Chiefs of Staff, that British inaction in the face of further German aggression would cause the outside world to 'conclude that our sun had set'.[24] The problem was that such cessions would in no way have met Hitler's requirements. For once his Propaganda Minister, Goebbels, was precisely correct in his 30 September 1938 diary entry on the Munich conference: 'The slogan from now on is: Rearm, Rearm, Rearm. This has been a victory of pressure, nerves and the media.'[25] The implication that Germany would have to fight to make more gains was essentially correct. Hitler had ceased to command any credibility with the British when Grigore Gafencu, the Romanian Foreign Minister, visited Berlin and then London in April 1939 and quoted to Chamberlain pacific sentiments that Hitler had made to him. Chamberlain, 'his face twitching mournfully', replied that Hitler was a liar.[26]

This repugnance against Nazi Germany was accompanied by a positive factor that boosted the martial spirit: the renaissance, to be tragically shattered the following year, of Britain and France as comrades in arms. By August 1939 the Anglo-French military relationship had reached a stage of intimacy in which the military delegations of the two countries that were to try to negotiate an alliance with Russia in Moscow could not only agree beforehand at a meeting in Paris to act as one team but also to signal to one another by nasal scratching if one delegation detected the slightest sign of the other slipping from agreed positions.[27] Even if Hitler had split the Anglo-Polish, as opposed to the Anglo-French, alliance – a not wholly impossible undertaking if he had not been absolute determined on war in the late summer of 1939 – war with the Western powers would only have been postponed, to be fought in even less favourable circumstances to the democracies than those of that year. With German policy on war and peace in the hands of one whom Vansittart had so aptly described years earlier as 'a half mad and ridiculously dangerous demagogue' there can be no reason for not accepting without reservation Alan Bullock's view on the occasion of the twentieth anniversary of the end of the Second World War in Europe: 'Looking back, with more that twenty years' hindsight, the only question I can see to ask is not whether there would be a war, but when, and at what cost.'[28]

Notes

1 Jan Karski, *The Great Powers and Poland 1919–1945: From Versailles to Yalta* (Lanham, MD, University Press of America, 1985), p. 379.

2 Andrew Roberts, *'The Holy Fox': A Life of Lord Halifax* (London, Macmillan, 1992), pp. 144–5.

3 *Ibid.*, pp. 139–40; Donald Cameron Watt, *How War Came: The Immediate Origins of the Second World War, 1938–1939* (London, Heinemann, 1989), pp. 615–17.

4 Wesley K. Wark, *The Ultimate Enemy: British Intelligence and Nazi Germany, 1933–39* (London, Tauris, 1985), pp. 217–18, 232–3.

5 P. M. H. Bell, *The Origins of the Second World War in Europe* (London, Longman, 1986), pp. 172–4.

6 John F. Kennedy, *Why England Slept* (London, May Fair, 1962), pp. 159–64; R. J. Q. Adams, *British Politics and Foreign Policy in the Age of Appeasement, 1935–39* (London, Macmillan, 1993), pp. 145–9; R. J. Overy, *The Origins of the Second World War* (London, Longman, 1987), table 1, p. 49.

7 R. A. C. Parker, 'Economics, rearmament and foreign policy: the United Kingdom before 1939 – a preliminary study', *Journal of Contemporary History*, 10:4 (1975), 637–47.

8 Watt, *How War Came*, pp. 432–4.

9 Gerhard L. Weinberg, *Germany and the Soviet Union 1939–1941* (Leiden, Brill, 1954), p. 44.

10 Watt, *How War Came*, pp. 96, 390–407; on Dahlerus's activities see article by Andrew Roberts in *Sunday Telegraph*, review section, 8 August 1999.

11 Gerhard L. Weinberg, *The Foreign Policy of Hitler's Germany: Starting World War II, 1937–39* (Chicago, IL, University of Chicago Press, 1980), pp. 378–80.

12 Esmonde M. Robertson, 'German mobilization preparations and the

treaties between Germany and the Soviet Union of August and September 1939' in Robert Boyce and Esmonde M. Robertson (eds), *Paths to War* (London, Macmillan, 1989), pp. 344–8; A. Alexandroff and R. Rosecrance, 'Deterrence in 1939', *World Politics*, 29 (1977), 404–24.

13 Weinberg, *Starting World War II*, pp. 592–3, 631; Watt, *How War Came*, pp. 560–7; Martin Thomas, *Britain, France and Appeasement* (Oxford, Berg, 1996), pp. 181–3.

14 Esmonde M. Robertson, *Hitler's Pre-War Policy and Military Plans* (London, Longmans, 1963), pp. 185–91.

15 Joseph Goebbels, previously unpublished diary extracts, (diary entry for 29 September 1938) 'The Road to War', *Sunday Times*, News Review, section 2, p. 3, 12 July 1992.

16 J. Néré, *The Foreign Policy of France from 1914 to 1945* (London, Routledge, 1975), pp. 240–1.

17 Karski, *Great Powers*, pp. 368–9; Anita Prazmowska, *Britain, Poland and the Eastern Front, 1939* (Cambridge, Cambridge University Press, 1987), p. 158; Sidney Aster, *1939: The Making of the Second World War* (London, Deutsch, 1973), remains an excellent survey of diplomacy during the last months of peace with the emphasis on British policy.

18 David Irving, *Hitler's War* (London, Hodder and Stoughton, 1977), pp. 7–20.

19 Christopher Hill, *Cabinet Decisions on Foreign Policy: the British Experience October 1938–June 1941* (Cambridge, Cambridge University Press, 1991), pp. 85–99, for a detailed study of British policy towards declaring war.

20 Watt, *How War Came*, p. 385; for a similar statement by a German historian see W. Deist, M. Messerschmidt, H-E. Volkmann and W. Wette, *Germany and the Second World War: Vol. I, The Build-up of German Aggression*, (Oxford, Clarendon Press, 1990), p. 730.

21 For example, John E. Dreifort, 'The French role in the least unpleasant solution' in Maya Latynski (ed.), *Reappraising the Munich Pact: Continental Perspectives* (Baltimore, MD, Johns Hopkins University Press, 1992).

22 Correlli Barnett, *The Collapse of British Power* (Gloucester, Sutton, 1984), p. 449.

23 Larry William Fuchser, *Neville Chamberlain and Appeasement: A Study in the Politics of History* (New York, Norton, 1982), pp. 113–14; R. A. C. Parker, *Chamberlain and Appeasement: British Policy and the Coming of the Second World War* (London, Macmillan, 1993), p. 134.

24 David Dilks, '"We must hope for the best and prepare for the worst": the prime minister, the cabinet and Hitler's Germany, 1937–39', *Proceedings of the British Academy*, 63 (1987), 309–52.

25 Goebbels, diary extracts, *Sunday Times*, 12 July 1992.

26 Grigore Gafencu, *Prelude to the Russian Campaign* (London, Muller, 1945), p. 232.

27 Fyodor Volkov, *Secrets from Whitehall and Downing Street* (Moscow, Progress Publishers, 1980), pp. 299–300.

28 Alan Bullock, 'The war that had to be', *The Spectator*, 17 May 1965; the semi-official German history of the war's origins (Deist et al., *Germany and the Second World War*, p. 4) agrees that the bringing about of this war was, to a quite exceptional extent, the responsibility of one man.

CHAPTER THIRTEEN

WORLD WAR

It is undeniable that Britain and France went to war with decidedly halfhearted ideas about how it should be waged. It is extraordinary that in May 1939 Nevile Henderson, the ambassador in Berlin, told his German colleagues, as he would have regarded them, that if war came it 'would be conducted defensively by the Western Powers'.[1] He was, nevertheless, only speaking the truth. The allies envisaged no action in the West to divert German forces from Poland, nor offensive action of any kind against the Third Reich on land or in the air. Only at sea would there be no deliberate avoidance of fighting the enemy. They feared German retaliation, perhaps with dreadful savagery. British government committees in the late 1930s agonised over what counter-measures might be possible if Germany dropped chemical or germ warfare bombs or both, which was regarded as a distinct possibility. In terms of protecting the country's population, they could think of little.[2] Even if that did not happen, they did not, now that war had actually started, want to embark on a competition of strategic bombing of British and German cities.[3] This coincided with some remarkable statements about the nature of the peace settlement that Britain should aim for, if not from the government itself, then from influential outside voices. In October 1939 the prestigious newspaper, *The Economist*, made an impassioned plea that Britain and France, not Germany, should pay Poland compensation for material damage caused by the German invasion and that there should be 'no arms inequality' for Germany.[4]

Well might Hitler have remarked to an official on the eve of his attack on Poland, when he at last accepted that Britain and France would declare war: 'In two months Poland will be finished; then we shall have a great peace conference with the Western Powers.' In

Britain pleas to the government for precisely that came from both predictable quarters – the Conservative extreme right[5] – and from less predictable ones. Twenty Labour MPs responded to a speech that Hitler made calling for peace after the conclusion of the Polish campaign by appealing for his offer not to be rejected out of hand.[6] In the government's view what stood in the way of anything like that was, quite simply, Hitler himself. Even Chamberlain saw little chance of peace unless Hitler was deposed, and Churchill's and also Halifax's presence in the new War Cabinet was an effective antidote to prime ministerial backsliding.[7] Despite some awareness of the difficulties of separating the person of Hitler from the Nazi movement, they would have been willing in late 1939 to make peace with a post-Hitler regime on a German nationalist agenda under which the Reich could keep 'German' areas of Poland while the Czechs would have to make do with a statelet probably confined to the German 'protectorate' of Bohemia and Moravia. This would have restored to the map a more or less real Poland and a somewhat bogus Czech entity. This was a ruthless but also realistic acid test in that Hitler's acceptance of such limitations on German power was rightly seen to be inconceivable. Thus peace would have to be preceded by his departure from office, to dignified retirement if that was what his successors wanted. France indicated a preference for a much grander programme of war aims, including even the dismemberment of Germany.[8] These minimalist war aims in the case of Britain reflected concern about how the war could be won at acceptable cost or even at any cost. Politicians felt some scepticism towards the more extreme claims about German economic weakness that were being made by some professional economists,[9] and towards the too neat Treasury forecast that the German economy would collapse within eighteen months whereas the British could last for two years.[10]

What were needed to transform the war that began in September 1939 into a world war that Germany could not win and would be very likely to lose were American and Soviet entry into the conflict. The precondition for both was, ironically, German near victory in the initial conflict. That was to give Hitler at least the option of attacking Russia and was to spur both the United States and Japan towards participation. In the United States the response to the European war was as favourable as the British and French could rationally have expected. Roosevelt's first pronouncement was that although Americans had to be neutral in deed, they did not have to be neutral in thought, and a Gallup poll showed a microscopic 0.2 per cent of Americans actually supporting Germany.[11] The United States persuaded the republics of Latin America to join with it in proclaiming a Pan-American Neutrality Zone in Atlantic waters off the Western Hemisphere in which the navies of the belligerents were expected not to operate, and this became of real value to the allies in November when Congress was persuaded to reverse its stand of the summer and allow belligerents to purchase war materials for cash in the United States and then 'carry' them home on their own ships, a facility, as already noted, that only the British and French would be able to utilise. At the same time, every possible safeguard was included to guard against this step taking the United States into war. These included that American ships could not visit belligerent ports nor its citizens travel on belligerents' ships. The administration mounted a massive and by no means hypocritical public relations campaign based on the argument that these amendments to the law were the best means to keep the United States neutral.[12] Even with these safeguards and this propaganda, the law might not have passed without lobbying from US business interests that wanted to sell to the allies. Only in the United States' unconcealed jealousy towards Nazi influence in Latin America, manifested most notably in attempts to organise German colonists and people of German descent, was there a hint of inexorable conflict. While the democracies at war still had to pay in cash for purchases in the United States, Congress in 1940 voted a loan of $500 million for Latin American countries to cushion the termination of their trade with Germany.[13] Seldom in diplomatic history can there have been a more unjustifiably alarmist warning than the one that the head of the German embassy in Washington sent to Berlin on 11 September 1939 that, 'Roosevelt is determined to go to war against Germany even in the face of resistance of his own country.' There was a curious, almost oriental, fatalism in the President's country if the recently established device of opinion polls are to be believed. While the 'phoney war' went on in Europe, these polls showed a consistent 63 per cent of Americans thinking that if Germany won there it would eventually attack the United States, yet few of these respondents favoured American entry into the war.[14]

Day to day dealings between the United States and the allies remained in the hands of the self-proclaimed 'realists' of the State Department, still obsessed with Britain as the main obstacle to American economic recovery, and their admirers including ambassador Kennedy in London who noted during the second week of war that Britain was a country of 'economic totalitarianism'. When, in July 1940, Britain temporarily closed the 'Burma Road' supply route to China at a time when it mattered very little in practical terms because of the monsoon season and in order to conciliate Japan while England faced the threat of invasion, Cordell Hull protested woodenly to the British ambassador, partly 'on account of the interest this Government, engaged as it is in international commerce, has in seeing all arteries and channels of trade kept open'. Exactly a year later Hull was still musing that the United States should be ready to be completely ruthless in forcing Britain not to follow its inclination to adopt 'the Hitlerian commercial policy'.[15] Britain maintained a vast number of employees in America – 12,000 by the end of 1941[16] – but they could have achieved little if, as was actually not the case, all American attitudes about foreign policy had been so entrenched.

The chief American diplomatic move during the 'phoney war' in Western Europe that lasted until April 1940 was the mission of the 'realist' Sumner Welles to European capitals the previous month. Roosevelt probably wanted to discourage Hitler from initiating serious military action while the State Department clique undoubtedly aimed at a compromise peace to be achieved by American mediation with the United States charging trade liberalisation as the price for its services.[17] Rarely can there have been a more counterproductive exercise. Privately, Hitler showed his contempt for the mission by signing the order for Denmark and Norway to be invaded the day before he saw Welles. On the other hand, the German leader was rattled by the fact that Welles visited Rome twice. He made a major effort to court Mussolini, including a meeting at the Brenner Pass in mid March at which the Italian, who was deeply unhappy about having had to observe neutrality, committed Italy to enter the war.

Hitler had no wish at this point to provoke the United States. He regarded eventual war with it as both inevitable and desirable, and a pseudo practical, though really science fiction, preparatory step had been taken as far back as 1937 when he and Goering ordered the development of aircraft that could bomb American east coast cities. Much effort was wasted on this absurd project.[18] After the start of war, the Fuhrer rejected appeals from his naval commanders for unrestricted submarine warfare in the Atlantic even when they presented him with evidence of the US navy helping the Royal Navy to locate German vessels. He remembered another lesson from the previous war when unrestricted submarine attacks had played their part in bringing the United States into war in 1917. The German press was ordered, after hostilities commenced, to cease its personal attacks on Roosevelt (who was actually totally indifferent to whether Nazi newspapers insulted him or not); and German representatives in the United States were told to go out of their way to avoid open identification with organised isolationist forces so that the latter could not be accused of being Nazi stooges. In fact, they did not always refrain from meddling and often did so with predictable crassness. There was even an attempt to induce John L. Lewis, the most prominent trade union leader in the country, to organise a general strike if the administration showed signs of intervening in the war.[19]

Then came the stunning German military victories in France and five small West European countries in the spring of 1940 and the replacement of Chamberlain as British Prime Minister by Churchill on 10 May, with Halifax remaining as Foreign Secretary and, with Chamberlain who remained in the government, joint second most senior political figure. As the prospect of France continuing to resist diminished in late May, some senior ministers in the British War Cabinet felt obliged to give some consideration to what was euphemistically referred to as a 'European settlement',[20] that is, a compromise peace with Hitler's Germany. This was the time when Cadogan noted in his diary, 'A miracle may save us: otherwise we're done.'[21] There was to be such a miracle in the popular imagination of the time and later, in the evacuation to England of 330,000 troops from Dunkirk after earlier expectations that it would only be possible to rescue 40–50,000 from capture in France.

Dunkirk did undoubtedly give Churchill a final and decisive argument against exploring what German peace terms might be.[22] However the real battle was fought out before the Dunkirk evacuation had succeeded. At Cabinet on Sunday 26 May, Halifax pressed for an approach to Mussolini and his still neutral Italy to mediate the end of the war. Churchill opposed this but it might have succeeded had it not been for the fact that Chamberlain sided with the new Prime Minister. The following day the Foreign Secretary returned to the advocacy of his view that any German peace terms should be examined, though he dropped the Mussolini idea. Churchill's achievement on this occasion was to resist Halifax successfully while also persuading him not to resign. The next day, 28 May, Halifax tried yet again, this time reviving his Mussolini proposal. Churchill continued to oppose: 'The Prime Minister thought that the chances of decent terms being offered to us at present were a thousand to one against.' The matter of war or attempted peace was then put before the full Cabinet which gave Churchill unanimous support after he had addressed it. The War Cabinet met again and Halifax admitted defeat. Although Churchill wisely did not say so, he really seems to have believed that Nazi domination of Europe – even a Europe in which Britain retained more of the features of independence that almost any other country except Germany – would have been so barbaric that it was better to fight on in a hopeless struggle to the death than compromise.[23]

In June and into July Churchill, having defeated his internal critics, sent false signals to Hitler that he might soon be willing to negotiate peace terms.[24] Towards the end of July this became less necessary as intercepts of German communications appeared to indicate clearly that there would be no early invasion.[25] By this time *The Times* had recently ceased to refer to Hitler as 'Herr'.[26] The Fuhrer's next 'peace offer' to Britain, in his speech to the Reichstag on 19 July, was rejected on the grounds that he could not be trusted and was not offering to give up German conquests. Despite this, German, or German-authorised, peace moves to Britain, mostly via Sweden, continued for a few months.[27] Britain and its dominions would not make peace, but stood alone unless, as Hitler did, one counts Norway which Germany had conquered but whose king and government declined to accept that they had lost and that they should seek terms from Berlin. (In August 1940, in the course of an audience that he granted the Norwegian traitor, Vidkun Quisling, Hitler remarked: 'It is an ironic fate that I have to wage war against the two countries for which I have had the greatest sympathy all my life – England and Norway.')[28]

The German victories in the spring–summer of 1940 made possible two gigantic moves that were to prove catastrophic for their perpetrators. One was by Germany against the Soviet Union, the other by Japan against the United States and Britain. To begin with the former, one must guard against treating the German onslaught into Russia in 1941 as inevitable in relation to the time at which it occurred. It was inevitable in a wider sense. Goebbels understood his master's mind when he wrote in his diary on 23 August 1939 as the

Nazi–Soviet pact was signed: 'The Bolshevik question is of lesser importance for the moment'.[29] The issue concerned how long the 'moment' to which Goebbels referred would last. At a luncheon in Berlin a few weeks after the end of the campaign in Poland, General Heinz Guderian, the commander of armoured forces, disappointed Hitler by expressing unqualified satisfaction when he asked him how the German army and people had responded to his pact with Russia. Hitler looked amazed and changed the subject. It took time for the politically naive general to realise that Hitler had been hoping that he would have said that they understood that it was a distasteful and, it was to be hoped, temporary necessity.[30] According to Martin Bormann, who probably knew Hitler's mind as well as anyone, even when he appeared to be most preoccupied with Western Europe his actions were governed by the 'primacy of his eastern policy'.[31]

And yet, as France staggered towards defeat, Hitler was not certain in his own mind what the next steps in that policy should be. His senior generals thought that the logical (and amoral) choice was between a war against the Soviet Union to occupy its western borderlands only, or a war in alliance with the Soviets to drive Britain out of the Middle East and the Persian Gulf region. Either campaign would have been within German capabilities and would have greatly improved the country's strategic and economic situation.[32] There were also attractions to simply continuing to operate the agreements that Germany and Russia had reached the previous year. Not only were the Soviets bartering raw materials that were doing much to counter the Royal Navy's blockade of Germany but also they were providing help in port and icebreaking activities for the German navy in its operations against Britain.[33] Against this had to be set not only fundamental Nazi aims but also the fact that Stalin was displaying a seemingly almost insatiable expansionist appetite. After his slightly hesitant occupation of eastern Poland, he attacked Finland during the Winter War of 1939–40 and, after the main Finnish defences had been overrun towards the end of the winter, would probably have completed his conquest of the country but for fear that Britain and France would use that as an excuse for 'switching the war': making peace with Germany and declaring war on Russia.[34] (They would not have made peace with Germany but might admittedly have been drawn into war with Russia.) In June Foreign Minister Molotov congratulated Germany on its 'splendid victories' in the West and almost casually informed it that the Soviet Union would be taking possession of the Baltic states of Estonia, Latvia and Lithuania and the Romanian provinces of Bessarabia and Bukovina. This was allowable under German–Soviet agreements except for Bukovina over which Germany forced Russia to confine its acquisitions to the northern half of the province.

Stalin now had everything that he could claim under the agreements (except Finland) and a little more besides, but he was manifestly unwilling to stop there. Hitler's 'Vienna award' in August, under which the Fuhrer ordered Romania to cede the greater part of another of its provinces, Transylvania, to Hungary provoked the first official Soviet protest to Germany since the conclusion of the Nazi–Soviet pact. The Soviets did not oppose Hungary's gain – they positively supported it – but they were furious about Germany's guarantee of the integrity of what remained of Romania. Russia wanted to squeeze Romania, possibly our of existence. In late 1940 it nibbled at Romanian territory in the Danube delta in disregard of the German guarantee.[35] This affected the one country in Europe, apart from Russia, from which Germany could obtain oil. Stalin went on to demand that Bulgaria must become a Soviet protectorate with a substantial Red Army garrison on its soil, not as an end in itself but so that he could seize Istanbul and the Straits between the Black Sea and the Aegean from Turkey. He justified all this by reference to the strategic defence needs of the Soviet Union, and yet he had also embarked on an energetic courtship of Yugoslavia, a neighbour of the greater German Reich but a country of no strategic importance to the Soviet Union.[36] Any German government would have been alarmed, though the grotesque element in this situation resides in the fact that Stalin really did not conceive of these demands as being directed against Germany but rather against Britain. He could never rid his mind of Lenin's teaching that Britain was the most dangerous and treacherous of the imperialist countries and one French, and therefore presumably neutral, observer has seen him at this time as obsessed with 'anglophobic demons'.[37] The evidence indicates that in 1940 Stalin wanted to control Romania, Bulgaria and the Straits because he was convinced that otherwise Britain might seize them at any time to launch a new Crimean war or a new intervention like the one that had followed the 1917 Bolshevik revolution.[38]

The Soviet side stuck to these demands when Hitler consented to receive Molotov in Berlin in November. This makes it impossible to test for certain whether there was any sincerity in Hitler's offer of partnership if the Soviet Union would exclude itself from any role in Europe west of its borders and confine its future expansion to Asia or whether, in the more probable view of one German historian, the Fuhrer merely wanted to 'bamboozle' Stalin into keeping up deliveries of Soviet raw materials until the eve of the invasion and until after Germany had largely ceased to provide anything in return.[39] If this was in fact the aim it was achieved with brilliant success. On 31 July, in an 'incredible' and 'boundless' overestimation of what Germany could accomplish, Hitler had ordered his military staff to prepare plans for a campaign against Russia, not with limited objectives but with that of the country's complete 'destruction' in the words of army Chief of Staff Halder.[40]

Some historians have made much – and probably too much – of the fact that Hitler did not follow his 'decision' of 31 July with a definitive directive to prepare for an invasion until 18 December. In all likelihood, all this means is that invasion was postponable beyond 1941 if two conditions could be met. The first was Stalin's assent, which was refused, to the terms that Hitler presented to Molotov in Berlin. The second was the implementation of what has been called a 'peripheral' military strategy in the Iberian peninsula, North West Africa and the Spanish and Portuguese islands in the eastern Atlantic. This means of ending the war with Britain and thereby lessening the urgency of a showdown with Russia would have required the cooperation of Spain or France or both, which might have been forthcoming if Hitler had been interested only in inflicting hammer blows on Britain, especially the capture of Gibraltar, the western gateway to the Mediterranean, which could then have been graciously handed over to Spain. Instead, the peripheral strategy brought out the messianic streak in Hitler. Besides striking at Britain, he was determined to prepare the defences of the nazi and fascist Europe that he was creating against an attack from the United States that, he remarked to Ribbentrop, might not come until 1970 or 1980. If the Italians, the Vichy French and Molotov were merely bemused by this, the Spanish dictator Franco was furious when he learnt that Hitler's grand design would not only deny him the whole of French Morocco – a non-negotiable part of his price for entering the war – because Germany wanted sovereign bases in some of its ports, but would also involve Spain in giving up one of the Canary islands that had been Spanish since the fifteenth century. In early December 1940 he refused to enter the war. Hitler was compelled to begin detailed work on his Russian campaign with Britain wholly undefeated and the south western flank of his European empire left exposed. Instead of being a preliminary to the conquest of Russia, the peripheral strategy took on the form of a sequel. In July 1941, expecting the war in Russia to be over within weeks, Hitler ordered that substantial elite forces should be transferred to South West Europe in time for Gibraltar to be captured by 15 October.[41]

Under these circumstances, Hitler was not being entirely insincere in telling his generals that, if Britain could not by direct means be defeated or even seriously damaged, it could be dealt with by the conquest of Russia which he described to Admiral Raeder as Britain's 'continental sword'. It would, therefore, be correct to say that the war with Britain and, to a lesser and uncertain extent, the revelation of Stalin's unacceptable ambitions dictated the *timing* of Hitler's war against Russia but not whether there would be such a war. That war represented, in the findings of the most authoritative modern German historical scholarship, a marriage of 'rational thought and dogma', of Nazi *Lebensraum* yearnings and a much older German dream of 'spatial unassailability' in the Eurasian heartland, of euphoria after the victories in Western Europe and the most vicious racism that found expression in military plans for a war of extermination and economic plans for the deliberate starving to death of tens of millions of people in occupied Soviet territory as its resources were plundered and exploited for Germany. Heavily influenced by anti-Semitism and a sincere belief that the Soviet regime was a front for Jewish power, the senior German military commanders accepted not unwillingly Hitler's orders about the character the war should take. For example, some initial preparation during war planning for treating Soviet prisoners of war in accordance with international law was quickly abandoned. The generals needed even less persuasion to accept Hitler's view that only with the resources of Russia under its control could Germany win its final war with Anglo-America or with the United States alone.[42] Hitler did not rule out the possibility that the defeat of Russia would do what the fall of France had failed to do and induce a Britain purged of Churchill to join in 'Europe's struggle against America' as Germany's 'junior partner'. He rejected the idea of Britain and the United States as 'brother nations', asking, 'So what? The German brotherhood of nations fought the most bitter internecine wars for centuries on end.'[43]

Some of Hitler's other motives for invading did not require a specifically Nazi mindset. He felt genuine resentment about Soviet economic demands during the early months of the war when Germany's position had been relatively weak, and, while ruling out a Soviet attack in the near future, was convinced that Stalin would eventually have sent the Red Army into Europe as 'at the time of the Huns' if he had not invaded first.[44] Some of his views, such as his belief in the insincerity of the Russians as allies because of the 'psyche of the Slavic folk-soul', were merely absurd and unpleasant.[45] It is, however, when one considers the bestiality that was planned from the first to accompany the invasion that currently fashionable theories about symmetry between Germany and its opponents in the origins of the Second World War, all of them functioning within the one international system, begin to break down. There was no equivalent elsewhere to the all-pervading moral depravity in Third Reich Germany. This was exemplified in early 1941 by the big German industrial firms. On the one hand, they besieged the Soviet embassy in Berlin for business contracts in case their government decided, after all, not to invade. On the other, they egged the government on in the hope of cheap gains and presented the government with lists of Russian resources that they wished to take over, requests for slave labour and so on.[46]

While these industrialists smiled about what they thought would soon be theirs, Stalin improved their chances by refusing to be 'provoked', that is, do anything about German invasion preparations. He was deluded that only some German generals and not Hitler could wish to invade and he remained deluded about British conspiracies and machinations, especially after the Deputy Fuhrer, Rudolf Hess, flew to Scotland in May.[47]

The irony is that even the most sweeping German victories in the Soviet Union would not have had the impact that Hitler hoped for on Britain. This was because, in the first place, British policymakers feared that the only alternative to a German–Russian showdown would be a revival of a nightmare that had haunted the Foreign Office in the years before 1914: a situation in which Russia would accept German domination of Europe in return for a free hand to challenge Britain in Asia – essentially what Hitler suggested to Molotov when they met in Berlin.[48] In the second place, the British took it for granted that German victory over Russia would be both swift and cheap and would be followed not by Hitler waiting for Britain to see reason, but by the Reich switching its victorious forces from East to West for a final onslaught against the United Kingdom. On 14 June 1941, having finally become convinced that Hitler would not offer Stalin the option of agreeing to a sweeping list of demands in an ultimatum as the alternative to war, the Chiefs of Staff issued a directive for the armed forces to be in the highest state of readiness to resist a German invasion of England around 1 September, following a successful campaign in Russia and allowing time to move troops to the West.[49] In its editorial response to the Barbarossa invasion after it was actually launched on 22 June *The Times* echoed conventional wisdom in referring to 'the momentary diversion of Hitler's forces towards the East'.[50] Russia suffered horrendous losses of territory, material resources and, above all, human life from the German attack but was not defeated. Nor, contrary to what seem to have been universal expectations in the Soviet elite immediately after 22 June, did Britain 'switch' and join Germany against Soviet Russia.

With the war expanded in Europe, in September 1941 United States military planners warned President Roosevelt that there was no possibility of Britain and Russia inflicting actual defeat on Germany.[51] By then the United States' entry into the war was a real possibility. The origins of the creation of that possibility go back to the German victories in the spring of 1940. For what it was worth, these, in conjunction with Chamberlain's replacement by Churchill, caused British policy to abandon its reservations about the United States as a desirable ally. The continuing British war effort only made sense on the hypothesis that America would join.[52] The United States was, needless to say, not to be easily moved, but it embarked on a dual policy of rearmament and aid for Britain that pointed in the direction of possible war entry. After resisting the President's call for an extra $2 billion defence appropriation in the winter of 1939–40, from May 1940 Congress voted three massive appropriations, culminating in one for nearly $5 billion in September. The aims at this stage were hemispheric defence and aid for those resisting Germany. These were reflected in the late summer of 1940 in the conclusion of a defence agreement with Canada and in the agreement with Britain in September by which the United States would transfer fifty destroyers, no longer of use to its navy, in return for bases on several British colonies in the Caribbean area and Bermuda. Initially, the United States had sought the bases without offering Britain anything at all in return.[53] The destroyers proved a sad disappointment in terms of practical usefulness. As David Irving has gleefully noted, they were valued by the Americans at a paltry $15 million for the whole lot, and Churchill himself had to accept that they were 'worthless hulks' that it would have been suicidal for the Royal Navy to try to use.[54] However, by late 1940 Britain, for its part, was placing orders in the United States, especially for aircraft, that it knew it could not pay for. British gold and dollar reserves were down to £3 million by the new year of 1941 and national bankruptcy was only staved off by a loan of £60 million from the Belgian government in exile in February.[55]

At the end of 1940 Roosevelt proposed the Lend Lease scheme to Congress under which the United States, 'getting away from a dollar sign' in the President's words, would aid countries at war with Germany with the question of recompense to be left flexible and for discussion after hostilities had been concluded.[56] The law was speedily enacted by Congress, though Britain was not actually to gain much under it for some time. What all this meant was that the United States was preparing to underwrite the British (and later Russian) war effort so that Britain at least would be able to continue to fight on almost indefinitely while the United States remained neutral. Other US actions pointed to an awareness that such neutrality might not be possible. Between January and March 1941 the 'ABC' (American–British–Canadian) talks by military planners of the three countries were held in Washington in which plans for some military cooperation were worked out for implementation if the United States entered the war, though it disappointed the British by refusing to interest itself in the defence of Singapore. Skeleton US bases were established in Scotland and Northern Ireland. There were signs of the emergence of a substantial interventionist coalition in American public life.[57] Nor were the forces of organised isolationism particularly impressive. The best known of them, the America First Committee, was virtually a Mid West regional organisation; two thirds of its members lived within a sixty miles radius of Chicago.[58]

By early 1941 the United States was waging what one historian has called 'clandestine political warfare' against Germany in parts of Europe and North Africa, including Portugal, Yugoslavia, Bulgaria and French Morocco.[59] To this might be added France itself because of the appointment at the end of 1940 of Admiral Leahy, a man very close politically to the President, as ambassador to the government at Vichy that had signed the armistice with Germany, which served notice that the United States would do everything that it could to dissuade France from reentering the war on the German side or from close collaboration with the German war effort, though that ceased to be a German priority after they invaded Russia. In March and April 1941 all German consulates and other agencies in the United States were closed down and severe measures were taken against all organisations and individuals having connections with Germany. The German embassy in Washington remained but was practically under siege. A propaganda war against Germany was initiated, including a scare story about the smuggling of 25,000 'storm troops' into Brazil.[60] This was likely to be very effective. A nation in which, only two years earlier, millions of people had treated a spoof radio show about an invasion from outer space as a factual news bulletin would have no difficulty in believing in the existence of a legion of ghostly storm troops roaming South America. At a press conference on 27 October 1941 Roosevelt himself joined in the fun by producing and declaring to be authentic a map purporting to be an official German plan to redivide South America from ten republics to only five in favour of those that were willing to make common cause with Germany, including an enlarged and renamed Colombia that would recover the Panama Canal. The map was a British forgery.[61] Whether Roosevelt knew that it was a forgery is impossible to say. In all probability, he did not wish to know. (This is not to overlook that Germany actually had a substantial espionage apparatus, especially in Brazil.)[62]

Of even greater importance in putting America and Germany on a collision course was the situation in the Atlantic. After lend lease officially began in March 1941 there was a logical argument for protecting the aid materials for Britain from U-boat attack as they crossed the ocean. Roosevelt was only prepared to go a certain distance in responding to that logic. In April he extended eastwards the Neutrality Zone proclaimed just after the start of the war and made arrangements with Britain to take over the garrisoning of Iceland to which Britain had sent troops after the German occupation of Denmark in 1940. Besides relieving Britain of one of the most minor of its burdens, the idea was that United States ships should carry lend lease and other goods to Iceland and unload them and they should then be transferred to British ships which alone would then be at risk from German submarines. Iceland could only be of limited utility. Many British ships would continue to come to United States ports. Roosevelt considered providing them with United States escorts to the edge of the Neutrality Zone but decided against such a step. At this time, and probably for much longer as well, the President was sincerely intent on keeping his country out of war.[63] As late as August, when he held a conference with Churchill at Placentia Bay, Newfoundland, that produced the worthy sentiments of the Atlantic Charter, Roosevelt vetoed a plea by Churchill that their joint communiqué should denounce Nazi Germany by name, and, on returning to Washington, be spoke with vehemence about the unthinkability of the United States going to war.[64]

During most of 1941 Hitler worked hard to keep America out of the war. With the Russian campaign approaching, he vetoed a plea from his naval chief, Admiral Raeder, for the German navy to operate in the Neutrality Zone and to have the right to inspect US vessels and sink them if they had supplies for the enemy.[65] The German invasion of Russia on 22 June produced a new surge in isolationist feeling in the United States. Many Americans who could narrowly stomach considering being allied with Britain could not, at this time, do so in relation to 'Bolshevik' Russia. However, it was at this time that the German government became convinced that Roosevelt's strategy was to goad Germany into war with the United States by provoking incidents in the Atlantic. They took some (and not illusory) comfort from the evidence of still massive isolationism in America, noting for instance with satisfaction that the House of Representatives approved by only a one vote majority (203–202) in August the extension of the Selective Service Act to provide for conscription for eighteen months, an issue on which the administration had virtually staked its reputation. Hitler gave the most draconian orders to Raeder that US ships, merchant or navy, must not be attacked even when they were caught signalling the positions of German submarines to the British navy.

These orders were repeated a number of times, the last only six days before Pearl Harbor. By then changes in United States policy had made it impossible to avoid incidents. In September Roosevelt responded to a warning from the Navy Department that the British were losing the Battle of the Atlantic by ordering the US navy to help protect British convoys from the U-boats. He was presumably also influenced by a plea from Churchill, couched in somewhat demeaning terms – the Prime Minister 'would be grateful if you could give me any kind of hope' – that his government was in danger of falling.[66] He also authorised work on a 'Victory Program' to work out the extent and nature of the war effort that the United States would have to make if the Axis powers were to be defeated. The Americans justifiably regarded what the British had told them about their ideas for winning the war, based on blockade, bombing and risings by subject peoples, as delusory.[67] The US navy became involved in the battle against the U-boats which were picturesquely referred to by Roosevelt as 'rattlesnakes', and quickly suffered quite heavy losses. In November Congress repealed, by the customary very small majorities, the main clauses in the Neutrality laws to enable US merchant vessels to enter combat zones and to carry materials of war to ports in friendly countries. It remains a mystery whether Roosevelt's aim was to maintain a serious British war effort precisely to enable the United States to stay neutral or whether, as his 'backdoor to war' critics alleged, he now wanted to do what Hitler believed he wanted to do and goad the Fuhrer into declaring war. What is certain is that Hitler was extremely unwilling to take such a step unless and until Japan made war on the United States.

We must therefore retrace our steps and examine events in the Far East to understand the final stage in the origins of the Second World War. Early in 1940 Japanese leaders were in one of their periodic moods of depression about the war in China and wondered whether they would have to terminate the enterprise. One of their reasons for being reluctant to do so was genuinely defensive. Their army had been defeated by the Red Army in two border wars in 1938 and 1939, and they were convinced that a final, all out war with the Soviet Union was inevitable. They were convinced of the need to retain their conquests in north China to defend in depth Manchuria and Korea which they were determined to keep forever. Then the German victories in Western Europe raised their spirits. They still feared the United States but no longer Britain alone. The war in China could go on and the question became less whether there should be a new expansionist move than which one: against Russia, as favoured by the army, or southwards, as favoured by the navy which was particularly interested in securing the oilfields of the Netherlands East Indies (now Indonesia). Such a move would not necessarily have meant war with the United States if the Japanese had confined themselves to attacking British and Dutch possessions. (Vichy France was unable to refuse Japanese demands to take military control of northern French Indochina in September 1940, though Japan did that as a means of preventing supplies reaching the Republic of China rather than as a preliminary to southern expansion.)

Japan received strong encouragement for a southern thrust from Germany and weak discouragement from the United States. On 20 May 1940, while the campaign in Western Europe was still going on, Germany hastened to inform Japan that it had no claim on the Netherlands East Indies, an invitation to the Japanese to regard it as theirs for the taking and based on typically Nazi thinking that Germany was entitled to dispose of Holland and its colonies as it wished by right of conquest.[68] In September, Germany, Italy and Japan went on to negotiate the Tripartite Pact, yet another piece of verbiage under which the signatories made no binding commitments to one another, though Germany did throw in the sweetener of definitively renouncing any claim for the return of the former German island colonies in the Western Pacific that Japan had gained as a result of the Great War.[69] Beyond that, there was a typically grandiose agreement in principle that the Japanese sphere of the future should include India, Australia and East Siberia as well as all East Asia. Hitler wrote to Mussolini that, despite 'misgivings', he believed that 'a close cooperation with Japan is the best way either to keep America entirely out of the picture or to render her entry into the war ineffective.'[70] The Japanese, for their part, hoped that it would distract American attention towards Europe. The Japanese records of the negotiation of the Tripartite Pact provide a remarkable insight into the black heart, the insane war for its own sake mindset, of Nazism: 'Germany in asking Japan to join the Axis, is envisaging a stupendous struggle with the British Empire, not to say all of Anglo-Saxondom, which includes America ... The present war may end before long, but this great war will go on for decades in one form or another.'[71]

In July 1940 Roosevelt had imposed token sanctions against Japan, embargoing the export of types of oil and scrap metal that it did not need. He refused any help to France to resist Japanese demands over Indochina. In September he took the more serious step of embargoing all scrap metal exports. Clearly not deriving much feeling of strength from the Tripartite Pact, Japan offered peace terms to the Chinese leader, Chiang Kai-shek, and its opposite, a deal with Russia if it would cease its limited aid to Chiang. The former's response was negative, while Stalin's terms for an agreement were absurdly extravagant. In the winter of 1940–41 Japan was under pressure, as already noted, from Germany to attack the British Empire in East Asia and especially Singapore, with Ribbentrop giving his expert opinion that the United States would remain neutral. The United

States actually waged a war of nerves in which they exaggerated the extent to which they felt an identity of interest with Britain. Britain itself chipped in by creating a war scare in February with the probable, but unsuccessful, purpose of inducing the United States to send ships to Singapore.[72] The Japanese concluded that it was very unlikely that they would be able to attack Britain alone.[73]

The British were not so certain. They feared that Japan might propose, and the United States might accept, an agreement to preserve peace in the Far East in return for the United States staying out of the European war.[74] Alternatively, they still feared Japan only attacking British and Dutch possessions and America remaining neutral. Their over-strident attempts to extract a firm promise of US intervention if they were attacked, most notably at the Churchill–Roosevelt meeting in August 1941, were counterproductive and caused the Americans to think that Britain was trying to push them into war in the East. Churchill was left to make a bravado statement after the meeting that if Japan attacked only the United States Britain would at once join the war.[75] Not until 1 December did Roosevelt remark casually to the British ambassador that it was 'obvious' that the United States would go to war if Japan attacked British or Dutch colonies.[76] Britain's ordeal thus ended nearly a week before Pearl Harbor. The release in 1994 of the official history of Britain's Naval Intelligence Division disproved the always implausible theory that Churchill knew about the impending Japanese attack and did not warn the United States.[77] On the contrary, in those last pre-Pearl Harbor days the Prime Minister still thought that Japan might turn against the Soviets and minuted the Foreign Secretary: 'We could not, of course, agree to an arrangement [with the United States] whereby Japan was free to attack Russia in Siberia.'[78]

In the spring of 1941 Japanese government thoughts about attacking the Western powers had become more intense. In March–April Foreign Minister Matsuoka Yosuke visited the Axis capitals and then Moscow. In the former he responded to Ribbentrop's obsessive enquiries about when Britain would be ousted from Singapore by assuring him that it was only a matter of time. In the latter he signed a neutrality pact with Stalin to cover Japan's northern and western flanks. The pact enshrined the status quo and Stalin only signed it very reluctantly, having grown accustomed to receiving something in return for his mere autograph; and only because he wished to send out a signal to Berlin that he was now ready to conclude a four power pact (Germany, Italy, Japan, and the Soviet Union) on German terms. This resulted from the mood of panic that had gripped Stalin since the unexpected, lightning success of the German campaigns in Yugoslavia and Greece in April. Six months earlier Hitler might have been interested but no longer by this time.[79] In the Japanese government most were less singleminded than Matsuoka. In April Admiral Yamamoto, the naval chief, warned the Prime Minister, Prince Konoe, that if there was war the navy would be able to do great things for six months or a year, but that if it continued for two or three years the outcome would be very uncertain.[80] Talks were initiated with the United States in Washington to probe the chances of preserving peace in that quarter.

Japan was also tempted to revive the idea of striking against Russia as the German government confided that it expected war with that country, though they would not inform Tokyo of the date. At the beginning of June Hitler recited a list of alleged Soviet sins to the Japanese ambassador and concluded: 'I personally, whenever I find that my partner (sic) has any hostile intentions, usually draw my sword before he does.'[81] The possibility that Japan might enter the German–Soviet war after it started on 22 June was lessened by Nazi, and especially Hitler's, racism. Whereas the comparatively minor figure of Ribbentrop constantly urged Japanese entry, Hitler radiated indifference. For eighteen months from July 1941 until after the German catastrophe at Stalingrad, he refused to meet the Japanese ambassador except on formal occasions. The simple, crude fact was that the German dictator wanted the crushing of Russia to be an 'Aryan' achievement without any significant 'yellow race' input.[82]

As well as this, the Japanese, after their mauling by the Red Army in 1939, never shared Hitler's confidence that the German campaign in Russia would be swift and victorious, and decided that they would only intervene on the 'umikaki' (ripe plum that falls to the ground) principle: if Soviet resistance was manifestly collapsing, they would move into Eastern Siberia. Japan began almost doubling its forces in Manchuria and a date, 29 August, was fixed for the start of war with Russia but only if the situation on the Soviet–German front was deemed hopeless for the Russians and only if they had withdrawn at least half their forces facing Japan in the Far East. By the end of July neither of these conditions had been met and Japan was impressed, rather than provoked, by the Soviet refusal to accede to any of a list of minor demands that it made in early August. Also, the navy never ceased to argue the case for southern expansion passionately and effectively. On 9 August all plans for an invasion of Eastern Siberia were abandoned. On the day before the Pearl Harbor attack the Japanese ambassador in Berlin was instructed to ask Germany, in effect, not to embarrass Japan by urging it to attack Russia in the East until the project on which Japan was about to embark was accomplished.[83]

The possibility cannot be ruled out that Japan would have drawn back from the brink in relations with the Western powers also but for the precipitate US action in embargoing all fuel exports in July in response to the Japanese occupation of southern Indochina, with the reluctant consent of the French authorities. This came hard on the heels of the breakdown of negotiations with the Dutch colonial authorities in the East Indies who refused to sell any oil to Japan.[84] The United States' action of a total embargo was taken by middle level officials – Roosevelt had wanted some fuel to continue to flow – but was so popular in the country that the President had to suppress any thoughts about modifying it. Even the arch isolationist, Senator Wheeler, unaware of the exact nature of what had happened, said that for the first time he agreed with Roosevelt.[85] Japanese stockpiles of fuel were inevitably limited; for instance, there was only enough for two years in the case of aviation fuel.

The United States proceeded to make what were, for Japan, impossibly steep demands before the embargo could be lifted, including that Japan should leave the Tripartite Pact, commit itself to free trade and evacuate all Chinese territory occupied since 1937. If Konoe had agreed to this he would undoubtedly have been assassinated, but he was replaced in any case by a more warminded government under General Tojo in the early autumn. This was followed by a final phase of American–Japanese negotiations. Japan was willing to offer real concessions, including even the evacuation of occupied areas of southern China, if the economic sanctions were lifted. The navy did not like this, but many in the army remained interested in reviving the project of war with the Soviet Union. It was the United States that was intransigent, demanding unconditional withdrawal from the whole of China. A more accommodating US policy might have produced dramatic results. In November Germany and Japan renewed the Anti-Comintern Pact of 1936 for a further five years and segments in Japanese ruling circles ensured that this was done with a maximum of celebratory publicity.[86] The option of turning against the Soviet Union, not the United States and Britain, remained almost until Pearl Harbor. Roosevelt undoubtedly did not want war in the Pacific but was trapped in a situation in which he could offer Japan no lifeline. United States policy had slipped rather casually into demanding of Japan that, like China under the Kuomintang government, it must accept an American defined and led international order or take the risks involved in war. The great American failure was the complete one not to anticipate an attack on their Pacific fleet at Pearl Harbor with which Japan intended to start its war. By the beginning of December the United States belatedly realised that war was imminent, but they were distracted by reports of Japanese naval movements toward South East Asia, especially the Philippines, and were convinced that Japan lacked the naval strength for simultaneous operations there and in the distant Pacific.

The very last chance of preventing a new war in the Pacific and, perhaps, of keeping the United States out of the war that was already going on in Europe would have arisen if Germany had been heavily discouraging to Japan. Instead, when in November Japan told Germany that it expected failure in its negotiations with the United States, would respond to such failure with hostilities and would appreciate an undertaking from Germany that it would not seek to resolve its problems with a United States that had been diverted to the Pacific, the Nazi government offered lavish assurance. Emboldened, Japan went on to ask Germany to promise to declare war on the United States if Japan attacked it; precisely such an assurance was given without quibble. Hitler was convinced that Roosevelt had the power to embark on war with Germany and was determined to do so. There were morale advantages in Germany declaring war first, but, above all, he was terrified of the United States and Germany being at war while peace reigned in the Far East because then the United States would have been able to concentrate all its resources against Germany. In a global war the United States would have to expend many resources against Japan, and any war effort that it made against Germany could be expected to be virtually cancelled out by the cessation of material aid to Britain and Russia. (The Americans 'will need it themselves', wrote Goebbels, echoing his master.) In any case, America was expected to need years to mobilise its vast resources,[87] and before that could be done, during 1942, Hitler hoped and expected to defeat all or most Russian resistance, to thrust into the Middle East and to link up with victorious Japanese armies in the region of Iran or North West India. The United States (and Britain if it continued to fight) would then find themselves confronted by an impregnable European and Asian fortress of the Tripartite Pact states. Even more immediately, Hitler looked forward to unrestrained and therefore victorious German tactics in the naval war in the Atlantic to bring Britain to its knees.

On 7 December the Japanese attacked at Pearl Harbor. The next day the United States declared war on Japan. On 10 December Goebbels recorded of Hitler: 'He is delighted at such a happy turn of events in dealings between the USA and Japan and about the outbreak of war.' On 11 December Germany, and Italy declared war on the United States. On 13 December Goebbels remarked of his Fuhrer's sensation that, as a result of the expansion of the war, a 'ton weight has been taken off him'.[88] Hitler, who bore overwhelming responsibility for plunging Europe into war, could also claim a significant share of the responsibility for the expansion of war over most of the world.

To conclude, there was a certain symmetry to the origins of the Second World War in terms of beginning and end. Between 1931 and 1933, by occupying Manchuria and by sending out indications that had whetted rather than satisfied its appetite for empire, Japan effectively took the Far East out of international society in the sense of a system in which peace was ensured by the non-warlike intentions of the major powers with interests in the area. Then the focus of instability shifted to Europe. Japan invaded China in 1937 and occupied large areas, but there is almost no possibility that that would have led to a wider conflict, involving the United States and the British, French and Dutch with their colonies in South East Asia, but for the outbreak of war in Europe, though a Japanese victory in China would very likely have been followed by a showdown war between Japan and the Soviet Union. On the one hand, the Western democracies felt too little interest in the fate of China to risk war with Japan on behalf of that country. On the other, Japan had too much respect for Western power, and even for British and French alone, to risk war with it if it was in a position to utilise all its resources against Japan. To pursue the theme of symmetry, after seven years or so between 1933 and 1940 in which events in Europe had increasingly claimed the major share of attention, the Far East returned to a position of central importance in 1940 and 1941, notwithstanding the further immensely important European event of the latter year, the outbreak of war between Germany and Russia. Japan decided that it was no longer too risky to strike at the European colonies in South and South East Asia. Their occupation would indeed have been almost child's play but for the fact that the United States was both threatening Japan with potentially crippling economic sanctions and was unwilling to stand by and let the British and Dutch colonies be overrun. This was despite a traditional American dislike for European colonial empires and despite years of unwillingness to help China even though it was regarded as a friend. It required the phenomenon of Japanese aggressiveness in East Asia and the Pacific and German and Italian aggressive war in Europe and North Africa to bring about a switch to global and internventionist thinking in the Roosevelt administration in Washington. The United States might have stayed neutral indefinitely if the status quo had been threatened only in the European and Middle East–North Africa context or only in the Far East if America's own possessions there had been left alone by Japan (as would have been technically feasible). Threats in both areas brought the United States into the Second World War and ensured that that war would end in victory for the forces opposed to the totalitarian right and not stalemate or even a German–Japanese victory, and created the conditions in which the United States would eventually be the only superpower.

Notes

1 Christopher Thorne, *The Approach of War 1938–39* (London, Macmillan, 1967), p. 162.
2 Report in *Daily Telegraph*, 28 February 1990.
3 For a fascinating account of the process by which these self-imposed restraints were set aside, see Frederick M. Sallager, *The Road to Total War* (New York, Van Nostrand Reinhold, 1969).
4 Victor Rothwell, 'Germany and Anglo-Soviet relations during the Second World War', *Crossroads* (New York), 25 (1987), 1–18, p. 13.
5 Richard Lamb, *The Ghosts of Peace 1935–1945* (Salisbury, Russell, 1987), pp. 130–2.
6 David Irving, *Churchill's War: Vol. One, The Struggle for Power* (Bullbrook, Australia, Veritas Publishing, 1987), pp. 203–4, 214.
7 Christopher Hill, *Cabinet Decisions on Foreign Policy: The British Experience, October 1938–June 1941* (Cambridge, Cambridge University Press, 1991), pp. 112–13, 116.
8 Nicholas Bethell, *The War Hitler Won: September 1939* (London, Allen

Lane/Penguin, 1972), pp. 356–8, 366–7, 389–91.

9   John Lukacs, *The Last European War: September 1939/December 1941* (London, Routledge, 1977), pp. 228–9.

10 Clive Ponting, *1940: Myth and Reality* (London, Cardinal, 1990), pp. 43–6, 218–20.

11 Bethell, *The War*, pp. 256–7.

12 Robert E. Herzstein, *Roosevelt & Hitler: Prelude to War* (New York, Paragon House, 1988), pp. 306–7.

13 Saul Friedlander, *Prelude to Downfall: Hitler and the United States 1939–1941* (London, Chatto & Windus, 1967), pp. 26–30; William Carr, *Poland to Pearl Harbor: The Making of the Second World War* (London, Arnold, 1985), pp. 14, 75.

14 Joseph P. Lash, *Roosevelt and Churchill, 1939–1941: The Partnership that Saved the West* (New York, Norton, 1976), pp. 33, 147.

15 Lloyd C. Gardner, *Spheres of Influence* (London, Murray, 1993), pp. 64, 97; David Dilks (ed.), *The Diaries of Sir Alexander Cadogan 1938–1945* (London, Cassell, 1971), p. 314.

16 Thomas E. Hachey (ed.), *Confidential Dispatches: Analyses of America by the British Ambassador, 1939–1945* (Evanston, IL, New University Press, 1974), p. 41.

17 David Reynolds, *The Creation of the Anglo-American Alliance, 1937–1941* (London, Europa Publications, 1981), pp. 69–72.

18 Gerhard L. Weinberg, *World in the Balance: Behind the Scenes of World War II* (Hanover, New Hampshire, University Press of New England, 1981), p. xiii.

19 Friedlander, *Prelude to Downfall*, pp. 49–51, 55–65, 100.

20 Andrew Roberts, *'The Holy Fox': A Life of Lord Halifax* (London, Macmillan, 1992), p. 218.

21 Dilks (ed.), *Cadogan*, p.288.

22 Ponting, *1940*, pp. 102–3; Reynolds *Creation*, pp. 103–6; Lamb, *Ghosts*, pp. 138–42.

23 John Lukacs, *Five Days in London, May 1940* (New Haven, CT, Yale University Press, 1999), pp. 112–22, 131, 148–55, 183–6, 190, 217; see also Hill, *Cabinet Decisions*, pp. 149, 163–8; Roberts, *Halifax*, pp. 213–28.

24 The subject of John Lukacs, *The Duel Hitler vs. Churchill: 10 May–31 July 1940* (London, The Bodley Head, 1990).

25 Irving, *Churchill's War*, p. 368.

26 Lukacs, *Five Days*, p. 131.

27 Lamb, *Ghosts*, pp. 216–17.

28 Ralph Hewins, *Quisling: Prophet without Honour* (London, W. H. Allen, 1965), p. 292.

29 Joseph Goebbels, previously unpublished diary extracts (diary entry

for 23 August 1939), *Sunday Times*, News Review, section 2, p. 3, 12 July 1992.

30 Heinz Guderian, *Panzer Leader* (London, Futura, 1974), pp. 84–5.

31 H. Boog, J. Forster, J. Hoffman, E. Klink, R-D. Müller and G. R. Ueberschar, *Germany and the Second World War: Vol. IV, The Attack on the Soviet Union* (Oxford, Clarendon Press, 1998), p. 41.

32 *Ibid.*, pp. 20–2.

33 Gerhard L. Weinberg, *Germany and the Soviet Union 1939–1941* (Leiden, Brill, 1954), pp. 71–85.

34 Geoffrey Roberts, *The Unholy Alliance: Stalin's Pact with Hitler* (London, Tauris, 1989), pp. 180–2.

35 Roberts, *Unholy*, pp. 190–3, 269; Lukacs, *Last European War*, p. 119; Grigore Gafencu, *Prelude to the Russian Campaign* (London, Muller, 1945), pp. 73–9, 302–6; Boog et al., *Germany and the Second World War*, pp. 109–13.

36 Esmonde M. Robertson, 'Hitler turns from the West to Russia, May–December 1940' in Robert Boyce and Esmonde M. Robertson (eds), *Paths to War* (London, Macmillan, 1989), pp. 371–2, for Yugoslavia.

37 Paolo Spriano, *Stalin and the European Communists* (London, Verso, 1985), pp. 157, 161, quoting Stéphane Courtois.

38 Gabriel Gorodetsky, *Grand Delusion: Stalin and the German Invasion of Russia* (New Haven, CT, Yale University Press, 1999), pp. 13–14, 17, 72–5, 81.

39 W. Deist, M. Messerschmidt, H-E. Volkmann and W. Wette, *Germany and the Second World War: Vol. I, The Build-up of German Aggression* (Oxford, Clarendon Press, 1990), p. 360; Boog et al., *Germany and the Second World War*, pp. 194–9.

40 Boog et al., *Germany and the Second World War*, pp. 4, 8, 251–4.

41 Norman J. W. Goda, *Tomorrow the World: Hitler, Northwest Africa, and the Path toward America* (College Station, TX, Texas A & M University Press, 1998), p. 187. See Goda's book generally for the subject matter of the paragraph to which this note refers.

42 Boog et al., *Germany and the Second World War*; the references are too numerous to cite.

43 Boog et al., *Germany and the Second World War*, p. 1046; *Hitler's Table Talk 1941–1944* (Oxford, Oxford University Press, 1988), pp. 26, 684–5; see also Deist et al., *Germany and the Second World War*, pp. 550–1.

44 *Hitler's Table Talk*, pp. 31, 183, 624.

45 Deist et al., *Germany and the Second World War*, p. 551.

46 Boog et al., *Germany and the Second World War*, pp. 166, 170.

47 Gorodetsky, *Delusion*, pp. 180–9, 264–74, 316–23; Valentin Berezhkov, *History in the Making: Memoirs of World War II Diplomacy* (Moscow,

Progress Publishers, 1982), pp. 147–8.

48 Gabriel Gorodetsky, *Stafford Cripps' Mission to Moscow 1940–42* (Cambridge, Cambridge University Press, 1984), pp. 51–5, 94–6.

49 *Ibid.*, pp. 137–43; H. F. Hinsley, 'British Intelligence and Barbarossa' in John Erickson and David Dilks (eds), *Barbarossa: The Axis and the Allies* (Edinburgh, Edinburgh University Press, 1994), p. 72.

50 W. P. and Zelda K. Coates, *A History of Anglo-Soviet Relations* (London, Lawrence and Wishart, 1943), pp. 679–80.

51 William Carr, *Poland to Pearl Harbor: The Making of the Second World War* (London, Arnold, 1985), pp. 140–1.

52 Reynolds, *Creation*, pp. 97–100.

53 *Ibid.*, pp. 121–32; Lash, *Partnership,* p. 203.

54 Irving, *Churchill's War*, pp. 400, 487–9.

55 Ponting, *1940*, pp. 205–14.

56 Lash, *Partnership*, pp. 260–3.

57 Reynolds, *Creation*, pp. 182–5, 198–9, 222–6, 253.

58 Jean-Baptiste Duroselle, *From Wilson to Roosevelt: Foreign Policy of The United States 1913–1945* (London, Chatto & Windus, 1963), pp. 276–7.

59 Lukacs, *Last European War*, p. 501.

60 Herzstein, *Roosevelt & Hitler*, p. 327.

61 Report, 'How Britain hoodwinked Roosevelt', *The Times*, 2 April 1985, p. 12.

62 See Stanley E. Hilton, *Hitler's Secret War in South America 1939–1945: German Military Espionage and Allied Counterespionage in Brazil* (Baton Rouge, LA, Louisiana State University Press, 1981).

63 Reynolds, *Creation*, pp. 147–50, 201–2, 211–13, 286–9.

64 Theodore A. Wilson, *The First Summit: Roosevelt and Churchill at Placentia Bay 1941* (London, Macdonald, 1970), pp. 211, 264–7.

65 Friedlander, *Prelude*, pp. 205–7.

66 Wilson, *First Summit*, p. 259.

67 Lash, *Partnership*, pp. 384–5.

68 Bernd Martin, 'The German–Japanese alliance in the Second World War' in Saki Dockrill (ed.), *From Pearl Harbor to Hiroshima: The Second World War in Asia and the Pacific* (London, Macmillan, 1994), p. 154.

69 Carr, *Poland*, pp. 104–8.

70 Goda, *Tomorrow*, p. 75.

71 Friedlander, *Prelude*, p. 133.

72 Nicholas R. Clifford, *Retreat from China: British Policy in the Far East 1937–1941* (London, Longman, 1967), pp. 152–3.

73 Carr, *Poland*, pp. 111–12.

74 Lash, *Partnership*, pp. 333–7.

75 Wilson, *First Summit*, pp. 85–93,162–70, 257–8.
76 Lash, *Partnership*, pp. 476–7, 483.
77 Report in *Daily Telegraph* (London), 1 August 1994.
78 Lash, *Partnership*, p. 468.
79 Gorodetsky, *Delusion*, pp. 150–3, 196–9.
80 Ikuhito Hata, 'Admiral Yamamoto's surprise attack and the Japanese navy's war strategy' in Dockrill (ed.), *From Pearl Harbor*, p. 65.
81 S. Budkevich, 'Japanese imperialists disappointed', *International Affairs* (Moscow), June 1966, 66–73.
82 Boog et al., *Germany and the Second World War*, pp. 1044–8; Bernd Martin, 'The German–Japanese alliance' in Dockrill (ed.), *From Pearl Harbor*, pp. 153–73; Bernd Martin, 'The German Perspective' in Akira Iriye (ed.), *Pearl Harbor and the Coming of the Pacific War: A Brief History with Documents and Essays* (Boston, MA, Bedford/St. Martin's, 1999), pp. 219–30.
83 Budkevich, 'Japanese imperialists'.
84 Friedlander, *Prelude*, p. 270; Carr, *Poland*, pp. 150–1.
85 Reynolds, *Creation*, pp. 234–6; Lash, *Partnership*, p. 407.
86 Ian Nish, *Japanese Foreign Policy 1869–1942* (London, Routledge, 1977), p. 246.
87 Goda, *Tomorrow*, pp. xix–xx.
88 Goebbels, unpublished diaries, *Sunday Times*, 19 July 1992.

BIBLIOGRAPHICAL GUIDE

Introductory

There are some useful edited collections. Patrick Finney (ed.), *The Origins of the Second World War* (London, 1997), groups together pieces that had already been published by twenty historians. The essays were originally commissioned for Robert Boyce and Esmonde M. Robertson (eds), *Paths to War* (London, 1989), and the two editions – essentially two different books – edited by Gordon Martel, *The Origins of the Second World War Reconsidered: The A. J. P. Taylor Debate After Twenty-five Years* (London, 1986), and *The Origins of the Second World War Reconsidered: A. J. P. Taylor and the Historians* (London, 1999). Taylor has been downgraded in the second edition in which he is not mentioned by some of the contributors, while others usually do so only to make the point that his once celebrated book has passed from being controversial to being discredited and disproved, at least in many key aspects. Two more specialised collections of essays are Gordon A. Craig and Felix Gilbert (eds), *The Diplomats 1919–1939* (Princeton, 1953), and Wolfgang J. Mommsen and Lothar Kettenacker (eds), *The Fascist Challenge and the Policy of Appeasement* (London, 1983). Two influential essays in book form by individual historians are Donald Cameron Watt, *Too Serious a Business: European Armed Forces and the Approach to the Second World War* (London, 1975), and R. J. Overy, *The Inter-War Crisis 1919–1939* (London, 1994).

The peace settlement and the 1920s

There are good short guides to the peace settlement and their immediate circumstances in Gerhard Schulz, *Revolutions and Peace Treaties, 1917–1920* (London, 1972), and Alan Sharp, *The Versailles Settlement: Peacemaking in Paris, 1919* (London, 1991). For key aspects see Harold I. Nelson, *Land and Power: British and Allied Policy on Germany's Frontiers 1916–19* (London, 1963); Lorna S. Jaffe, *The Decision to Disarm Germany* (London, 1985) and Bruce Kent, *The Spoils of War: The Politics, Economics, and Diplomacy of Reparations 1918–1932* (Oxford, 1989). On the entire period from the armistice to 1933 there is still only Sally Marks, *The Illusion of Peace: International Relations in Europe 1918–1933* (London, 1976) which needs to be used with care. The only slightly older Raymond J. Sontag, *A Broken World 1919–1939* (New York, 1971), has a finer feel for the period. On the early 1920s see Anne Orde, *Great Britain and International Security 1920–1926* (London, 1978), and W. Kleine-Ablbrandt, *The Burden of Victory: France, Britain and Versailles, 1919–1925* (Lanham, MD, 1995). On the later 1920s Jon Jacobson, *Locarno Diplomacy: Germany and the West 1925–1929* (Princeton, NJ, 1972), remains unsurpassed. On the peace settlement's most famous creation see George Scott, *The Rise and Fall of the League of Nations* (London, 1973), and F. P. Walters, *A History of the League of Nations* (London, 1952). F. L. Carsten, *Britain and the Weimar Republic* (London, 1984), and Martin Gilbert, *Horace Rumbold* (London, 1973) show why the demise of the German republic caused little regret in official British quarters. For a more balanced view of German policy in this period see Marshall M. Lee and Wolfgang Michalka, *German Foreign Policy 1917–1933: Continuity or Break?* (Leamington Spa, 1987), and John Hiden, *Germany and Europe 1919–1939* (London, various edns.).

Hitler and early Nazi foreign policy thinking

Rohan D'O. Butler, *The Roots of National Socialism 1783–1933* (London, 1941) and Woodruff D. Smith, *The Ideological Origins of Nazi Imperialism* (New York, 1986) make for instructive comparative reading. For Hitler's foreign policy thinking in the early stages of his political 'career' see D. Aigner, 'Hitler's ultimate aims – a programme of world domination?' in H. W. Koch (ed.), *Aspects of the Third Reich* (London, 1985); Geoffrey Stoakes, 'The evolution of Hitler's ideas on foreign policy, 1919–1925' in Peter D. Stachura (ed.), *The Shaping of the Nazi State* (London, 1978) and Geoffrey Stoakes, *Hitler and the Quest for World Dominion* (Leamington Spa, 1986). For the wider context in which Nazi ultimate goals, though only very vaguely hinted at, could appeal to many voters see Peter Fritzche, *Germans into Nazis* (Cambridge, MA, 1998), and part I by Wolfram Wette of the book written by Wette and others referred to in the next section. Among the many biographies of Hitler William Carr, *Hitler: A Study in Personality and Politics* (London, 1978) retains interest from having been written by a foreign policy-rearmament specialist. Ian Kershaw, *Hitler 1889–1936: Hubris* (London 1998) and *Hitler 1937–1945: Nemesis* (London, 2000) together constitute the most recent study.

Bibliographical guide

Nazi Germany: foreign policy and rearmament

For an introduction see the relevant chapters of Gordon A. Craig, *Germany 1866–1945* (Oxford, 1978) and John Hiden, *Republican and Fascist Germany* (London, 1996). The most important single work for all aspects of German war preparations is the monumental Wilhelm Deist, Manfred Messerschmidt, Hans-Erich Volkmann and Wolfram Wette, *Germany and the Second World War: Vol. I, The Build-up of German Aggression* (Oxford, 1990). There is a still useful supplement to it in Norman Rich, *Hitler's War Aims: Ideology, the Nazi State, and the Course of Expansion* (London, 1973). One of the above-mentioned, Deist, has also written a short study, *The Wehrmacht and German Rearmament* (London, 1981), to which also may be added a couple of older, still useful books: E. M. Robertson, *Hitler's pre-War Policy and Military Plans* (London, 1963) and William Carr, *Arms, Autarky and Aggression* (London, 1972). There is an invaluable collection of documents in J. Noakes and G. Pridham (eds), *Nazism 1919–1945: Vol. 3 Foreign Policy, War and Racial Extermination* (Exeter, 1988). Rearmament was the central theme of the peacetime Third Reich and the problems that it created have been extensively explored: Avraham Barkai, *Nazi Economics: Ideology, Theory, and Policy* (Oxford, 1990); Thomas Childers and Jane Caplan (eds), *Reevaluating the Third Reich* (some chapters), (New York, 1993); Tim Mason, *Social Policy in the Third Reich* (Oxford, 1993) and his *Nazism, Fascism and the Working Class* (Cambridge, 1995); and R. J. Overy, *War and Economy in the Third Reich* (Oxford, 1994). Ian Kershaw, *The 'Hitler Myth': Image and Reality in the Third Reich* (Oxford, 1987), explains the dictator's considerable success in rising above the tensions that rearmament created in the minds of many Germans. On foreign policy, the major work for the early years is Gerhard L. Weinberg, *The Foreign Policy of Hitler's Germany: Diplomatic Revolution in Europe, 1933–36* (Chicago, IL, 1970). There is also some pre-war material in Weinberg's *Germany, Hitler and World War II* (Cambridge, 1995). Short studies include Hiden, *Germany and Europe* (see above section on the peace settlement and the 1920s); Lionel Kochan, *The Struggle for Germany 1914:45* (Edinburgh, 1963) and Klaus Hildebrand, *The Foreign Policy of the Third Reich* (London, 1973). The title of John Weitz, *Joachim von Ribbentrop: Hitler's Diplomat* (London, 1992), speaks for itself.

Britain (before 1938)

There are many overview studies, including Paul W. Doerr, *British Foreign Policy 1919–1939* (Manchester, 1998); Roy Douglas, *World Crisis and British Decline, 1929–56* (London, 1986); Robert Holland, *The Pursuit of Greatness 1900–1970* (London, 1991); David Reynolds, *Britannia Overruled* (London, 1991) and, more specifically on the 1930s, R. J. Q. Adams (ed.), *British*

Appeasement and the Origins of World War II (Lexington, 1994), William R. Rock, *British Appeasement in the 1930s* (London, 1977) and Peijian Shen, *The Age of Appeasement: The Evolution of British Foreign Policy in the 1930s* (Stroud, 1999), which is the most recent study but not the most reliable. For contrasting views of whether Britain was a 'real' great power see Correlli Barnett, *The Collapse of British Power* (Gloucester, 1984) and Anthony Clayton, *The British Empire as a Superpower, 1919–39* (London, 1986). See also the essays in David Dilks (ed.), *Retreat from Power: Vol. One 1906–1939* (London, 1981); Peter Catterall (ed.), *Britain and the Threat to Stability in Europe, 1918–45* (Leicester, 1993) and the classic Paul Kennedy, 'The tradition of appeasement in British foreign policy, 1865–1939' in his *Strategy and Diplomacy 1870–1945* (London, 1983). A selection of books on important aspects can only be semi-arbitrary: R. J. Q. Adams, *British Politics and Foreign Policy in the Age of Appeasement, 1935–39* (London, 1993); Maurice Cowling, *The Impact of Hitler: British Politics and British Policy 1933–1940* (Cambridge, 1975); N. J. Crowson, *Facing Fascisim: The Conservative Party and the European Dictators 1935–1940* (London, 1997); Andrew J. Crozier, *Appeasement and Germany's Last Bid for Colonies* (London, 1988); N. H. Gibbs, *Grand Strategy: Vol. I, Rearmament Policy* (London, 1976); Joseph A. Maiolo, *The Royal Navy and Nazi Germany, 1933–39* (London, 1998); G. C. Peden, *British Rearmament and the Treasury 1932–1939* (Edinburgh, 1979); A. R. Peters, *Anthony Eden at the Foreign Office 1931–1938* (Aldershot, 1986); Gaines Post, Jr., *Dilemmas of Appeasement: British Deterrence and Defense, 1934–1937* (Ithaca, NY, 1993); Michael L. Roi, *Alternative to Appeasement: Sir Robert Vansittart and Alliance Diplomacy, 1934–1937* (Westport, CT, 1997); Gustav Schmidt, *The Politics and Economics of Appeasement* (Leamington Spa, 1986) and Wesley K. Wark, *The Ultimate Enemy: British Intelligence and Nazi Germany, 1933–1939* (London, 1985).

France

For general studies see Anthony Adamthwaite, *Grandeur and Misery: France's Bid for Power in Europe 1914–1940* (London, 1995); Robert J. Young, *France and the Origins of the Second World War* (London, 1996) and the older J. Néré, *The Foreign Policy of France from 1914 to 1945* (London, 1975). More recent is Robert Boyce (ed.), *French Foreign and Defence Policy, 1918–1940* (London, 1998). On the Anglo-French relationship, see P. M. H. Bell, *France and Britain 1900–1940: Entente and Estrangement* (London, 1996); Nicholas Rostow, *Anglo-French Relations, 1934–36* (London, 1984); Martin Thomas, *Britain, France and Appeasement: Anglo-French Relations in the Popular Front Era* (Oxford, 1996) and Neville Waites (ed.), *Troubled Neighbours: Franco-British Relations in the*

Twentieth Century (London, 1971). On France and East Central Europe, Timothy A. Komjathy, *The Crises of France's East Central European Diplomacy, 1933–1938* (New York, 1976) and Nicole Jordan, *The Popular Front and Central Europe: The Dilemmas of French Impotence, 1918–1940* (Cambridge, 1992). On defence and rearmament, Martin S. Alexander, *The Republic in Danger: General Maurice Gamelin and the Politics of French Defence, 1933–1940* (Cambridge, 1992). On the Popular Front period, John E. Dreifort, *Yvon Delbos at the Quai D'Orsay* (Lawrence, KS, 1973).

Italy

For a general survey see H. James Burgwyn, *Italian Foreign Policy in the Interwar Period, 1918–1940* (New York, 1997). Philip V. Cannistraro (ed.), *Historical Dictionary of Fascist Italy* (Westport, CT, 1982) is a splendid source of information. On relations with the western powers in the 1930s, see Frank Hardie, *The Abyssinian Crisis* (London, 1974); Richard Lamb, *Mussolini and the British* (London, 1997); Denis Mack Smith, *Mussolini's Roman Empire* (London, 1977) and Esmonde M. Robertson, *Mussolini as Empire-Builder: Europe and Africa 1932–36* (London, 1977). For the 'axis' partnership with Germany, see Elizabeth Wiskemann, *The Rome–Berlin Axis* (London, 1966 revised edn.), and Mario Toscano, *The Origins of the Pact of Steel* (Baltimore, MD, 1967). There is an apologia for the Duce in Luigi Villari, *Italian Foreign Policy under Mussolini* (London, 1959). Brian R. Sullivan in Martel (ed.), chapter 10 (2nd edn.; see introductory section above) explains the somewhat illusory nature of Italy's importance.

Central Europe

This area became of greatest importance to war origins in the later 1930s, for which see Anita Prazmowska, *Eastern Europe and the Origins of the Second World War* (London, 2000) and the section on the later 1930s below. What follows is a small selection for the inter-war period generally: G. Batonyi, *Britain and Central Europe 1918–1933* (Oxford, 1998); Jan Karski, *The Great Powers and Poland 1919–1945: From Versailles to Yalta* (Lanham, MD, 1985); Josef Korbel, *Poland between East and West, 1919–1933* (Princeton, NJ, 1963); Antony Polonsky, *Politics in Independent Poland 1921–1939* (Oxford, 1972); Carl Tighe, *Gdánsk: National Identity in the German–Polish Borderlands* (London, 1990) and Bela Vago, *The Shadow of the Swastika: The Rise of Fascism and Anti-Semitism in the Danube Basin, 1936–39* (London, 1975).

Bibliographical guide

Crises in the later 1930s

The most important single work, though concentrating on one country, is Gerhard L. Weinberg, *The Foreign Policy of Hitler's Germany: Starting World War II, 1937–1939* (Chicago, IL, 1980). J. T. Emmerson, *The Rhineland Crisis, 7 March 1936* (London, 1977) is an able study of a watershed event. On the Impact of the Spanish Civil War, see Michael Alpert, *A New International History of the Spanish Civil War* (London, 1994), and Christian Leitz and David J. Dunthorn (eds), *Spain in an International Context, 1936–1939* (Oxford, 1999). On the more subterranean efforts to stave off the catastrophe, see Richard Lamb, *The Ghosts of Peace 1935–1945* (Salisbury, 1987). The published literature on the crises of 1938 and 1939 makes selection even more difficult than usual. Much work on British policy has focused on Neville Chamberlain, including Larry William Fuchser, *Neville Chamberlain and Appeasement* (New York, 1982); R. A. C. Parker, *Chamberlain and Appeasement* (London, 1993); Frank McDonough, *Neville Chamberlain, Appeasement and the British Road to War* (Manchester, 1998) and John Ruggiero, *Neville Chamberlain and British Rearmament* (London, 1999). For his increasingly important Foreign Minister, see Andrew Roberts, *'The Holy Fox': A Life of Lord Halifax* (London, 1991), and for his envoy in Berlin see Peter Nevile, *Appeasing Hitler: The Diplomacy of Sir Nevile Henderson* (London, 1999). For his most famous critic, see R. A. C. Parker, *Churchill and Appeasement* (London, 2000). The policies of all the countries that were affected by the great Czechoslovak crisis are examined in a special issue of *Diplomacy and Statecraft*, 10: 2 and 3, July/ November 1999, edited by Igor Lukes and Erik Goldstein, and in Maya Latynski (ed.), *Reappraising Munich: Continental Perspectives* (Baltimore, MD, 1992). For Czechoslovakia itself, see Elizabeth Wiskemann, *Czechs and Germans* (London, 2nd edn. 1967); J. W. Bruegel, *Czechoslovakia before Munich: The German Minority Problem and British Appeasement Policy* (Cambridge, 1973) and Norman Stone and Eduard Strouhal (eds), *Czechoslovakia: Crossroads and Crises, 1918–1988* (London, 1989). For an assessment of the strategic consequences of Munich see Williamson Murray, *The Change in the European Balance of Power, 1938–1939* (Princeton, NJ, 1984). For France in 1938–39 see Anthony Adamthwaite, *France and the Coming of the Second World War* (London, 1977). For Poland as it moved to the forefront of events, see Anna M. Cienciala, *Poland and the Western Powers 1938–1939* (London, 1968) and Anita Prazmowska, *Britain, Poland and the Eastern Front, 1939* (Cambridge, 1987). Donald Cameron Watt, *How War Came: The Immediate Origins of the Second World War, 1938–1939* (London, 1989) is the most important book for the subject described in its title. Useful supplements are the essays in Roy Douglas (ed.), *1939: A Retrospect after Forty Years* (London, 1983); Sidney Aster, *1939: The Making of the Second World War* (London, 1973), which is essentially about British policy; Simon Newman, *March 1939: The British Guarantee to Poland* (Oxford, 1976) and John Hiden and Thomas Lane (eds), *The Baltic and the Outbreak of the Second World War* (Cambridge, 1992).

The Soviet Union and the communist movement

There are overviews in R. Craig Nation, *Black Earth, Red Star: A History of Soviet Security Policy, 1917–1991* (Ithaca, NY, 1992), and Caroline Kennedy-Pipe, *Russia and the World 1917–1991* (London, 1998). The fading and ultimate ending of the Cold War brought about a change in Western historiography of Soviet foreign policy from the view of the Soviet regime as an ideological crusade that had taken over a country to one of the regime as a nation state, pursuing ordinary national aims. On the early period of the 1920s this may be gauged from comparing Elliot R. Goodman, *The Soviet Design for a World State* (New York, 1960) with Jon Jacobson, *When the Soviet Union Entered World Politics* (Berkeley, CA, 1994) – titles alone that say much. On the 1930s, the 'normal state' thesis has Geoffrey Roberts, *The Unholy Alliance: Stalin's Pact with Hitler* (London, 1989); the same author's *The Soviet Union and the Origins of the Second World War* (London, 1995) and Michael Jabara Carley, *1939: The Alliance that Never Was and the Coming of World War II* (Chicago, IL, 1999) firmly in its grip. For a more balanced view that takes more account of Marxist–Leninist ideology and the peculiarities of Russian history see E. H. Carr, *The Twilight of the Comitern, 1930–1935* (London, 1982); Robert C. Tucker, *Stalin in Power: The Revolution from Above 1928–1941* (New York, 1990) and Jonathan Haslam, *The Soviet Union and the Struggle for Collective Security in Europe, 1933–39* (London, 1984). For two key aspects, see Walter Laqueur, *Russia and Germany: A Century of Conflict* (London, 1965) and Tim Rees and Andrew Thorpe (eds), *International Communism and the Communist International 1919–43* (Manchester, 1998).

The Far East (to 1939)

Japanese policy is well served by several general studies, including Michael A. Barnhart, *Japan and the Wider World since 1868* (London, 1997); William Beasley, *Japanese Imperialism* (Oxford, 1987); Akira Iriye, *Japan and the Wider World* (London, 1997) and Ian Nish, *Japanese Foreign Policy 1869–1942* (London, 1977). For Japanese–American relations, see Walter LaFeber, *The Clash: US–Japanese Relations Throughout History* (New York, 1997). For the Washington conference of 1921–22 and its aftermath see the special issue of *Diplomacy and Statecraft*, 4:3 (1993), edited by Erik Goldstein and John Mauer. See also Roger Dingman, *Power in the Pacific* (Chicago, IL, 1976) and Akira Iriye, *After Imperialism* (Cambridge, MA, 1965). For the

Manchurian crisis of 1931–33 and its aftermath, see Sadako Ogata, *Defiance in Manchuria* (Berkeley, CA, 1964), Christopher Thorne, *The Limits of Foreign Policy* (London, 1972) for the responses of the Western powers and Dorothy Borg, *The United States and the Far Eastern Crisis, 1933–1938* (Cambridge, MA, 1964). For Britain and the inter-war Far East, see Wm. Roger Louis, *British Strategy in the Far East 1919–1939* (Oxford, 1971); Ann Trotter, *Britain and East Asia 1933–1937* (Cambridge, 1975) and Robert Bickers, *Britain in China 1900–1949* (Manchester, 1999). For the chequered relationship between Nazi Germany and Japan, see John P. Fox, *Germany and the Far Eastern Crisis 1931–1938* (Oxford, 1982). For the Sino-Japanese conflict, see Youli Sun, *China and the Origins of the Pacific War, 1931–1941* (London, 1993) and Akira Iriye, *The Origins of the Second World War in Asia and the Pacific* (London, 1987), and his essay on 'Culture in Japanese foreign affairs' in T. G. Fraser and Peter Lowe (eds), *Conflict and Amity in East Asia* (London, 1992).

The United States (to 1939)

Alexander J. Groth, *Democracies against Hitler: Myth, Reality and Prologue* (Aldershot, 1999) goes some way to explaining why the American democracy was slow to react to the Nazi threat. It may be studied in conjunction with Patricia Clavin, *The Failure of Economic Diplomacy: Britain, Germany, France and the United States, 1931–36* (London, 1996), which is enlightening on why Nazi Germany was not at the forefront of American policymakers' minds early in the Roosevelt presidency. For the story as it continued, see David F. Schmitz and Richard Challener (eds), *Appeasement in Europe: A Reappraisal of US Policies* (Westport, CT, 1990). On the bilateral German-American relationship, see Arnold A. Offner, *American Appeasement: United States Foreign Policy and Germany, 1933–1938* (Cambridge, MA, 1969). For two diametrically opposed views of Roosevelt's conduct of foreign policy, the first favourable and the second extremely adverse, see Robert Dallek, *Franklin D. Roosevelt and American Foreign Policy, 1932–1945* (New York, 1979) and Frederick W. Marks III, *Wind over Sand: the Diplomacy of Franklin Roosevelt* (Athens, GA, 1988). Relations with Britain were central to United States foreign policy in this period. See Ritchie Ovendale, *'Appeasement' and the English Speaking World 1937–1939* (Cardiff, 1975), which also includes the dominions in its coverage; David Reynolds, *The Creation of the Anglo-American Alliance, 1937–1941* (London, 1981); D. Cameron Watt, *Succeeding John Bull: America in Britain's Place 1900–1975* (Cambridge, 1984); William R. Rock, *Churchill and Roosevelt: British Foreign Policy and the United States, 1937–1940* (Columbus, OH, 1988); Ian Cowman, *Dominion or Decline: Anglo-American Naval Relations in the Pacific, 1937–1941* (Oxford, 1996) and B. J. C.

McKercher, *Transition of Power: Britain's Loss of Global Pre-eminence to the United States, 1930–1945* (Cambridge, 1999), though the title is completely misleading for the 1930s. To reinforce the point, Edward M. Bennett, *Recognition of Russia: An American Foreign Policy Dilemma* (Waltham, MA, 1970) illustrates the excessive importance attached to gestures in American foreign policy of that decade.

From European to world war

Two important general works are John Lukacs, *The Last European War September 1939/December 1941* (London, 1977) and William Carr, *Poland to Pearl Harbor: The Making of the Second World War* (London, 1985). For the very start of the war, see Nicholas Bethell, *The War Hitler Won* (London, 1972). For Britain's crucial decision not to seek peace terms in 1940, see John Lukacs, *The Duel: Hitler vs. Churchill* (London, 1990), and his *Five Days in London, May 1940* (New Haven, CT, 1999); Christopher Hill, *Cabinet Decisions on Foreign Policy: the British Experience, October 1938–June 1941* (Cambridge, 1991) and Sheila Lawlor, *Churchill and the Politics of War, 1940–1941* (Cambridge, 1994). For the looming German–American confrontation, see Saul Friedlander, *Prelude to Downfall: Hitler and the United States 1939–1941* (London, 1967); Robert E. Herzstein, *Roosevelt and Hitler: Prelude to War* (New York, 1989), and Norman J. W. Goda, *Tomorrow the World: Hitler, Northwest Africa, and the Path toward America* (College Station, TX, 1998). For the faltering steps towards an Anglo-American alliance, a selection from the huge literature might include some of the books on relations between the two in the section on the United States to 1939 above, plus Lloyd C. Gardner, *Spheres of Influence: The Partition of Europe, from Munich to Yalta* (London, 1993); Theodore A. Wilson, *The First Summit: Roosevelt and Churchill at Placentia Bay 1941* (London, 1970) and Joseph P. Lash, *Roosevelt and Churchill, 1940–1941: the Partnership that Saved the West* (New York, 1976). For the extension of the war to include the Soviet Union, there are two important collective books. These are Bernd Wegner (ed.), *From Peace to War: Germany, Russia and the World, 1939–1941* (Providence, RI, 1997), and Horst Boog and five other authors, *Germany and the Second World War: Vol. IV, The Attack on the Soviet Union* (Oxford, 1998), though Joachim Hoffmann's somewhat notorious contribution, in which it is argued that Stalin was preparing to invade Hitler's Europe and was only prevented from doing so because Hitler struck first, cannot be taken seriously; certainly not since the publication of Gabriel Gorodetsky, *Grand Delusion: Stalin and the German Invasion of Russia* (New Haven, CT, 1999), which is probably definitive on the Russian side, though not always convincing on the German. See also the essays in John Erikson and David Dilks (eds), *Barbarossa: The Axis and the Allies* (Edinburgh, 1994); Pavel Sevostyanov, *Before the Nazi Invasion: Soviet Diplomacy in September 1939–June 1941* (Moscow, 1984) for how the Soviet Union wished the story to be told during its last years; Paolo Spriano, *Stalin and the European Communists* (London, 1985) for evidence of how the weirdness of Stalin's mind affected Soviet foreign policy; E. E. Erickson III, *Feeding the Eagle: Soviet Aid to Nazi Germany* (New York, 1999) for Stalin's aid programme to Germany before the invasion; and Patrick R. Osborn, *Operation Pike: Britain versus the Soviet Union, 1939–1941* (London, 2000) for the abysmal state of relations with Germany's main enemy. For the extension of the war to include Japan, see Akira Iriye (ed.), *Pearl Harbor and the Coming of the Pacific War: A Brief History with Documents and Essays* (Boston, MA, 1999); Dorothy Borg and Shumpei Okamoto (eds), *Pearl Harbor as History: Japanese-American Relations, 1939–1941* (New York, 1973); Waldo H. Heinrichs, *Threshold of War: Franklin D. Roosevelt and American Entry into World War II* (New York, 1988), and some of the essays in Saki Dockrill (ed.), *From Pearl Harbor to Hiroshima* (London, 1994). For British policy, see Anthony Best, *Britain, Japan and Pearl Harbor: Avoiding War in East Asia 1936–1941* (London, 1995). For the South East Asian aspect, see Nicholas Tarling, *Britain, Southeast Asia and the Onset of the Pacific War* (Cambridge, 1996), and Jonathan Marshall, *To Have and Have Not: Southeast Asian Raw Materials and the Coming of the Pacific War* (Berkeley, CA, 1995), which discusses how American policymakers became convinced that the United States could not risk allowing Japan to take possession of the resources of that region.

INDEX